John Muir

THE OKLAHOMA WESTERN BIOGRAPHIES
RICHARD W. ETULAIN, GENERAL EDITOR

John Muir

APOSTLE OF NATURE

By Thurman Wilkins

UNIVERSITY OF OKLAHOMA PRESS : NORMAN AND LONDON

By Thurman Wilkins

Clarence King: A Biography (New York, 1958; 2d edition, revised and enlarged with the help of Caroline Lawson Hinkley, Albuquerque, 1988)

Thomas Moran: Artist of the Mountains (Norman, 1966)

Cherokee Tragedy: The Ridge Family and the Decimation of a People (New York, 1970; 2d edition, revised, Norman, 1986)

John Muir: Apostle of Nature (Norman, 1995)

This book is published with the generous assistance of The McCasland Foundation, Duncan, Oklahoma.

Library of Congress Cataloging-in-Publication Data

Wilkins, Thurman.
    John Muir : apostle of nature / by Thurman Wilkins.
       p. cm.—(Oklahoma western biographies ; v. 8)
    Includes bibliographical references (p.   ) and index.
    ISBN: 0-8061-2712-0 (cloth : alk. paper)
       1. Muir, John, 1838–1914. 2. Naturalists—United States—
Biography. 3. Conservationists—United States—Biography.
I. Title. II. Series.
  QH31.M78W54 1995
  333.7'2'092—dc20
  [B]

                             95–11426
                              CIP

John Muir: Apostle of Nature is Volume 8 in *The Oklahoma Western Biographies*.

The paper in this book meets the guidelines for permanence and durability of the Committee on Production Guidelines for Book Longevity of the Council on Library Resources, Inc. ∞

1 2 3 4 5 6 7 8 9 10

For Sophie and Mary K

Contents

Illustrations

FIGURES

Series Editor's Preface

IN this thoroughly researched and sprightly written biography, Thurman Wilkins shows why John Muir remains a major figure in American intellectual and environmental history. A pioneering force in influencing others to pay more careful attention to people-land relationships, Muir, like Henry David Thoreau, followed his own preachments in his emblematic life as a naturalist and conservationist.

Wilkins does a fine job of briefly outlining Muir's active life, especially his joyful ramblings throughout North America and elsewhere in the world. The author appealingly depicts Muir's enthusiasm, his nature skills, and his tireless devotion to conservation causes. No one will read this story without being drawn to Muir's ebullience and his authentic attachment to the natural world.

Readers also will be attracted to the author's straightforward approach. He tells in detail where Muir went, what he saw, and what he did, without allowing the story to drag. A seasoned biographer with well-received earlier life stories of Clarence King and Thomas Moran, Wilkins displays a keen sense of pace in telling this story. He likewise clearly illustrates the personality of his subject through numerous apt quotations from Muir's voluminous writings.

Here, then, is a smoothly fashioned biography of an important Westerner. Overall, Wilkins furnishes a lively, coherent introduction to John Muir's active life as well as to his notable efforts in behalf of conservation and preservation and the establishment of parks and wilderness areas. In placing Muir's life in the larger contexts of national and regional cultural and environmental history, Thurman Wilkins achieves the major goals of volumes in the Oklahoma Western Biographies series.

RICHARD W. ETULAIN

University of New Mexico

Preface

HAVING grown up in southern California, where I was a mountain buff as a schoolboy, I learned about John Muir when I was very young. On a number of occasions I stayed with friends at Muir Lodge in the Big Santa Anita Canyon of the San Gabriel Mountains (which we called the Sierra Madre Mountains more often than not), and at those times I learned of Muir's connection with the Sierra Club, to which the lodge belongs. On my frequent hikes in the San Gabriel and San Bernardino ranges, as well as on one extended outing in the Sierra Nevada, I was fascinated by the water ouzel, among the birds my companions and I observed. I was delighted, then, to encounter Muir's essay on the ouzel when I read *The Mountains of California* as a high school student. I wasn't then acquainted with David Starr Jordan's characterization of it as "the best bird biography in existence," but it struck me as a literary gem, and I read it several times, prizing it above *Stickeen*, which was required reading in my high school English program.

John Muir's books have continued to hold my attention over the years, and so it followed naturally that, when invited to contribute to the Oklahoma Western Biographies series, I should have suggested Muir as my choice of subject. The resulting short biography joins a recent surge of books and articles about the prime movers of the American conservation movement, works that reflect the nation's impulse to live more in harmony with the earth, as well as to understand the roots of the complex environmentalism of the present day.

Muir's personality was intricate and paradoxical, but in such a brief narrative as this it is necessary to focus attention more restrictively than a longer book would allow. I have therefore placed my emphasis as accurately as I have found possible on Muir the practical doer, who was at the same time a romantic idealist and even somewhat of a mystic. The book shows him in action, basically in chronological order, first as schoolboy and farm youth, then as college student, inventor, botanist, geologist, mountaineer, explorer, literary naturalist, fruit grower, and finally a leader of the preservationist wing of the American conservation movement. Above all, Muir was a lover of nature—in the estimation of John Burroughs "probably the truest lover of nature . . . that we have ever had"; and that inspired and inspiring devotion led him to fight for years for the preservation of American forests, a theme that vies in importance with his dedicated work on behalf of national parks.

The ultimate objective of this narrative, then, is to demonstrate how Muir, in the words of Eleanor Roosevelt, to a large degree "started the concept of conservation" (at least that aspect of it known as "preservationism"); how having trained himself as a botanist and geologist, he could best be remembered for his lyric responses to the order and harmony of nature and for his leadership in the movement to preserve the American wilderness—how indeed he could be, and has been, described in understandable hyperbole as an undeniable "father" of the forest reservations and system of national parks in the United States, notwithstanding all other workers for those causes. The impulse for yet another book about Muir is that the recent searching reassessment of his life and work places him at the very cutting edge of present-day environmentalism, his concept of wilderness exerting as much vitality today as when he lived and worked.

I must acknowledge that my first debt in connection with this book is to John N. Drayton, Editor-in-Chief of the University of Oklahoma Press, who, during our discussion about a project I had broached to him, suggested that, instead, I write a volume for the recently inaugurated Oklahoma Western Biographies. That was fortunate, for before I could have finished the book I had suggested, an excellent volume on the identical subject was published by the University of Nebraska Press.

In the work on John Muir that followed I have contracted obligations to many people. Professor Richard Etulain, Editor of the series in which the book will be published, has been constantly helpful, making constructive suggestions, and reading the manuscript whenever I needed guidance. My thanks goes to T. H. Watkins, Editor of *Wilderness* magazine, for instructive comments after he, too, had read the manuscript. To my former wife Sophie Wilkins, translator from the German and former editor at Alfred A. Knopf, I am also grateful for reading the entire manuscript and making important suggestions, while the latest person to read the whole manuscript was Lucy Lippard, prolific author, who gave me valuable advice.

Next I must thank Caroline Lawson Hinkley for her faithful aid with my researches and for her lending her photographic expertise to the making of several photos for illustrating the volume. Clifford Nelson and Todd Hinkley, both of the U.S. Geological Survey, have helped me with what seemed to me thorny geological problems, reading parts of the manuscript more times than once when necessary. I am grateful, too, to Daniel Wilkins, Professor of Astronomy at the University of Nebraska, Omaha, for pertinent suggestions and sending me needed research materials. I must likewise acknowledge the valuable article on Muir's glaciology sent to me through Clifford Nelson by Dennis R. Dean, who publishes regularly on the history of geology.

At the same time my appreciation extends to King Gillette, Don Gillett, and Whitney Scobert (all cousins, as well as distant relatives of Clarence King, a staunch ally of J. D. Whitney in the glacier controversy of the 1870s with John Muir). This sympathetic trio, along with their wives, Kay, Leila, and Elva respectively, have furnished me with a helpful assortment of research items, including the standard guide to place-names in the Sierra Nevada and the map of Kings Canyon and Sequoia national parks that provided the basis for the simplified version reproduced on pages 120–21 below. I am likewise indebted to Francis and Nell Donohoe and their daughters Kitty and Moira, all of whom lived for years in Yosemite Valley, for sharing with me their understanding of special traditions of the valley.

My research base for this volume has been the Bandon City Library, and I am deeply grateful to Judy Romans, Chief Librarian, and to her staff, especially Frances Ledbetter, Carol Pitman, and Susan Dissette—all of whom have been assiduous in helping me with my numerous requests. Others to whom I am indebted include Deanne Hall, M. J. Fisher, David K. Blackburn, Jack Harris, Brita Mack, Inga Khoury, Roberta Waddell, Kathryn Talalay, William F. and Maymie B. Kimes, Ronald Limbaugh, Richard Ogar, Andy Kraushaar, Kay and Richard O'Grady, and George Steddom, a former mayor of Bandon.

Many libraries have sent me information and lent me research materials—including the Southwestern Oregon Community College Library, the Southern Oregon State College Library, the University of Oregon Library, the Bancroft Library, the University of the Pacific Libraries; the University of Colorado Library, Boulder; the USGS Library, Reston; the USGS Library, Denver; the Library of Congress, the State Historical Society of Wisconsin, the University of Nebraska Library, Omaha; the Oregon State Library, the Sierra Club, the Henry E. Huntington Library, the Yale University Library, the California State Library, the John Muir National Historical Site, the Historical Society of California, the Archives of the American Academy of Arts and Letters, the Reed College Library, and the Columbia University Library.

I beg indulgence from both individuals and institutions for any names I may have inadvertently omitted. I beg, too, that any errors of fact that I may have committed through ignorance or accidence in the following pages may be forgiven. I also trust that I may be credited with having invented no detail in this account of John Muir's life, nor of having intentionally resorted to any dubious source. And now as I close this preface, let me heartily thank Mildred Logan, Associate Editor of the University of Oklahoma Press, for so conscientiously seeing this manuscript through the press.

THURMAN WILKINS

Bandon, Oregon

Prologue

THE forests of America . . . must have been a great delight to God; for they were the best he ever planted. The whole continent was a garden, and from the beginning it seemed to be favored above all the other wild parks and gardens of the globe." Thus, in "The American Forests," an essay of 1897, John Muir evoked the myth of America as Paradise Regained, a trope that echoed the impression Captain Arthur Barlowe, agent of Sir Walter Raleigh, had given in his account of a voyage to North Carolina in 1584. Barlowe had portrayed the New World as a boundless garden of "incredible abundance." But his expansive reaction represented only one pole in antithetical notions of America. When the *Mayflower* rode off Cape Cod in December 1620, William Bradford registered a diametrically opposed impression of the forest that he viewed across the waves—"hideous and desolate wilderness, full of wilde beasts and wilde men."

Optimistic views like Barlowe's were often shattered by the harsh realities of settling America, whereas pessimistic ones like Bradford's prevailed more often than not in the minds of pioneers who faced the primeval forest with fear and aversion, and thus they evolved into the dominant notion that settlers held of wilderness during the forepart of the new country's history. It was an indisputable reality that those on the frontier lived too close to the wilderness to develop any genuine esteem for it, and under such circumstances the hostile cast of their attitude regarding it can be readily understood, as well as the fact that their goal was its total conquest. This goal was nurtured by a crucial component of their view of wild nature—a conviction rejected by John Muir—that the Creator had made nature (trees, plants, minerals, wildlife, indeed all natural objects) primarily for human use, and therefore it behooved people to use nature without stint and without regard for anything except their own benefit. It followed from such an outlook that only those things deemed useful were considered good (or as Cotton Mather put the matter, "What is not useful is vicious"); and since so much of the wilderness did not appear to exist for human benefit, but was perceived as rather a thwarting evil, the advance of the pioneers spelled general devastation for wild nature. In the course of this despoilment, as Muir once pointed out, "The early settlers, claiming Heaven as their guide, regarded God's trees as only a larger kind of pernicious weeds."

Still holding the same general view of nature, subsequent pioneers settled the Far West so rapidly after the Civil War, destroying wilderness wholesale as they advanced, that the census of 1890 found the frontier had ceased to exist by that epochal date. This startling fact was popularized by a Wisconsin professor named Frederick Jackson Turner and his followers, who soon became the dominant historical school of the day, generalizing that the pioneers' struggle to conquer the frontier had led to their developing such romantic and desirably American virtues as independence, manliness, individualism, confidence in the common man, and even the impetus toward democracy.

However that may be, with awareness now dawning on the public consciousness that the frontier was no longer an active factor in American life, a widespread nostalgia began to generate in its favor; and at the same time there emerged a new regard for wilderness (encouraged to a tangible degree by the essays of John Muir), a positive idealization that replaced the time-worn attitude that wilderness was something to be deplored, a reprehensible antagonist of the national hero that Fenimore Cooper's Leatherstocking had long exemplified. Thus, toward the close of the nineteenth century a growing portion of the American people intensified their glorification of the frontiersman on the one hand and his environment on the other, at the ironic moment in history when wild nature had become relatively depleted.

Several historical developments contributed to the reevaluation of whatever wilderness that still remained in the Far West.

First, there were certain postwar physical changes. The booming industrialization that had followed the Civil War, coupled with an exploding birthrate, triggered a shift in population from the rural areas, a movement encouraged by the spread of labor-saving agricultural equipment and by drought in the West. The uprooted farm population made its exodus from the countryside and joined streams of immigrants from Europe in a vast descent upon U.S. cities—a shift that transformed the very fabric of American life. The magnitude of that change is aptly illustrated by the fact that from the period of the Civil War until 1900, the urban population multiplied four times over, whereas the rural population merely doubled.

A concomitant of this gravitation to the city was a hastening of the reaction against the former condemnation of wilderness, while at the same time a tendency manifested itself to project upon the city the antipathy formerly reserved for wild nature. A sentiment of that sort informed the aspersion cast by Horace Greeley in 1871 on the teeming megalopolis in which he worked and which he demeaned as "the living wilderness of New York City." Such reactions against the urban milieu, dirtier and smellier than ever, served to heighten public regard for the wilds as a logical antidote to all the dispiriting conditions of the congested municipalities.

At the same time the crowding of people into the cities produced another reaction—a darkening of the public mood and a profound discontent with a civilization driven by business values and a *laissez-faire* so unrestrained that the acquisitive instinct ran riot and developed what Mark Twain called "an age of money lust, hardness, and cynicism," and—as Twain himself might have added (and Muir emphatically did)—a determination to exploit the remaining wilderness for all the "commodities" it afforded. In reaction, the people beset by this somber mood were ripe for the appeal of all things primitive, certainly for the appeal of wilderness, and at the same time for that of the American Indian, whose perceived virtues of virility, hardihood, and warlike capacity the popular mind had associated with untamed nature. It followed, then, that a change in the public regard for the Indian encouraged a change in the American attitude toward wilderness, and vice versa.

The publication in 1881 of Helen Hunt Jackson's *A Century of Dishonor* and of her novel *Ramona* three years later focused attention effectively on Indians, airing their grievances as they had never been aired before. Jackson's books, moreover, prompted hosts of Americans to join her in actively sympathizing with the native inhabitants (as Muir had learned to do on meeting the Native Americans of Alaska), not in sentimentalizing them according to the noble savage stereotype, but in looking at them with a considerate eye. She identified the main causes of their troubles not as "savageness" but as disease, whiskey, the culture shock of exchanging freedom for the demoralization of reservations, and the frauds perpetrated against Native Americans by white people, not the least of which was the cynical drive launched by the federal government during the Civil War to take possession of Indian western lands by military force.

The compassionate case that Jackson made, besides stimulating timely empathy with the plight of the natives, touched off a stream of books and articles that documented, in the following decades, white America's multitudinous sins against them. At the same time indigenous peoples were studied scientifically by the Bureau of [American] Ethnology, at first under the direction of Major John Wesley Powell. Also, several organizations were launched to promote Indian welfare, and they worked to great advantage. They also fostered white understanding, and the more the white public came to appreciate Native Americans, the better Caucasian Americans felt about the wilderness that they identified with the natives. A more favorable attitude toward the native peoples did its share in paving the way for the wilderness cult that would emerge at the end of the century.

Another development that coincided with the drift to the cities was the reintensification after the Civil War of the long-enduring conflict between science and religion, as a result of delayed reaction to the publication in 1859 of Charles Darwin's *Origin of Species*. The conflict was aggravated considerably by the appearance in 1871 of *The Descent of Man*, undermining as it did

the accepted views of human origin. There was little let-up thereafter in the pressure that Darwinism exerted against the outlook
of traditional religion, for during the Gilded Age and afterward
such effective publicists as Thomas Henry Huxley, Herbert Spen-
cer, John Fiske, and Robert Ingersoll advocated the doctrine of
natural selection more energetically than ever.

To compound the difficulties of orthodoxy, vigorously pursued textual criticism of the Bible, as well as the comparative
study of the other great religions, especially Vedanta and Bud-
dhism, raised numerous questions about the infallibility of the
Christian scriptures. As a result, the cause of religion seemed to
founder for many people, pressed as it was by both science and
scholarship. In 1893 Nathaniel S. Shaler, professor of geology at
Harvard, made a statement highly suggestive of the situation:
"My first contact with natural science in my youth and early manhood had the not uncommon effect of leading me far away from
Christianity. Of late years a further insight into the truths of nature has gradually forced me once again towards the ground from
which I had departed." The pattern of Shaler's experience was far
from unique; for in the face of the pervasive malaise of spirit
caused by the Darwinian and other onslaughts against traditional
religion, wilderness (as well as nature in general) frequently assumed a special value as a restorative to shaken faith. This became
another reason why demands now multiplied for the federal government to protect the last remaining wilderness. Such preservationists as John Muir often spoke of wilderness in terms of "tran-
scendental temples" in which to pray and worship God.

The drift to the cities also ran parallel with the late nineteenth century's burgeoning of nature literature in the United
States, a decisive factor promoting the popularity of wilderness.
One of the most significant events in this development was the
republication of the works of Henry David Thoreau in 1893–94,
with the result that Thoreau received the public recognition that
he had failed to gain during his lifetime. His pleas for the preservation of wilderness (even the establishment of national parks,
which he called "national reservations" in 1858 and which he had
recommended for the protection of wild animals and for the

public's "inspiration") were not lost on his many new readers, and his works assumed the leading position in the contemporary American school of nature writing.

The flowering of nature appreciation that Thoreau's works encouraged grew into a literary groundswell and made a crucial contribution to the advent of the aforesaid back-to-nature cult at the century's turn. A conspicuous component of this surging literary wave was a spate of novels with nature themes, such as *A Kentucky Cardinal* by James Lane Allen, the popularity of which was exceeded only by that of such atavistic narratives as Jack London's *Call of the Wild*. But perhaps the most distinctive part of this nature-oriented groundswell was the natural history essay, a genre that preoccupied scores of writers like Ernest Seton Thompson (or Ernest Thompson Seton, as he also signed himself) and achieved a popularity outdone only by the leading fiction of the day. It reached its zenith in the essays of John Burroughs and John Muir, but as fashionable as the works of Burroughs and Muir might be, neither writer could supplant Thoreau as America's leading literary naturalist.

Meanwhile, the love of wildness preached by the literary naturalists was reinforced by the "wild images" that were now produced by landscape painters who ventured west to carry on the tradition of such pioneer painters of the American frontier as George Catlin, Karl Bodmer, Jacob Miller, and John Mix Stanley. Albert Bierstadt, the first and most prominent of this second wave of artists, visited the Rocky Mountains in 1859 as a guest of the survey party of Frederick W. Lander, and on this expedition he found a subject for his brush that guaranteed the making of a career specializing in gigantic canvases. Bierstadt's inclinations and the demands of the time meshed neatly and led to a full-blown vogue for his enormous panoramas of the Rocky Mountains and the Sierra Nevada, including Yosemite Valley, which he considered his quintessential subject. At the same time, in joining Lander's survey and spending a season in the Sierra Nevada with Clarence King's Fortieth Parallel Survey, he followed a pattern fashionable with other artists as well. For example, Gilbert Munger, afterward lionized in England, spent two seasons—1869

and 1870—with the King survey in Utah and California; and
Sanford R. Gifford, who had toured Europe with Bierstadt as an
art student, passed the summer of 1870 with the U.S. Geological
and Geographical Survey of the Territories under Dr. Ferdinand
V. Hayden.

The year after, Thomas Moran joined Hayden on an expedition to the Yellowstone country, along with the photographer
William Henry Jackson. The watercolor sketches that Moran made
of the natural features there bolstered Jackson's photos as visual
evidence of Yellowstone's grandeur in the campaign of 1872 to
make the region a national park. In 1873 Moran joined the survey
led by Major John Wesley Powell, famous for his epic descents of
the Green and Colorado rivers. The principal result of Moran's
venture with the Powell survey was his immense painting of the
Grand Canyon that Congress purchased for ten thousand dollars
to hang in the Senate lobby along with an earlier panorama that
Moran had painted of Yellowstone, both monumental testimoni-
als that wilderness had at last become a proper object for national
respect. Moran continued to devote his attention to western
wilderness, his canvases finding congenial company in the land-
scapes painted by two artists on the Pacific coast—Thomas Hill
and William Keith, the latter an intimate friend of John Muir.
The work of all such artists demonstrated how, in the later decades of the nineteenth century, landscape painting fortified literature as a means of making Americans aware of the beauties of
their western wilds.

Photography served a similar purpose, often involved with
the western surveys, as Jackson had been with Hayden's expedi-
tions to the Yellowstone country. Jackson remained with Hayden
for several years, going out season after season to photograph
terrain the survey parties mapped and studied, and in the process
he became, according to popular perception, the best photographer of the American West, his collection of negatives reaching a
total of thirty thousand. Timothy O'Sullivan also took remarkable pictures as the official photographer of the King survey, and
Jack Hillers served ably as the photographer of the Powell survey.
On the Pacific coast such picture-takers as Carleton E. Watkins

and Eadweard Muybridge did outstanding work as well, especially when photographing Yosemite Valley. The work of all such photographers aroused wide popular interest, particularly when made into views for the ubiquitous stereoscope, and exerted strong influence in promoting the popularity of the Western scene.

There was at the same time a noticeable correlation between the nineteenth-century movement for wilderness protection and the movement to create municipal parks for the purpose of retaining oases of natural beauty within the cities as countermeasures to urban filth and overcrowding. The city park idea seems to have stemmed from efforts to render cemeteries more attractive. The idea caught on, and in time attractively landscaped graveyards located well beyond the limits of the cities became fashionable places to visit; and in the words of Andrew Jackson Downing, a leading landscape architect, "People seem to go there to enjoy themselves, and not to indulge in any serious recollections or regrets."

The step from landscaped cemeteries of popular resort to landscaped city parks (sometimes with zoos) was a natural one. Already Philadelphia had begun to purchase the land that later became Fairmount Park, four thousand acres in extent. At about the same time Boston had hired a landscape architect to beautify its Common, a former cow pasture; and in Washington, D.C., the wilds along Rock Creek remained unspoiled, waiting to become Rock Creek Park as late as 1890. But the most spectacular effort to preserve natural beauty within a metropolitan area was the creation in Manhattan of the 840-acre pleasure ground of Central Park. It was landscaped between 1857 and 1861 by Frederick Law Olmsted (a student of Downing's), assisted by Calvert Vaux.

Then after a Civil War interim as secretary general of the U.S. Sanitary Commission (the predecessor of the American Red Cross), Olmsted headed west, to become the first chairman of the board of commissioners to administer Yosemite State Park, which Congress had ceded to California in 1864 and which was to become the haunt of John Muir by the end of that decade. Though only a state park and only ten square miles in area, Yosemite emerged in the normal course of events as the real beginning of America's national park system. The second unit of the system, though the first national park to be so designated, was Yellowstone, created in 1872. Unlike the case of Yosemite, the motives of those who secured the establishment of Yellowstone as a national park placed less weight on the aesthetic, cultural, or spiritual merits of wilderness than they did on forestalling private acquisition and exploitation of the geysers and other natural wonders there.

Likewise, the Adirondack Forest Reserve of 715,000 acres was set aside by New York State in 1885, to be "kept forever as wild forest lands," not for the purpose of preserving wilderness, but to insure a steady flow of water for the Hudson River and the Erie Canal. It was only later that the truth dawned on certain perceptive people (to some degree through the stimulus of John Muir's essays) that perhaps the most important value of the creation of both Yellowstone National Park and the Adirondack Forest Reserve had been the preservation of the wilderness within their bounds. Thereafter, the preservation of wilderness, in accordance with Muir's prescription, was regularly made a principal *raison d'être* for all new national parks.

Meanwhile, Olmsted returned to his career as landscape architect, and his achievements aptly epitomized the accomplishments of his entire profession during the postwar era when the city parks conception came of age in response to urban growth of such proportions that it threatened to doom multitudes to lives starved of natural beauty. Olmsted advocated the retention of stands of wildwood outside every city, reminiscent of Thoreau's proposal that every Massachusetts township "have a park, or rather primitive forest, of five hundred or a thousand acres." Thus, the municipal parks movement resonated heartily with the growing appreciation of wilderness in the later decades of the nineteenth century; in the last analysis, the difference between recreation in an urban park and recreation in a national park or wilderness area was largely a matter of degree. The two movements reinforced each other nicely.

Limited area and resources might prevent a city park from providing as much wildness as nature-hungry patrons might desire, and in that case the unsatisfied devotees might find themselves bound for the White Mountains or the Adirondacks or even the western wilderness. Travel in the West had been facilitated by the thirty-four wagon roads that the U.S. Topographical Engineers had constructed between 1850 and 1860 through nine future states beyond the Mississippi. But not until the Pacific railroads were completed did the inundations of sightseers begin. The tourism that the railroads promoted (both the boon and the bane of John Muir) capitalized on the wild and monumental scenery of the West, and as a result of vigorous advertising, the trains brought enormous throngs of visitors to the western wilds, including the brand-new national parks. Tourism, then, proved a powerful means of popularizing wilderness during the latter part of the nineteenth century.

The foregoing developments, variously combined and recombined, led to the century-end rise of the aforesaid back-to-nature wilderness cult. From the first the cult fed on the popular nature fare that abounded—no fewer than fifty periodicals devoted to wildlife had broken into print—and it was closely linked with a contemporary boom in sports and other health-promoting activities such as cycling, hiking, and camping out; and one of its features was a craze for birdwatching, to satisfy which publishers in Boston and New York sold seventy thousand textbooks about birds in half a dozen years. At the same time the cult embraced the shibboleths of manliness and virility and espoused the "strenuous life," as preached by Theodore Roosevelt, who had practiced it in the Bad Lands of Dakota and who in 1888 had helped to organize the Boone and Crockett Club for its sedulous promotion.

The cult's perception that the American wilderness was rapidly disappearing prompted its loud demands for the preservation of the remnants that still survived—demands that coincided with the efforts of a preservation movement that had long been under way and which had helped, in fact, to generate the wilderness cult itself. The movement had its champions, and a leader among them was the reddish-bearded, blue-eyed nature essayist John Muir, who had long preached the benign effects of wilderness. "Climb the mountains and get their good tidings," he had once written. "Nature's peace will flow into you as the sunshine into the trees. The winds will blow their freshness into you, and the storms their energy, while cares will drop away like autumn leaves."

At first Muir's clarion call to preserve remaining wilderness areas remained an integral part of the program of a single fledgling conservation movement. But as time passed, the mainstream of the movement assumed a more and more utilitarian character, usurping "conservation" as its exclusive designation and defining it as a scientific process whereby the nation, through farsighted planning, might wisely and efficiently administer the use of the natural resources of the public domain (timber-cut allocations, multipurpose river developments including those for hydroelectric power, and the controlled management of grazing lands, to name but three representative spheres), all "for the greatest good of the greatest number for the longest time." It would soon become apparent, however, that a fundamental contradiction existed between this gospel of utility, no matter how judicious and restrained, and the call to preserve wilderness intact (with all the wildlife therein) through its being, in John Muir's words, "reserved, protected, and administered by the Federal government for the public good forever." Thus, in the wake of the schism that inevitably developed, the preservationists would persevere only as a separate wing of the conservation movement (especially as the scope of the movement steadily widened), not always distinct in its special identity, but with John Muir ever acknowledged as its most outspoken mover and shaper.

John Muir

CHAPTER I

Dunbar Days

WHEN John Muir was a boy in Dunbar, Scotland, during the 1840s, his high spirits led his father to fear he was "gey daft." Daniel Muir did not realize that John was resolution incarnate and a boy who would never accept defeat. When he was punished—and that was often, for Daniel was a stern disciplinarian—Johnnie never flinched, and Daniel would throw up his hands and say, "The verra Deevil's in yon one." At the same time Johnnie's mother Anne was a kindly woman, whose tender embrace would comfort her son in all his troubles, as when in his third year he thought he had swallowed his tongue. He had told her it was in his stomach, but she had taken him in her arms and answered with a soothing laugh, "Nae, laddie." It was in his mouth, she added, for how could he talk without it? Both parents, however, took skeptical views of Johnnie's growing fondness for "scootchers," the Scottish term for deeds done on a dare.

One scootcher involved the former laboratory of Dr. Charles Wightman, who had owned the Muirs' house, but who had died soon after Daniel bought it. The doctor had left an assortment of retorts and beakers in an upstairs room, the windows of which the Muirs had boarded up because of the excessive Scottish window tax. No one went into the room because of the darkness there. Besides, the Muirs' housemaids claimed that Dr. Wightman's ghost haunted it, a fact that made it a favorite "scootchering" place for Johnnie and his younger brother Davie. On a dare one or the other boy would dart into the darkness and touch a beaker or two, then dart out again before the ghost could show itself.

The boys were particularly proud of another scootcher involving their third-story bedroom. One night Johnnie crept out of the dormer window, held the sill with one hand and dangled over the edge of the slate roof. He put Davie through the same dare and claimed that Davie had also brought it off. Then he climbed to the rooftop of the dormer and sat there with the wind billowing out his nightgown like a sail while he gazed across the fields to the Lammermuir Hills. When he dared Davie to follow suit, Davie did so until he slipped and froze.

"I canna get doon! Oh, I canna get doon!" he wailed.

"Dinna greet [cry], Davie," Johnnie called back. "Dinna greet, I'll get ye doon. If you greet, Fayther will hear, and gee us baith an awfu' skelping [thrashing]."

Johnnie grasped Davie's feet and pulled him down inside the window, but as he did so, both boys were in momentary danger of falling from the roof. On visiting the house a half-century later, John Muir was so impressed by the slickness of the slates and the pitch of the roof that he exclaimed, perhaps to make a good story, that "with all my after experience in mountaineering . . . what I had done in daring boyhood was now beyond my skill."

Johnnie also clambered about the ruins of Dunbar Castle, which stood at the edge of town on the shore of the often stormy North Sea—a castle built a thousand years before by the militant Picts. The castle would receive due notice in *The Story of My Boyhood and Youth,* in the first chapter of which Muir would describe the town of his birth, a "royal burgh" of five thousand people. He would give his impressions of the townsfolk and the environs, including the wild seashore with waves rolling in from the North Sea, and the Firth of Forth stretching away to the northwest in the direction of Edinburgh. There was also Dunbar Harbor with its fishing boats of all sorts and sizes, as well as the outlying moors and meadows, the hills and hayfields—all a colorful backdrop for his young protagonist, the idealized "bairn" named Johnnie Muir. In the Scots dialect his surname Muir meant "moor" or wild expanse of wasteland, a highly apt name for one whose love of all things wild would last throughout his life.

Johnnie was the third child and first son of Daniel Muir and

Dunbar Castle, long the seat of the earls of Dunbar, later the home of Mary, Queen of Scots, and two of her husbands, first Lord Darnley and then the earl of Bothwell. Over these ruins John Muir climbed when a boy. Courtesy of Mr. and Mrs. William F. Kimes. From John Muir Papers, Holt-Atherton Department of Special Collections University of the Pacific Libraries. Copyright 1984 Muir-Hanna Trust.

Anne (or Ann) Gilrye. Anne was the youngest of ten children, all dead of tuberculosis except herself and an older sister named Margaret Rae. Their father was David Gilrye, whose surname was a shortened version of Gilderoy, prominent in the border lore of Scotland. David's wife was Margaret Hay of the proud Hay clan, notable for its distinguished men and for the impending fact that its hereditary chieftain, the Marquis of Tweeddale, would long serve Queen Victoria as Lord-Lieutenant of Scotland.

Daniel Muir, a tall, handsome man, was of mixed English and Highland stock, of the Gordon Clan, but his family was of humble circumstances, and when orphaned and in the care of an older sister, his life was hard. Throughout his youth he had to work on a worn-out croft, then rebelled and ran away from home in his twenty-first year. In adolescence he had joined an evangelical splinter of Presbyterianism and dedicated the rest of his life to an austere Calvinist concept of God. For several years he would move from sect to sect in an effort to find a spiritual home.

Meanwhile, he joined the British army, like his father before him (the first John Muir), and rose to the rank of sergeant-major. His duties brought him to Dunbar as a recruiter. There he met a young woman who had inherited a grain business, which she managed ineptly. Daniel wooed her and, on winning her hand, prevailed on her to purchase his release from the army. He assumed management of the business and, with brisk industry, perseverance, and scrupulous honesty, converted it into a thriving concern. His wife then died, and a year or so later the widowed corn merchant turned his eyes to Gilrye Place across the High Street from his corn store. The object of his attention was the twenty-year-old Anne Gilrye, who became his wife in spite of opposition from her father, a well-to-do retired "flesher," the Scots term for butcher. David Gilrye was a staunch Church of Scotland man, comfortable with established Presbyterianism, and the breach was wide between him and Daniel on religious grounds. "Yon wants a body to think and act his way," David said of Daniel. "An ye don't, he says ye're nae a true Christian."

Anne Gilrye adjusted gracefully to the severe life imposed on her by her husband's hidebound religiosity. John later described her as "a representative Scotch woman, quiet, conservative, of pious, affectionate character, fond of painting and poetry." On another occasion he told a friend that she was "gentle [and] well educated for her time . . . and was an ardent lover of natural scenery. . . . She tried to second [our] father's sternness, and to scold [us] mischievous lads into decorum, but could never really scold, however hard she tried." She was gray-eyed, tall of stature, and strong in her quiet way. She was sustained by an inner calm that kept her unruffled while Daniel bustled and stormed and played the family tyrant. Soon children came, first Margaret in 1834, then Sarah two years later. John was born on April 21, 1838. David came next, then Daniel, Jr., and then twin sisters, Mary and Annie. Later in America would be born the eighth child, named Joanna.

Anne Gilrye Muir, John Muir's mother as she looked in 1863 when she followed John's lead in rebelling against her husband's religious ban on "graven images," interdicted by the Bible. From John Muir Papers, Holt-Atherton Department of Special Collections University of the Pacific Libraries. Copyright 1984, Muir-Hanna Trust.

Meanwhile, Daniel's grain business continued to prosper, while in his spare time he played a violin that he had devised in his youth, gospel hymns and border ballads being his specialty. "My first conscious memory," John wrote years later, "is the singing of ballads, and I doubt not they will be ringing in my ears when I am dying." As the children grew older, they were encouraged to sing, and the whole family gained a local reputation for its musical gifts. All this continued till Daniel's religious zeal crossed the hazy line into fanaticism, leading him to abandon such worldliness as "fiddle" music and even to banish pictorial art, including pictures on the walls, as "graven images" interdicted by the Bible.

In spite of his father's bigotry, a touch of the idyllic characterized the first two or three years of Johnnie Muir's life. His mother was always there as a refuge when difficulties arose. Then, too, there was Grandfather Gilrye, grizzled and beetled-browed, with whom Johnnie walked day after day along the High Street. The old man would point out signs on the buildings and spell out the letters, thus teaching Johnnie the rudiments of reading. His grandfather also taught him how to tell time by naming the numbers on the dial of the townhall clock and explaining how the hands indicated the hours and minutes.

One memory would remain especially clear in John Muir's mind—that of a walk with his grandfather into the countryside to a hayfield, where they rested on a small haycock. Suddenly Johnnie heard "a sharp, prickly, stinging cry." When he called it to his grandfather's attention, the old man said that all he could hear was the sound of the wind. But Johnnie dug into the haystack until he uncovered a mother field mouse with a half-dozen tiny babies clinging to her teats. In that moment the wondrous world of nature began to open for Johnnie Muir.

When going on three, he entered "the auld Davel Brae Skule" of Mungo Siddons, in a gray stone building that bore a curious resemblance to a church. He went dressed in a perky kilt of Gordon plaid with a four-penny primer hanging in a green bag from his neck. He progressed rapidly, having learned his letters from Grandfather Gilrye's informal instruction, and was soon reading stories, some of which, like "Llewellyn's Dog," he read over and over till he had them by heart.

The days at the Davel Brae School, however rewarding, were not without their grimmer moments. It was a cherished principle of Scottish pedagogues that sparing the rod spoiled the child, and so the "taws," a small, thonged whip, was often applied. Whippings were so thorough that John Muir never forgot how the dominies had proved the "all-sufficing Scotch discovery . . . that . . . a close connection [existed] between the skin and the memory, and that irritating the skin excited the memory to any required degree." But frequent thrashings did not stultify Johnnie, nor did the dominies' methods prove otherwise counterproductive. His memory was prodigious, and he soaked up his lessons by seeming to photograph the print of the textbooks on the plates of his mind.

Johnnie's phenomenal memory was exercised at home as well as at school, for Daniel required him to learn the scriptures by heart. Sometimes Johnnie would falter in reciting what he had memorized from the Bible, and then his father thrashed him, having perfected "the Scotch method of making every duty dismal." But as with the taws at school, Johnnie's anger and revulsion did not drive him to rebel. He took his punishment in stride and later claimed that the whippings were "admirably influential in developing not only the memory but fortitude as well." But he would feel hard about the thrashings all his life, and in a letter dated a year before his death, he confessed: "I have good reason . . . to hate the habit of child-beating, having seen and felt its effects in some of their worst forms in my father's house." Notwithstanding his feelings about the "skelpings," Johnnie memorized for Daniel so many daily stints of scripture that by the age of eleven he had learned "by heart and by sore flesh" three quarters of the Old Testament and the New Testament from Matthew through Revelation.

Meanwhile, the playground of the Davel Brae School presented its own special rigors. Fist fights among the scholars occurred there every day. "After attaining the manly, belligerent age of five or six years," Muir later reminisced, "very few of my schooldays passed without a fist fight, and half a dozen was no uncommon number." No doubt this pugnacious atmosphere fostered the extreme contentiousness that would mark John Muir throughout his life, the aggressive hair-splitting that would cause his father to label him "a contumacious quibbler." But this trait would make him "a gude fechter" not only in fights on the playground but also in later battles for the causes close to his heart. Johnnie first earned his reputation as a good fighter while attending the Davel Brae School. He sustained it after moving on at the age of seven or eight to the grammar school of Dominie Lyon next door.

There he learned French, English, and Latin grammar and sponged up the course work in history, spelling, arithmetic, and geography. The natural history selections that he read included pieces by the Scottish ornithologist Alexander Wilson on the fishhawk and the bald eagle of America. He also read John James Audubon's essay on the passenger pigeon in the New World, where flocks stretched for miles and darkened the sky like thunderclouds.

At the grammar school Master Lyon, like Mungo Siddon at the elementary school, applied the taws with great thoroughness, not only for classroom lapses but also for fisticuffs on the playground. The playground afforded informal education that made for the Scottish character of fortitude and endurance. One game in particular would stand out in John Muir's memory in afteryears, a contest in which two opponents bared their legs for lashing with switches of knotweed till sheer pain made one of the boys cry, "Enough!" At other times Johnnie and his schoolmates acted out the deeds of William Wallace and Robert the Bruce. They also enacted the wild exploits of Bothwell, husband of Mary, Queen of Scots, and the flight of Edward II of England to the old castle after the Scots had drubbed him at Bannockburn.

At the castle the boys dared the scootcher of climbing down into the grottoes that had once served as dungeons but were now invaded by the North Sea. Or they scaled the mouldering crags of the castle like the bighorn sheep that Muir would later admire on the summits of California. "I must have been born a mountaineer," he wrote to his mother in later years, "and the climbs and 'scootchers' of boyhood days about the old Dunbar Castle and the roof of our house made fair beginnings." "That I did not fall," he marveled on another occasion, "and finish my rock-scrambling in those adventurous boyhood days seems now a reasonable wonder."

The boys had heard of so many ancient battles fought about the castle walls that they attributed every old bone that cropped up to some antique warrior who had fallen there. In scrambling over the weathered ruins, they never wondered what might happen to their own bones if they should fall, for they had developed climbing skills that defied disaster, although they took chances "that no cautious mountaineer would try." They also ventured chances in a playground operation that bore a resemblance to real warfare and was "greatly more exciting than personal combat." They chose leaders and formed into opposing armies. In winter they found plenty of ammunition in the damp snow that abounded in that season, and in summer they resorted to sand and grass sod. They shouted battlecries like "Bannockburn! Bannockburn! Scotland forever!" and closed for battle. "For heavy battery work," Muir later wrote, "we stuffed our Scotch blue bonnets with snow and sand, sometimes mixed with gravel, and fired them at each other as cannonballs." But all of this was merely child's play, compared with a later and more exciting sport that involved real gunpowder.

In his autobiography Muir described how the "laddies" fashioned guns from old gas pipe and mounted them on lengths of board, how they pooled their pennies for gunpowder and cut up scraps of lead into slugs for bullets. While one boy aimed the improvised gun, another would apply a lighted match to its touchhole. Armed with these weapons, they would troop along the seashore and fire at the gulls and geese that sailed overhead. Sometimes they would dig a hole in the sand and tamp a handful of powder around a makeshift fuse, to which they would warily touch a match. "This we called making earthquakes," John explained. Sometimes they went on a spree and tamped more than the usual amount of powder around the fuse, thereby singeing their hair and giving their faces powder burns they could not wash away. "Then, of course, came a correspondingly severe punishment from both father and teacher."

Daniel Muir took a jaundiced view of the boys' gunpowder games, as well as their clambering over the crags of the castle, their loitering about the harbor or along the seashore, and their forays into the glens of the Lammermuir Hills. He believed no good could come from such unsupervised play, in which the boys' minds might be corrupted, and in which they might pick up bad language (as indeed they did). Daniel ordered them to play in the walled garden behind the house on Saturdays and during vacations. "Play as much as you like [there]," he told them, "and mind what you'll get when you forget and disobey."

The lure of wild nature proved too strong, however, with larks and mavises calling. Disobey they did almost every Saturday and almost every day of vacation, and resigned to the "skelpings" that inevitably followed, they would steal away to join their companions on the beach or in the sunny, green fields. They would spend day after day listening to the skylarks, or running from ten to twenty miles at a stretch along East Lothian roads and lanes, or watching vast storms beat against the rocky headlands of the coast.

On coming home from such adventures—or from school—Johnnie and Davie would join the family for tea. Then they would run across the street with their schoolbooks to Grandfather Gilrye's house. They enjoyed meeting with the old man, for not only did he hear their lessons in a helpful spirit, but he also told them about his life and about their ancestry. He knew there was English in the Muir line, and he may have told Johnnie that he and his sisters Mary and Annie may have received their blue eyes and auburn hair from their English forebears, either on the Muir side or in the Gilrye or the Hay lines. John tended to discount his Anglo-Saxon ancestry, but came in time to sense something English in his heart, for he would fall in love with Milton and the English Romantics almost as much as with Robert Burns.

On February 18, 1849, Daniel Muir interrupted Johnnie and

Davie's session at Gilrye Place. "Bairns," he said, "you needna learn your lessons the nicht, for we're gan to America the morn!" Sometime during the past year Daniel had made the arbitrary decision, evidently without consulting his wife, to emigrate to the New World. His motivation was involved with his having recently joined the Campbellite sect or the Disciples of Christ, often known simply as Christians. The sect had originated in America, where it flourished, one of the many offshoots of the Great Revival. A few converts lived in Dunbar, and what had attracted Daniel to them was their professed aim to revive the simple ways of the primitive Christian Church as they were believed to have existed in the wake of Christ's ministry.

Doubtless Johnnie and Davie had only the haziest notion of the reasons for their father's decision, but how they rejoiced! At school Johnnie had read of maple trees in America that produced the most delicious sugar. He clapped his hands and promised to send their grandfather a box of maple sugar packed in gold dust, for this was the year of the California Gold Rush.

Many times later it would come to Johnnie in America that his grandfather had known whereof he spoke when he had said on giving each of them a gold sovereign, "Ah, poor laddies, poor laddies, you'll find something else ower the sea forbye gold and sugar. . . . You'll find plenty hard, hard work." The hardships the old man foresaw prompted him to insist that, until Daniel had built a suitable house, Anne Muir should remain behind at Gilrye Place, along with Margaret, Dannie Jr., and Annie and Mary. Daniel had made preparations for the voyage, packing great iron-bound boxes with all kinds of paraphernalia, much of it useless, as matters would prove. The largest box weighed four hundred pounds when full and would encumber them like the proverbial albatross throughout the trip.

Daniel Muir, along with Sarah, Johnnie, and Davie, boarded the train next morning for Glasgow, where they took passage on "a blunt-prowed, wave-beating ship" that was moored in the Clyde. The voyage would last for forty-five days, with the seas often so high and wild that Daniel and Sarah remained below deck, seasick, for most of the crossing. Brisk gales struck several times, but the boys, especially Johnnie, delighted in the storms. The light-hearted pair enjoyed full run of the vessel, talking with the sailors and learning about ropes and knots and spars, a new experience, for though they had watched many a ship sail into Dunbar Harbor, this was the first time they had ever been aboard one.

The captain asked them to his cabin, where he inquired about their schooling. He was surprised at how perfectly they pronounced English when they read aloud from one of his books, for Londoner that he was, he did not realize that only pure English was used in Scottish schools. The favor of the captain and crew helped make the days speed by for the brothers, and on April 5 the ship dropped anchor in New York Harbor, which teemed with confidence men and with gold seekers ready to ship for the Isthmus of Panama or to round the Horn for the goldfields of California.

CHAPTER 2

Fountain Lake and Hickory Hill

ONTARIO was Daniel Muir's first destination in America, but several Campbellites aboard ship advised him to forget Canada. If the inclement weather wasn't reason enough, the woods there were so heavy that a man might wear his life away in clearing a few acres. But the compelling reason why Daniel switched his goal to the United States was the news that many Campbellites had settled in the new states of Michigan and Wisconsin, and as Daniel was ambitious to become a lay preacher among the Disciples, he assumed that Michigan or Wisconsin would be a fertile field for his ministrations.

So on leaving New York City, he headed with the "bairns" up the Hudson River to Albany, then along the Erie Canal to Buffalo. There a grain dealer told him that most of the wheat he handled came from Wisconsin, and that information served as the clincher, since Daniel wished to become a wheat farmer himself. After steaming across Lake Erie and up Lake Huron and down Lake Michigan, the Muirs arrived at the thriving settlement of Milwaukee. There Daniel was advised to go to Kingston, a small town a hundred miles to the northwest, where he could find an agent to help him spy out a farm. Daniel hired the help of a farmer who had just sold his crop and planned to return to Kingston with an empty wagon. Daniel paid him thirty dollars to haul their belongings, not only the heavy iron-bound boxes, but also an array of pots and pans, a stove, a harvest cradle, and a scythe, among other things that Daniel had bought along the way.

The farm site that Daniel located in Buffalo Township near the Fox River surrounded a small glacial lake, with water lilies floating gracefully on the water near the shore. There were fish— "pickerel, sunfish, black bass, perch, shiners, [and] pumpkinseeds." Dragonflies flew over the ripples in a glancing dance, and the fish snapped them up whenever they skimmed too near the surface. In an upsurge of long-suppressed poetic fancy, Daniel named the lake Fountain Lake for all the springs that fed it, and the farm itself the Fountain Lake farm. There, until a house could be built, the Muirs moved into a one-story shanty of burr oak logs that Daniel had thrown up with the help of neighbors.

For a few months after their arrival, Johnnie and Davie ran free and unrestrained, immersed in the wonders of Wisconsin. "This sudden plash into pure wildness—baptism in Nature's warm heart—how utterly happy it made us!" John recalled in old age. He would never forget the wild creatures they observed that first summer, in particular the pair of blue jays that mysteriously moved their eggs during the night after the boys had disturbed their nest. Somehow the jays typified the wild creatures with which Johnnie's heart beat in warm rapport that first summer, but there were other things that, in their own special ways, made his first months memorable at Fountain Lake. The pony, for instance.

In Scotland their father had promised the boys a horse in America. As always, Daniel kept his word and bought a pony from a Kingston storekeeper, who had taken him in trade from a Winnebago Indian. Daniel paid thirteen dollars for him, "a stout handsome bay with long black main and tail." It was a bargain, for the pony was docile and obedient, trained to stop the moment one said, "Whoa." Sometimes he stopped so abruptly that Johnnie or Davie sailed over his head. But the boys soon became excellent riders, managing the pony without a bridle or a saddle. They named him Jack, and he became their frequent companion during their first, free summer at Fountain Lake and later whenever they enjoyed any leisure.

Daniel, however, could never forgive the habit Jack developed of nipping the cows on the rump as he drove them to the barnyard. One day Daniel became so exasperated that he threatened to shoot the pony and, before relenting, even sent Johnnie to the house for a gun. Unable to overcome his prejudice against Jack, he finally sold him for a pittance to a farmer to ride to the

California goldfields. The boys felt betrayed; but selling Jack, they decided, was vastly better than shooting him.

One animal Daniel finally did shoot was a puppy named Watch, which the boys had acquired soon after their arrival at Fountain Lake. He was so goodnatured that they often played with him, and on one occasion Johnnie lightheartedly tied his father's bullwhip to the dog's tail. Watch ran off for a romp, and when he returned, the whip was missing. It happened that Daniel was preparing to haul lumber for the new house and needed the whip, and when he asked Johnnie where it might be, Johnnie gave a straightforward answer. His explanation made his father so angry that he sent Davie to the woods for a switch. "The old Scotch fashion of whipping for every act of disobedience or of simple playful forgetfulness was still kept up in the wilderness," John later explained, "and of course many of those whippings fell on me. Most of them were outrageously severe, and utterly barren of fun." But that was not the case on this occasion. Davie lingered over his task and, on coming back, handed Daniel a burr oak sapling ten feet long. Daniel demanded angrily what kind of switch that was. But Davie innocently lowered his eyes, and Daniel merely flung the sapling out of doors.

As time went on, Watch grew overly fond of chickens, and neighbors accused him of raiding their hencoops. Ever a dispenser of justice, Daniel convicted the dog and executed him, and the eight chicken heads found in his stomach sustained the sentence. "So poor Watch was killed because his taste for chickens was too much like our own," John would comment when an old man.

Meanwhile, the first wonderful summer waned, and Daniel put Johnnie and Davie to work helping a Yankee hired man to clear the land. The boys, especially Johnnie, were ordered to haul brushwood grubbed from the "opens" to make plow-land. They fired the heaps of brush, and the piles burned so fiercely that Daniel found in the flames a pretext for religious instruction. "Now, John . . .," Muir would later quote him as saying, "just think what an awful thing it would be to be thrown into that fire:—and then think of hellfire, that is so many times hotter."

But the exhortation had little effect on Johnnie, whose heart was filled with "the heavenly fire of faith and hope" that banished all thought of dying, much less of going to hell.

In the meantime, throughout that first summer and fall, the carpenters Daniel had hired worked hard on the new house, an eight-room, two-story frame building that would long be acknowledged as the best house in the township. It was ready for the Muir reunion in November when Anne and the other children arrived. They settled down in the new quarters, which Sarah had fitted out with lace curtains and decorated with asters and goldenrods. The household routine was resumed as before, and the family situation remained fundamentally unchanged, with Daniel ever playing the tyrant and Anne the refuge, loving and ready to comfort the children.

It was inevitable, in such a situation, that the children's psychology should be affected. Davie was rather a coward in contrast with Johnnie. But the latter did not escape a certain psychological distortion at his parents' hands. Johnnie continued to welcome the comforting arms of Anne Gilrye as an anodyne to his father's thrashings and had, over the years, developed what twentieth-century psychologists would call a rather pronounced Oedipus complex. He would ever appreciate "mothering," and there would always be older women ready to serve as surrogate mothers.*

---

*Muir's first substitute mother seems to have been a neighbor, Mrs. Jean Galloway, the mother of David Galloway, who became Johnnie's brother-in-law upon marrying Sarah in 1856. Then came Mrs. Frances Pelton of the Mondell House at Prairie du Chien. Then there was also Jeanne C. Carr, wife of Professor Ezra S. Carr, and the woman who, as some would say, was the love of John Muir's life, exerting more influence over him than anyone else except his parents. The idealized devotion he bore Jeanne Carr was only palely reflected in his relations with other women ready to mother him, Professor Catharine Merrill of Indianapolis, for instance, or Mrs. A. G. Black (the wife of the Yosemite hotelkeeper, who, Muir wrote in 1874, "has fairly mothered me"), or Mrs. Clara McChesney of Oakland, a sympathetic woman who protected him as earnestly as a mother from rumors of involvement with not only Mrs. Carr but also Elvira Hutchings of Yosemite—rumors that threatened to burgeon into scandal. But the crux of this matter was that he did not marry until middle age and then found it hard—at least at first—to give his full love to his wife, Louie Wanda Strentzel. The seeds of such difficulty were probably sown in his childhood and adolescence, as when Anne Gilrye's mothering recommenced on her arrival from Dunbar.

The Muirs would cultivate the Fountain Lake farm for eight years, during which time the soil wore out, so that when David Galloway and Sarah took over the farm in 1857 it would gouge them for fertilizer to keep the land productive. While the farm remained in Daniel's possession, Johnnie, as the oldest boy, did more than his share of the heavy work, though Davie was kept busy too, and even the older girls had to toil in the fields, to the detriment of their health. John worked from morning till night; that meant a thirteen-hour day in wintertime. Years later, in his autobiography, he would put the matter pointedly: "We were all made slaves through the vice of over-industry."

Roused from bed at six in winter, Johnnie would ease his chilblained feet into his frozen boots, then fall to such chores as feeding the horses and cattle, fetching water from a nearby spring, and bringing in wood for the kitchen stove—all prebreakfast chores. After a frugal meal the more taxing labors of the day began, like building fences and chopping trees. The time for rising was even earlier in the summer—four o'clock for a seventeen-hour day—and "when we arose from our clammy beds," John later recollected, "our cotten shirts clung to our backs as wet with sweat as the bathing-suits of swimmers, and remained so all the long, sweltering days." He would add that their work was extra hard in summer—"mowing, hoeing, cradling wheat, hauling it to the barns, etc. [We had] no rest in the shade of trees on the side of the fields. When tired we dared not even go to the spring for water in the terrible thirst of the muggy dog-days, because the field was in sight of the house and we might be seen." Daniel made it his practice to sit by the window while reading his Bible.

Not even illness exempted the young Muirs from the farm labor. "We were held to our tasks as long as we could stand," John later wrote. He recalled that once he had suffered from mumps and could swallow only milk; but though weakness made him reel and fall among the sheaves, his work was in no way lightened. "Only once," he remembered, "was I allowed to leave the harvest field—when I was stricken down with pneumonia." Yet Daniel refused to call a physician, for he believed "that God

and hard work were by far the best doctors." Through that
doctrine of hard work, Johnnie had been put to the plow when
he was twelve, his head barely reaching above the plow handles,
but his competitive spirit drove him to rival the hired hands, so
that in time no one else could plow a straighter furrow. For years
thereafter it would be his lot to do the lion's share of the plowing. But he was also, as he later recalled, "foolishly ambitious to
be first in mowing and cradling, and by the time I was sixteen [I]
led all the hired men."

The same determination he showed as a field worker was
exemplified to a remarkable degree by an incident at Fountain
Lake, where he had learned to swim by imitating the frogs. It
happened on a Fourth of July, one of the few holidays that Daniel
allowed his children, and Johnnie celebrated it by going swim-
ming. After a turn in shallow water he decided to try a deeper
part of the lake, and there he met with trouble. "I sank, strug-
gling, frightened and confused," he wrote. He managed to gain
the surface, "but before I could breathe enough to call for help,
[I] sank back again and lost all control of myself." He sank and
rose several times, then sucked some water into his lungs and
began to drown. Suddenly, then, he remembered that he could
swim underwater like a frog; and doing so, he made his way
toward the shore. At last his feet touched bottom, and he could
bring his head above water and call for help.

This incident proved so humiliating that the next day Johnnie
returned secretly to the lake and dove repeatedly into the deepest
water. Each time he dove he shouted, "Take that!" Never again,
he claimed, would he lose control of himself in water, and it was
his firm belief that "never was victory over self more complete."

The discipline illustrated by Johnnie's repeated diving into
Fountain Lake was the same that enabled him to accomplish a
measure of reading and study under the harsh conditions of his
life in Wisconsin. Schooling for him there had been nonexistent,
except for two or three months at a log house called the Eddy
School. But it was his good fortune to have a few friends with
literary interests, especially the "Twa Davies," as he called David
Taylor and David Gray.

Sometime in 1854, along with the Twa Davies, Johnnie had helped to build a corduroy road over a morass called Weird Slough. During the project Johnnie was captivated by the lilt of the poetry that "the Twa" recited while they worked. They encouraged him to memorize poetry, especially the verse of Milton, the English Romantics, and Robert Burns. They also encouraged him to read novels, in particular those by Charles Dickens and Sir Walter Scott. But neither poetry nor fiction was part of the parched routine of the Muir household, and except for Milton, Johnnie had to read such matter on the sly. Daniel declared that such books were "the spawn of Satan, the Deevil's ain buiks o' lies."

Understandably, this proscription of reading touched off a minor rebellion in Johnnie against his father's bigotry, and he borrowed forbidden books from friends. Two such volumes were travel accounts by Mungo Park and Alexander von Humboldt, works that fascinated him; and in his enthusiasm he read a passage from Park's *Travels in the Interior of Africa* to his mother. Responding to his excitement, she said, "Weel, John, maybe you will travel like Park and Humboldt some day." Daniel overheard her remark and expostulated vehemently: "Oh Anne! Dinna put sic notions in the laddie's heed." Daniel's opposition merely fanned John's appreciation for works like those of Park and Humboldt, an enthusiasm that grew the more he rebelled against Daniel's condemnation of books.

Another cause for rebellion occurred when Daniel rode Nob, a favorite workhorse, so hard to reach a camp meeting on time that it developed pneumonia and died a lingering death. John was incensed that a Christian could treat a horse so cruelly. Compared with this outrage, Daniel's offense in selling Jack seemed trifling. In judging his father, John acted on a principle that had crystallized in his mind that dumb animals were "earthborn companions and fellow mortals." Daniel's religiosity had much to answer for, not merely for his callous treatment of animals, but also and especially for his incessant flogging of his "bairns" for their souls' sake. John's views against cruelty to children had grown unshakable, and he later wrote to a friend: "When the rod is falling on the flesh of a child, and, what may oftentimes be worse, heartbreaking scolding falling on its tender little heart, it makes the whole family seem far from the Kingdom of Heaven. In all the world I know of nothing more pathetic and deplorable than a heartbroken child, sobbing itself to sleep after being unjustly punished by a truly pious and conscientiously misguided parent."

In 1855, when John was seventeen, a further cause of tension between him and his father occurred when Daniel bought a piece of land twice as large as the Fountain Lake farm. For John it would be hardly less than a disaster, since opening a new farm would mean more of the same grinding toil—"heartbreaking chopping, grubbing, stump-digging, rail-splitting, fence-building, barn-building, house-building"—that had already stunted his growth, or so his tall family believed. They called him the "runt of the family," for he was only five feet nine inches tall.

In 1857 the Muirs moved to their new farm, called Hickory Hill. But there was no water at hand, and to make some available for the house that had been built on the low, sloping hill that gave the farm its name, a well had to be dug, and to be near the house it had to be dug on the hill itself. As the oldest son, John was assigned the job of digging it. At first the task was easy enough—digging through ten feet of topsoil, but after that he had to contend with a fine-grained sandstone. After blasting ineffectually with gunpowder, it became necessary to chip out this rock with a hammer and a mason's chisel, requiring that John pound away day after day in all ill-ventilated shaft, a yard or two across. Into this he was lowered and out of it he was drawn up in a wooden bucket by Daniel, who merely gave orders and never once went down into the shaft, a fact that would rankle in John's mind for years to come.

After chipping away for months, John reached the eighty-foot level, ten feet before he would strike "a fine, hearty gush of water"; and here he met with near disaster. It was customary on being lowered to the bottom of the shaft for him to put the chippings of the previous afternoon into the bucket to be hauled up. But on this occasion carbonic acid gas or "choke-damp" had collected in the well, and on breathing it he grew faint. His silence alerted his father, who called down: "What's keeping you so still?"

"Take me out," John gasped.

"Get in the bucket," Daniel ordered, "and hold on."

John lost consciousness as his father hauled him up; and when he was visited in his sickroom by William Duncan, a neighbor who had been a miner and a stonemason in Scotland, he described the accident to the ex-miner. "Weel, Johnnie," Duncan said, "it's God's mercy that you're alive. Many a companion of mine have I seen dead with choke-damp, but none that I ever saw or heard of was so near to death in it as you were and escaped without help." Duncan promptly showed them how to flush the well of the poisonous fumes, so that John might resume his chipping.

After the well was dug, the endless work of opening the Hickory Hill farm resumed, the hardest work falling on John as the oldest son—grubbing brush, burning brushwood, girdling and felling trees, digging out stumps—all the weary labor that had worn him down at the Fountain Lake farm. Later interminable rail-splitting occupied any time he had free from plowing and planting. "Father," he once suggested, "was not successful as a rail-splitter."

It was a pleasure to outdo his father—a double pleasure to outdo him at his own game and argue him down on some religious point. This John sometimes did, as when Daniel tried to foist on the family the fad of vegetarianism and graham or whole wheat bread that he had taken up. He insisted that meat be banished from the table. Anne Gilrye resisted, but Daniel remained unyielding until John pointed out that Jehovah had bade the ravens bring not only bread but also *flesh* to Elijah in his hiding place beside the Brook Cherith. "And the ravens brought him bread and flesh in the morning," John quoted, "and bread and flesh in the evening; and he drank of the brook." Since Daniel held the Bible as the final authority on every matter, he yielded in his demand, but perhaps threw in the aside he had used on other occasions that John was "a contumacious quibbler, too fond of disputation."

Sometime along the way, and during his scant spare time, John began a serious study of mathematics. "I [had] learned arithmetic in Scotland without understanding any of it," he wrote, "though I had the rules by heart." Now he reviewed arithmetic, working out problems on chips of wood from chopped trees, and went through algebra, geometry, and trigonometry one after another. Such study led him to a fascination with the pendulum, which gave him the secret of the clock. He constructed several clocks, and they were original enough to be called "inventions." But they were not his only inventions, for he made creative use of the time he gained when his father gave him permission to rise as early as he wished.

John had persisted in reading after family worship, and on growing tired of ordering him to bed night after night, Daniel had added one evening, "If you *will* read, get up in the morning . . . as early as you like." The next morning John sprang from bed and rushed downstairs to see how much time he had won. The kitchen clock said one o'clock, and that meant he had gained five hours. "I can hardly think of any other event in my life, any discovery I ever made that gave birth to joy so transportingly glorious as the possession of these five frosty hours." But at one in the morning in an unheated house in the dead of a Wisconsin winter, it was much too cold to read, as John had intended; it was necessary to keep physically active merely to keep warm.

In the cold John retreated to the cellar, with its tools brought from Scotland, and there by candlelight he worked on his inventions, to which he had first applied himself at Fountain Lake. Now came the model of a self-setting sawmill that he had devised in his head. The sound of his labor disturbed Daniel, whose bed stood directly above John's working space, but in view of the permission he had given his son, two weeks passed before he asked what John was doing down there. Making things, John replied, because it was too cold to read. "I did not vary more than five minutes from one o'clock all winter," he later wrote, "nor did I feel any bad effects whatever [from] so little sleep."

Among his clocks was one huge enough to be seen from the fields if mounted on the barn, as John had intended, but that

Daniel forbade, because it might attract too much attention from the neighbors. Another of John's inventions was an enormous thermometer, constructed from a three-foot iron bar, whose contraction and expansion were multiplied by a series of hoop-iron levers. He mounted this instrument on the side of the house, where it proved sensitive enough to register the heat from an observer's body when approached within five feet.

John's inventory of inventions included "water-wheels, curious doorlocks and latches, thermometers, hygrometers, pyrometers, clocks, a barometer, an automatic contrivance for feeding the horses at any required hour, a lamplighter and firelighter, [and] an early-or-late-rising machine." One of his clocks, whittled from shagbark hickory, was "shaped like a scythe to symbolize the scythe of Father Time," and to its pendulum he gave the shape of a bunch of arrows to suggest the flight of time. But no doubt the most spectacular application of the clock was in what he called his "early-rising machine."

This was a mechanism that tilted his bed upright at an appointed moment, tipping him to his feet and making in the process such a racket that it woke the entire family. It was the din of the early-rising machine that caused John's father to ask what on earth he had made. John replied that he didn't know what to call it. It had several purposes, "but getting people up early in the morning is one of the main things it is intended for; therefore it might . . . be called an early-rising machine."

At this point John's destiny seemed to lie with invention, and William Duncan, the ex-miner, encouraged him to display a sampling of his work. "Now, John," he said, "if you wish to get into a machine-shop, just take some of your inventions to the State Fair, and you may be sure that as soon as they are seen they will open the door of any shop in the country for you."

But they were only made of wood, John protested.

"What does it matter what they're made of when they're so out-and-out original?" Duncan exclaimed. "There's nothing else like them in the world."

Duncan's praise encouraged John to take his advice, though he could expect no support from his father. True to form, Daniel had a lecture ready: "[He] tried to assure me," John later wrote, "that when I was fairly out in the wicked world making my own way I would soon learn that although I might have thought him a hard taskmaster . . . , strangers were far harder." But John was ready to face the world. With the gold sovereign his grandfather had given him in 1849, and with another gold coin from his mother, and with about ten dollars he had earned from raising wheat on a patch of abandoned ground, but with nothing from Daniel (who said, "No; depend entirely on yourself"), John set out with three of his inventions—two clocks of shagbark hickory and a thermometer made from an old washboard. David drove him in a farm wagon to the railroad station at Pardeeville, nine miles from Hickory Hill. It was 1860, a year that not only marked a crossroads in John's life but was also a portentous one for the United States. Abraham Lincoln had been nominated for the presidency, and the Civil War loomed over the horizon.

CHAPTER 3

Madison Years

SOON several townsfolk of Pardeeville collected around John's inventions, speculating on their purposes, and one yokel decided that the larger clock was "a machine for taking the bones out of fish." Later the inventions aroused so much enthusiasm on the train that John won the privilege of riding the cowcatcher to the capital. There at the Temple of Art in the state fair grounds, he was welcomed by the superintendent and assigned space in which to display his devices. Their success with the fairgoers was immediate, a reporter from the *Wisconsin State Journal* noting on September 25, 1860: "While at the Fair Grounds this morning we saw some very ingenious specimens of mechanisms, in the form of clocks, made by Mr. JOHN MUIR, of Buffalo, Marquette County. . . . We will venture to predict that few articles will attract as much attention as these products of Mr. Muir's ingenuity." Another newspaper, the *Evening Patriot,* was even more enthusiastic, concluding that the devices "could only have been executed by genuine genius."

Both notices reached Hickory Hill almost at once, and just as promptly Daniel fired back a characteristic letter exhorting John to beware of vanity. John claimed that he had scarcely glanced at the notices, but of the incident he later wrote, "Strange to say, father carefully taught us to consider ourselves very poor worms of the dust, conceived in sin etc., and devoutly believed that quenching every spark of pride and self-confidence was a sacred duty, without realizing that in so doing he might at the same time be quenching everything else."

Meanwhile, the early-rising machine, which John assembled on the spot, using one of his clocks, was his most spectacular success, with the young sons of Professors Carr and Butler of the

state university vying with each other for the excitement of being
turned from bed at an appointed moment; and when Mrs. Carr,
the professor's wife and a judge of the exhibits, arrived at John's
display, she was impressed enough to recommend a special award.
The citation of the awards committee read: "The clocks presented by J. Muir exhibited great ingenuity. The Committee
regard him as a genius in the best sense, and think the state
should feel pride in encouraging him." John was under no illusion about the significance of his inventions; yet, as he later remarked, they "opened all doors for me and made marks that have
lasted many years, simply, I suppose, because they were original
and promising."

One door they opened was that of an inventor named Norman Wiard. Wiard had developed a steam-powered iceboat, with
which he hoped to open winter travel on the ice-bound upper
Mississippi. His machine shop and foundry were located at Prairie du Chien, a hundred miles west of Madison; and if John
would go there and serve as mechanic on the *Lady Franklin,* as
the boat was called, Wiard would give him instruction in mechanical drawing, training in the foundry, and the use of an ample collection of technical books. Naively, John rejected several
more substantial offers in favor of Wiard's proposal and rode to
Prairie du Chien on the iceboat, which was mounted on two flat-
cars. For weeks the boat held the public spotlight. But its promise
exceeded its performance. On its maiden trial, as well as on two
subsequent ones, it failed. Moreover, John received only one lesson in mechanical drawing and found the foundry work as dull as
farm labor.

No doubt the best thing to happen to him at Prairie du Chien
was his having taken a room at the Mondell House, a center of
the town's social life, where the young people accepted him tol-
erantly regardless of his acting like a prig in condemning their
kissing games. He did chores for his room and board at the
Mondell House. There, too, he formed a close friendship with
Mrs. Frances Pelton, the proprietor's wife, who became a kind of
substitute mother for him, neither the first nor the last. John also
took a lukewarm interest in her niece, Emily Pelton, a relation-

ship that would come to nothing beyond their remaining long-time friends. But kind as the Peltons were, he decided after a few months to return to Madison, where the University of Wisconsin beckoned from its hill above the fair grounds.

For the last twenty years or so the United States had enjoyed an era of intellectual ferment and discovery. Natural science had flourished, its principal medium of publication being the *American Journal of Science and Arts,* usually called "Silliman's Journal" after Benjamin Silliman, its founder and first editor. There was also much scientific popularization, especially in the fifties, when lectures and lyceums flourished and when increasing numbers of books and magazines were published. The leaven produced by such developments had long been quietly at work when John returned to Madison in January 1861.

At the same time the political situation in the United States had grown more ominous. As the inauguration of Abraham Lincoln approached, confusion grew in Washington in direct proportion to secession sentiment in the South, where seven states were ready to join a new Confederacy before March 4, 1861, the date on which Lincoln was due to take the oath of office. The obvious drift toward war would reach its climax on April 12 with the shelling of Fort Sumter in Charleston Harbor; after which President Lincoln would call for seventy-five thousand volunteers, an act that would edge Virginia and three other wavering states into the Confederacy, insuring that the die would be cast.

The attention of Wisconsin, like the rest of the nation, was rivetted on those dire events, and in Madison the state legislature would pause on May 1 to review a Wisconsin military unit uniformed in flamboyant Turkish style, and the enthusiasm would mount so high among the university students that eight of them withdrew from classes that day to enlist. John would feel no sympathy for their zeal; he would remain a convinced pacifist and consider the Civil War a stupid tragedy, as uncalled for as all the fratricidal strife of Scottish history.

Meanwhile, John took various odd jobs at Madison. "I was thus winning my bread," he later wrote, "while hoping . . . to make money enough to enter the State University. This was my

ambition, and it never wavered." One day a student told him that
he could board himself at the university for as little as a dollar a
week. Thereupon he nerved himself for an interview with the
acting chancellor, Professor John Sterling. He learned that tu-
ition for a twenty-week term came to only thirty-two dollars, in
addition to ten dollars for room and fuel.

There was no admission problem. John entered the preparatory division, taught by the same faculty who taught the college-
level courses. But because of his excellent schooling in Scotland,
his effective spare-time reading and study, his prodigious memory, and his general maturity, he did not have to stay there long.
Within a few months he joined the 180 students who constituted
the student body of the university. He was classified as a freshman in the scientific program, but he never became a regular
student. "Instead [I] picked out what I thought would be most
useful to me," he later wrote, "particularly chemistry, which
opened a new world, and mathematics and physics, a little Greek
and Latin, botany and geology."

In afteryears Jeanne Carr would confirm that instead of taking the regular program he "daintily picked such crumbs of literature and science as suited his needs." One of the rare certainties
of the incomplete registrar's records is that during his two and a
half years at the university John was never considered more than a
first-year student. But he worked diligently at his courses, those
in science under Professor Ezra S. Carr and those in the human-
ities under Professor James Davie Butler.

Though he had left home looking like a bumpkin in home-
made clothing, he was not ill dressed at the university whenever
he chose to spruce himself up; for before he left Prairie du Chien,
Daniel had relented and sent him a small trunk of "store-bought"
clothes. But his beard had grown so shaggy that a fellow student
had advised him to burn it off. The beard, of course, helped to set
him off as a character, whose gaucheries were exemplified by an
incident at a reception at Professor Sterling's house. The workings
of a grand piano there so piqued John's curiosity that he climbed
inside the instrument for a closer look. Such eccentricities, however, did not demean him in the estimate of his fellow students, as

shown by a revelation made to his brother David in later years by an alumnus who described John "as hero of the university," about whom the students had developed "traditions."

Notwithstanding his popular esteem or his store-bought clothes, John was so impoverished that he was forced to subsist on graham crackers, an occasional baked potato, mush, and water. "When I was in college," he later remembered, "I nearly starved. I lived on fifty cents a week, and used to count the crackers." Yet the deficiencies of his diet did not prevent him from excelling in his studies, especially in chemistry. According to his roommate, Charles E. Vroman, "He was acknowledged by common consent to be the most proficient chemical student in [the] college." To supplement the university's inadequate laboratory, John fitted up one of his own in his second-floor room at North Hall, buying the chemicals, beakers and other items from his own meager resources.

In time John's room became as much a campus showplace as he was himself a campus character. Students and professors alike visited it and even brought guests. "The room was lined with shelves, one above the other, higher than a man could reach," Vroman would remember. "These shelves were filled with retorts, glass tubes, glass jars, botanical and geological specimens, and small mechanical contrivances. On the floor, around the sides of the room, were a number of machines of larger size, whose purposes were not apparent at a glance."

One of these was the "loafer's chair," innocent looking, as if inviting visitors to take their ease. But its appearance was deceptive; under the seat was concealed an old horse pistol, charged with a blank cartridge. When the innocent guest sat down and leaned back, he would activate a hidden spring that pulled the pistol's trigger. Up he would start at the sudden explosion, provoking hilarious laughter. John had rigged up a signal system to alert students next door that a "verdant-looking chair victim" had arrived, so that they might "happen in" to enjoy the sport. John himself was vastly amused by it, being, according to Vroman, "a keen participant in frolics and college pranks."

Of continued interest was the early-rising machine, but its

The intricate "study desk" that John Muir invented in 1861 while a student at the University of Wisconsin at Madison. It is now on permanent display at the State Historical Society of Wisconsin. Courtesy of the State Historical Society of Wisconsin, neg. no. WHi(D487)9783.

noise disturbed the sleep of John's neighbors. At their complaints he discontinued its use. But if it now fell into eclipse, he devised sometime in 1861 his most intricate invention, the climax of all so far, his "study desk." It stood on slender legs whittled into the shapes of tiny books. Its slanted top involved a bisected wheel that worked in connection with smaller cogwheels underneath to move a cart filled with texts John wished to study. At a set moment a clock in the desk would buzz, and the desk went into operation. The book previously studied dropped into the cart below. Then the next book was pushed up into place, where it remained as long as John had allowed for that particular lesson. It was his practice to load the cart with volumes, then set the mechanism for a prescribed period for each book. His roommate later remembered how Muir would sit "as if chained, working like a beaver against the clock and the desk."

What most intrigued Jeanne Carr on her visit to John's room, however, was a device to measure the growth of plants. For the experiment he had chosen a Madeira vine that flourished in the sunniest window of his room. He had threaded a needle with a long hair of a female student, and according to Mrs. Carr, it "made the record faithfully upon a paper disk marked to indicate minute spaces with great exactness." It chronicled the growth of a climbing stem for each hour of the day, with motive power supplied by one of John's whittled clocks.

No doubt what contributed most to Mrs. Carr's admiration for John's device for measuring the growth of plants was her love of botany, a devotion suggested by a friend, who described her as "a young, pretty woman with tawny hair, a sweet expression and a charming voice [who] was always going about botanizing." Without question her delight in plants helped cement the affinity that would develop between her and John; and the same was true on his part, for though he was not yet a formal student of botany, he had loved plants and flowers since his Dunbar days. But an even more important stimulus to his response to her was the attractiveness of her personality and character. She was a native of Vermont, well educated and remarkably gifted, and everyone considered her a social and intellectual leader in Mad-

Jeanne C. Carr, whom Muir met in Madison, Wisconsin, in 1860, and who became his guide and confidante both in Wisconsin and in California, exerting unrivaled influence over him. Courtesy of Alfred A. Knopf.

ison. As their friendship grew, she would encourage John to read more literature, especially the works of the Transcendentalists (she happened to be a personal friend of Ralph Waldo Emerson); and in other ways she would become John's guide and mentor, even kindling in him the later drive to become a published author.

But their relationship soon became more than intellectual. They were drawn to each other emotionally, more so perhaps on

her part; for it may well be, as Frederick Turner suggests, that
"John Muir was the great love of Jeanne Carr's life." For John's
part, since she was twelve years his senior, now in her middle
thirties, she was one of his surrogate mothers, no doubt the most
beloved of all, his "spiritual mother," as he called her.

His success as Dr. Carr's student, his friendship with the son
who had helped demonstrate the early-rising machine at the state
fair, but above all the feeling he had inspired in Jeanne Carr made
him a welcome visitor at the Carr house. He might indeed have
become a permanent lodger there, had Jeanne Carr had her way.
As she later wrote, "I was anxious to make him at home in my
family; and would have felt it a privilege to do so, for the benefit
of my children, but no quail ever hid her nest more effectually—
or [more] truly enjoyed its privacy." But if John shied from living
in their house, he yet accepted the Carrs' encouragement to
spend his leisure reading in their well-stocked library.

There he first encountered the works of Emerson and Thoreau, a prelude to his thorough study of them years afterward.
There, too, he probably read Louis Agassiz's *Études sur les glaciers* and *Système glacière,* for he remembered the French he had
learned in Dunbar well enough to read the language. In the Carr
library he may have first met with *Origin of Species,* though he
did not read it intensively until years later. Darwin had broken on
the world too recently for his theory to be yet current in the
American hinterlands; but under Professor Carr's guidance John
learned its basic principles and accepted them to the point of
recognizing that the earth was dynamic, with its species still
developing. This meant, he perceived, that creation had taken
place in such a way that it could be better understood through a
study of science than by a close reading of Genesis. In this spirit
he probably read at the Carr library other extracurricular books,
probably mostly of a scientific character, that would help to
shape his career.

Professor Carr, "a handsome, clean-shaven man in his early
forties," had been trained as a physician; but after teaching medicine for a while he had turned to chemistry and geology. He had
attended Louis Agassiz's lectures on glaciology at Harvard, but

his chief claim as a geologist was his recent service on James
Hall's geological survey of Wisconsin. Besides Lyell's *Principles*
and the works of transitional geologists like Edward Hitchcock,
Dr. Carr assigned to his geology class the reports of the latest
state geological surveys. But above all he stressed personal field
work, the actual examination of the land and its features for
whatever story they had to tell. The glacial relics of Wisconsin
seemed of special interest to him, and the field trips on which he
took his students opened for John a lifetime fascination. "I shall
not forget the Doctor, who first laid before me the great book of
Nature," he wrote to Mrs. Carr two years after leaving the university. "He has . . . shown me where mines of priceless knowledge lie and how to reach them." John was thus acutely aware of
his intellectual debt to Dr. Carr. But in the long run he realized
that the influence of the doctor's wife was far, far greater.

Mrs. Carr's enthusiasm for botany notwithstanding, John credited his introduction to that science not to her but to a fellow
student named Milton Griswold. One day in June 1862, after
John had returned to the university from a stint of school teaching ten miles away (necessitated by a lack of funds), he met
Griswold under a large locust tree near North Hall. The tree was
in bloom, a fact that prompted Griswold to exercise his penchant
for imparting gratuitous information on botany; and in *My Boyhood and Youth* John would claim that what Griswold revealed to
him that day marked a turning point in his life. Plucking a locust
blossom, Griswold asked, "Muir, do you know what family this
tree belongs to?" John shook his head. Griswold then asked what
flower the locust blossom resembled, and John suggested that it
looked like a pea flower.

"That's right!" Griswold said, adding that the locust belonged to the pea family, and he immediately began to expatiate
on the common features of (and the interrelationships between)
such plants as the pea, bean, and vetch. His talk aroused a deep
interest in John, especially when Griswold demonstrated how to
identify a specimen by pulling it to pieces, noting each part, and
then shuffling through the analytic tables of a botany manual.
To be able thus to classify plants into species, genus, and order

underscored a lesson Dr. Carr had driven home in his science courses—that the whole world was unified by harmonious design. John told his student friend that what he had demonstrated was "perfectly wonderful." Then he added, "I am going to get me a Botany at once."

Griswold's lesson sent him to the woods and meadows in search of "plant glory." "I wandered away at every opportunity, making long excursions round the lakes, gathering specimens and keeping them fresh in a bucket in my room to study at night after my regular class tasks were learned." And when John went to work for David Galloway later that summer, he would set out before the day's chores began to search for flowers to classify after the day's work in the fields was over. The sorting and classifying, with help from the copy of Wood's *Botany** that he had bought in Madison, would last until midnight. Heretofore his "daftness" over flowers had stemmed from their outward beauty. "Now my eyes were opened to their inner beauty," John wrote, "all alike revealing glorious traces of the thoughts of God, and leading on and on into the infinite cosmos."

Except for this new enthusiasm for botany, John Muir might have become a medical doctor. The possibility of entering that profession was much on his mind during his later days in Madison, as a result of the Civil War as he saw it manifested in and around the university. Not long after the fall of Fort Sumter the fair grounds had been transformed into Camp Randall, filled with tents and drilling men and soon surrounded by saloons and brothels. Irregular though John himself might be in his church attendance, he had become zealous early in the war in a kind of religious commitment, ministering to the young men in uniform. He read the Bible to them, prayed with them, and counseled them against the temptation of the bars and bordellos.

But as the war wore on, the camp filled with sick and wounded soldiers from the battlefields. Illness increased from the messes of tainted sowbelly and the hardtack crawling with weevils. In addition many soldiers came down with smallpox and typhoid fever,

---

*Alphonso Wood, *Classbook of Botany* (New York: Barnes and Burr, 1861).

John Muir's first photo-
graph, taken in 1863 at
the end of his studies at
the University of Wiscon-
sin and before he "ske-
daddled" to Canada to
avoid the draft. From
John Muir Papers, Holt-
Atherton Department of
Special Collections, Uni-
versity of the Pacific Libraries. Copyright 1984
Muir-Hanna Trust.

and the hospital was crowded to overflowing. John continued his
ministrations, disheartened over the plight of the men he sought
to help. As a consequence, he felt he must do something personally to help alleviate human misery and so decided to become a
physician. The University of Wisconsin had no medical school,
however; and so he made plans to take the medical course at the
University of Michigan at Ann Arbor.

John remained in Madison through the spring semester of
1863, when a new development disturbed his mind, the prospect
of the draft. Lincoln had found it impossible to fill the gaps in

the Union armies with volunteers, so a conscription bill had been engineered through Congress. John duly registered, and the drawing began on July 13, 1863, an event so unpopular that it provoked a bloody riot in New York City, where aroused mobs destroyed the draft headquarters and gutted the offices of the *New York Tribune*. To John's relief his name did not come up, and it was also passed over in subsequent drawings.

But after a long botanical and geological excursion down the Wisconsin River valley into Iowa, John found the conscription situation had changed. Sometime in February Lincoln had ordered another draft, the drawing to commence on March 10; and John dared not risk the chance of his name coming up on this occasion. There were too few eligible men remaining in his region, and convinced pacifist that he was, the thought of having to kill revolted him to the very core. So after a spell of helping David Galloway with farm work at Fountain Lake, he decided to "skedaddle" to Canada, where his brother Daniel had gone before.

A further reason for his decision was that no letter had ever reached him from Ann Arbor on whether he had been accepted for the medical school there. But the fundamental reason was that he considered himself more Scottish than American, as indeed he was (he would not become an American citizen until he was sixty-five years old). He even thought seriously of shipping back to Scotland. "My Scottish highlands," he had written two years before, ". . . can have no substitute. *Scotland* alone will ever be Scotland to me. My love for my own Scottish land seems to grow with every pulse so that I cannot see the name or hear it but a thrill goes to every fiber of my body." But on March 1, 1864, he caught the train at Portage, bound for Canada and "the University of the Wilderness."

CHAPTER 4

Canada and Indianapolis

IT would appear that, when John Muir "skedaddled," he struck out directly for the Canadian border, proceeding through Michigan to Sault Sainte Marie, where he crossed into Canada with his copy of Wood's *Botany* and a volume by Humboldt in his pack. He was swashing about the Ontario swamps as early as April 1864, and some time thereafter occurred the highlight of his Canadian experience—his finding the rare orchid *Calypso borealis* or "Hider of the North." This discovery produced an epiphany-like effect that he would treasure for the rest of his life.

He lost no time in describing the blossom to Jeanne Carr, who passed his letter on to Professor Butler; and after adding a remark or two of his own, the professor sent John's description to the *Boston Recorder.* Forty-five years later Muir would indicate that "as far as I know [these] were the first of my words that appeared in print." Then he went on to describe the discovery once again—how he had splashed through a great tamarack swamp all day and begun to despair of reaching dry land before dark. "But when the sun was getting low and everything seemed most bewildering and discouraging, I found beautiful Calypso on the mossy bank of a stream." The isolated snow-white flower impressed John as the acme of "simple purity" and as "the most spiritual of all the flower people I had ever met." He was so overcome with emotion that he knelt beside it and wept from the fulness of his joy.

By May he had penetrated the wilderness as far as Simcoe County, Ontario, beginning on May 18 a three-week tour of some three hundred miles through both Simcoe and Grey counties. Between June and the end of August he continued to botanize through the southern reaches of Ontario, zigzagging in his course like a butterfly, the only disconcerting thing to happen to him being a brush with wolves in a grove of maple trees. Their dismal howling wakened him near midnight one night when his fire had burned low. He quickly rose to build it up again, and to judge from their long-drawn howling some of the wolves were close at hand. "But the nearest of all," Muir later wrote, "was much [closer] than I was aware of," for through the bushes illuminated by the rebuilt fire an enormous gray wolf rushed past him so alarmingly nearby that he involuntarily hurled at it a branch that he had picked up to feed the flames. That ended all sleep for the night. But it was the only time in Muir's Canadian wanderings that "the deep peace of the wilderness [was] savagely broken."

The last of August found him botanizing near Niagara Falls, and on September 2 he met his brother Dan there. The meeting had been prearranged by their family, who had mailed to each the whereabouts of the other. Thereafter they roamed the wilds together, interrupting their study of plants to work temporarily for a pittance, living on loaves of bread they bought from house-wives in lonely cabins. That autumn a letter from their mother overtook them, announcing another draft. Not only on her own authority but also on Daniel's, she ordered Dan, still a minor, to remain in the safety of Canada. Then she pleaded with John to stay with him, and Muir gladly complied.

During their wanderings Dan suggested that they go to a place where he had worked on first coming to Canada, a factory combined with a sawmill that was located near Georgian Bay. On reaching the bay, Muir was impressed with "the forests about its shores with their ferny, mossy dells" and decided that the region was a location favorable for study. So in need of money and content to remain for some time in the vicinity, he and Dan applied for work in the factory.

The owners, William Trout and Charles Jay, welcomed Dan back and soon recognized John's value as a mechanic. The fac-tory, situated near the small town of Meaford, needed a new addition, and its construction was the first work to be done. The Muir brothers helped until the late spring of 1865, when Dan returned home, the war having come to an end. John himself considered returning to the university at Madison, but finally stayed on at Trout's mill, where after a brief botanical excursion he signed a contract to produce thirty thousand broom handles for a company in Toronto. At Muir's suggestion the contract authorized him to make improvements in the plant's machinery and in recompense to receive half the profits that such improvements might bring in. By February 1866 he matured designs for a more efficient lathe and a mechanism to bore rake teeth. "It was a delight to see those machines work," William Trout later declared, himself the holder of several patents. When finished, the thirty thousand broom handles, along with twelve thousand rakes, were stored for seasoning in every niche and corner of the factory.

On the night of March 1, 1866, a storm blew sparks from the chimney of Trout's log house onto the factory roof. The wind fanned them into flames, and before they were discovered, the building was ablaze and soon burned to the ground. Trout and Jay invited Muir to help rebuild it, offering him a partnership, but he declined, having differed with them on how to worship God and claiming to love nature too much to remain in work "that involves the destruction of God's forests." The partners gave a note for his share of the burned rakes and broom handles, and between them, they raised cash enough for his fare back to the United States.

Muir chose Indianapolis as his destination, because it was an important rail center with machine shops where a mechanic could find work. Besides, it lay in the heart "of one of the richest forests of deciduous hardwood trees on the continent," a forest ideal for botanizing in one's spare time. He soon found a job at a factory for carriage parts, a firm known as Osgood, Smith & Co., "full of circular saws and chucks and eccentric and concentric lathes," so that he felt entirely at home. The firm, said to be the largest company of its kind in the country, advertised as its specialty the Sarven patent wheel.

Muir assumed charge of a circular saw, at ten dollars a week. His mechanical skill led by the weekend to his taking charge of all the circular saws, with wages raised to eighteen dollars a week.

Soon afterward he suggested a mechanism to produce parts of the Sarven wheel automatically. In addition he proposed improvements in the wheel itself. As a result his wages went up to twenty-five dollars a week. "Circumstances over which I have had no control," he wrote to his sister Sarah, "almost compel me to abandon the profession of my choice, and to take up the business of an inventor." At the same time he took pains to spend Sundays in the hardwood forest that surrounded the city.

By summer the Carrs and Professor Butler had opened social doors for him in Indianapolis by arranging that he meet the prominent Merrill-Moores family. Butler had written to tell the middle-aged spinster Catharine Merrill, one of the first women professors in America, that if she would only go into the fields with Muir, she would find that "Solomon could not speak more wisely about plants." Intrigued, she invited Muir to the Merrill house, where he was met by her young nephew, Merrill Moores. Moores later remembered that "a tall, sturdy man with blue eyes and a clear ruddy complexion . . . asked if Mrs. Moores and Miss Merrill lived there. He had a marked Scotch accent . . . and he at once impressed me as the handsomest man I had ever met."

Muir made an equally favorable impression on Catharine Merrill, and when she went to the woods with him, she found Professor Butler's claim was true. Thereafter she and her sister, Julia Merrill Moores, took Muir up enthusiastically. He became a frequent visitor, entertaining them with tales of his Canadian adventures. He also described his work at Osgood, Smith and the machine he had invented there that could "automatically make wooden hubs, spokes and felloes and assemble them into a fully completed wheel, lacking only the metal tire to be attached by hand." They asked if he had taken out a patent on his device.

"No," he replied, "all improvements and inventions should be the property of the human race. No inventor has the right to profit by an invention for which he deserves no credit. The idea of it was really inspired by the Almighty."

Catharine Merrill soon brought together a company of youngsters and adults to follow him into the forest every weekend. When asked to teach a Sunday school class, he agreed, provided he could do so in his own way, not as Bible study, but as nature study with the woods and the fields as classroom and such thoughts of God as trees, grass, rocks, and flowers as the subject matter. He had come to prefer reading about God in the details of nature, he would say, rather than in the Bible. He scintillated out of doors, but in the parlor, on realizing that he was the intended center of attraction, he grew shy and reticent and would soon leave. "It's too bad," Mrs. Moores once said after the other guests had departed. "They will never realize how wonderful he is."

Judson Osgood and Samuel Smith fully realized his worth, however, and remembering his original explanation that he intended to stay only long enough to earn funds sufficient to finance a tour of South America, they resolved to keep him by "progressive inducements." This led in the fall of 1866 to their selecting him, as their most perceptive employee, to make a detailed time-and-motion study of the plant. Muir detested waste of any sort, and so, although he had no model to guide him, he accepted the assignment and became a pioneer efficiency expert. He made a thorough study of operations throughout the plant. Belts and saws, lathes, and the men who ran them preoccupied him completely.

Sometime in December he gave Smith and Osgood the results of his survey, his data having taken the form of two charts. The first and smaller one, called "Beltology," reported on the devitalizing effects of temperature variations on leather held under tension. The chart also pointed out the loss of energy caused by worn belt joinings. The second, entitled "Chart of One Day's Labor," analyzed the fluctuations in a day's productivity—how work began poorly in the morning before the men were ready "to take hold." It then reported the tapering off before and after the noon break. But by far the worst decline occurred in the early evening. "Lamplight labor," Muir concluded, "is not worth more than two thirds daylight labor"—prescience, perhaps, of the eight-hour day.

Muir's time-and-motion study must have pleased Osgood and Smith, for as another inducement to keep him, they hinted of an eventual partnership. But if Muir seemed destined to settle down as a master mechanic and inventor, a stroke of dismal luck on March 6, 1867, changed the course of his life forever. As usual, he worked into the evening on that date. A new belt had stretched during the day's operation and had to be tightened. Muir began to loosen the lacings with the tang end of a file, but his hand slipped, and the tang pierced his right eye at the edge of the cornea. Stunned, he walked to the window, with his eye covered by the hollow of his hand. Dim light glimmered through the pane, and in the muted illumination he could see the aqueous humor leak into his cupped palm. In a few moments the sight of the injured eye faded completely, and he was heard to murmur, "My right eye is gone, closed forever on all God's beauty."

He managed to walk home. "But in a few hours," he wrote, "the shock sent me trembling to bed, and very soon by sympathy the other eye became blind." The next day a local doctor concluded that Muir's right eye was doomed, but that sight would in due time return to the left. This diagnosis was later modified by a specialist brought by the Merrill family to evaluate Muir's condition. After his examination the European-trained oculist declared, "You are young and healthy, and the lost aqueous humor will be restored and the sight also to some extent; and [with] your left eye after the inflammation has gone down and the nerve shock is overcome—you will be able to see about as well as ever." Indeed Muir did recover his sight as predicted, though there would remain a permanent cast in his right eye.

Meanwhile, many friends visited him in his darkened room, including Osgood and Smith, who came to tell him that they were planning to build a new shop and place him in charge of it. Catharine Merrill and the Mooreses also came to see him, and he chatted with children of his Sunday school class; and when more light was permitted in his room, they took turns at reading to him. It was a time of stocktaking, too, and he resolved conclusively to leave the factory. He was on the wrong track, he concluded. He needed to make a fresh beginning and get on with his real career, the study of nature. "I could have become a millionaire," he later said, "but I chose to become a tramp." He dwelt on plans for a walking tour through the southern states to study the flora there, and flourishing anew was his old ambition to explore the tropical forests of the Amazon, an aspiration well expressed by his exclamation, "How intensely I desire to be a Humboldt!" Then when his eyesight had improved enough for regular letter-writing, he informed the Carrs, "I read a description of the Yosemite Valley last year, and have thought of it almost every day since." Thus, California also became a place he dreamed of visiting, and that reminded Jeanne Carr of how a psychic friend had prophesied that John Muir would eventually land in Yosemite Valley.

On leaving his room in April 1867, he made a heartening trip to the woods, whose beauty confirmed his decision to leave the factory. In this determination he must have felt reassured by the letter he now received from Jeanne Carr. "I have often in my heart wondered what God was training you for," she wrote. "He gave you the eye within the eye, to see in all natural objects the realized ideas of his mind. He gave you pure tastes and the sturdy preference of whatever is most lovely and excellent. He has made you more an individualized existence than is common, and by your very nature, removed you from common temptations. He will surely place you where your work is." Wherever his work might be, John remained certain that it was not at Osgood, Smith; and so he finally resigned his position there and in the company of eleven-year-old Merrill Moores set off on a walking tour to Portage, Wisconsin, where David had gone into business and where John demonstrated how rude he could be when so inclined.

The demonstration occurred after David had introduced him to a fundamentalist minister, who in the course of their conversation put down the theory of evolution by haughtily declaring that he had never seen a chair evolve into a chairman. John abruptly turned his back on the parson and refused to speak to him for the rest of the evening. He made it clear that his purpose in returning to Wisconsin was not to humor stupid preachers but to spend some time with his family before setting out on his ramble through the South and, as he hoped, through the rain forests of the Amazon, his return to the University of the Wilderness.

CHAPTER 5

The Thousand-Mile Walk

"I never tried to abandon creeds or code of civilization," John Muir jotted on the flyleaf of a book; "they went away of their own accord, melting and evaporating noiselessly without any effort and without leaving any consciousness of loss." He probably underestimated the stress of the process. But his reaction against Campbellism and the shackles of creationism did not mean abandonment of his profound belief in God. It simply meant that Muir was no longer concerned with fundamentalist Christian dogma and would remain so for the rest of his life. He would ignore church and seek in nature the fulfillment of his religious impulse, leading to a notable measure of mysticism.

Predictably, his emerging "creedless" attitude brought greater censure than ever from Daniel on John's visit to Hickory Hill in the summer of 1867. Daniel considered his son's preoccupation with science a blasphemy, and they constantly clashed. It made no difference that John perceived God in every detail of nature. "Father," he shot back on one occasion, "I've been spending my time a lot nearer the Almighty than you have!" The final break came at their parting on a steaming day in August when Daniel interrupted John's farewells to his mother and sisters. "My son," he blurted out, "hae ye nae forgotten something?"

"What have I forgotten, Father?"

"Hae ye no forgotten to pay for your board and lodging?"

John was startled, but he quickly handed his father a gold coin. Then he said quietly, "Father, you invited me to come for a visit. I thought I was welcome. You may be very sure it will be a long time before I come again." Indeed the two would meet again only when Daniel lay upon his deathbed.

On September 2, 1867, John began his walk to the Gulf of

Mexico, after a journey by rail to Jeffersonville, Indiana. He crossed the Ohio River and strolled through the city of Louisville. A few miles beyond the limits of the city he spread his map on the ground and "rough-hewed" a course, his plan "simply to push on in a general southward direction by the wildest, leafiest, and least trodden way I could find." Specifically, the route of his "floral pilgrimage" would lead through Kentucky, Tennessee, the western tip of North Carolina, Georgia, and Florida.

He now opened a journal by writing on the inside cover of a medium-sized notebook, "John Muir, Earth-Planet, Universe." The journal, Muir's first surviving one, resulted from Professor Butler's advice to keep a "commonplace book," and it would be edited after his death by his literary executor William F. Badè and published as *A Thousand-Mile Walk to the Gulf.* Besides daily events, it recorded a new set of values that crystallized during Muir's long walk and shaped the pattern for his development as a zealous apostle of nature. Meanwhile, he observed at the outset of his excursion, "I bade adieu to all my mechanical inventions, determined to devote the rest of my life to the study of the inventions of God"—a pithy augury of his career to come.

As was his custom throughout his wanderings, he traveled light. Aside from his plant press, he carried all his belongings in a rubberized bag—a change of underwear, his journal, some soap, a towel, a comb and brush, his map, and four books: Wood's *Botany,* the New Testament, *Paradise Lost,* and Burns's poems.

On September 9, after a visit to Mammoth Cave, he bade goodbye to leafy, green Kentucky. The next day he came to the Cumberland Mountains of Tennessee, the first genuine mountains his feet had ever trod. He toiled upward for six or seven hours; then on more level ground a lone horseman overtook him and asked where he had come from and where he was going. The rider then offered to carry his bag. Muir replied that it wasn't a burden, but the stranger was so insistent that John finally yielded; whereupon the rider spurred his horse forward and, as soon as he thought he was out of sight, began to rummage through the contents. He was so disenchanted with what he found there,

The route of John Muir's thousand-mile walk to the Gulf in 1867, based on the map published in his volume *A Thousand-Mile Walk to the Gulf.*

however, that when Muir overtook him he handed the bag back
and rode abruptly off the way he had come.

Muir now discovered that the war had all but depopulated
the land between the Cumberlands and North Carolina. Lodgings were hard to find, and often he had to sleep in the open air.
One evening he was lucky enough to secure the hospitality of a
shaggy, dark-haired blacksmith, whose wife had prepared a supper of cornbread and bacon. After saying grace, the blacksmith
looked across the table and asked, "Young man, what are you
doing down here?"

Muir replied that he was studying plants, at which the blacksmith expressed dismay that a seemingly strong-minded man
could do nothing "better than wander over the country and look
at weeds." Seeing that his host was a religious man, Muir said,
"You are a believer in the Bible, are you not?"

"Oh, yes," the blacksmith answered.

Then take Solomon, Muir suggested. He was a strong-minded
man, but thought it well enough to study plants. "We are told
that he wrote a book about [them], not only of the great cedars
of Lebanon, but of little bits of things growing in the cracks of
the walls." But John's clincher was the advice of Jesus: "Consider
the lilies of the fields, how they grow."

Evidently that convinced the blacksmith that gathering plants
was a legitimate occupation. But he suggested that Muir was ill-
advised to cross the Cumberlands on foot. The war was over, true
enough, but roving guerillas made the mountains far from safe.
He advised Muir to give up his walking tour until the South
became more orderly again.

The next day the blacksmith's warning appeared to be well-
founded. Near sundown Muir saw ten horsemen riding abreast.
They reined up and watched him, their unkempt hair reaching to
their shoulders, their horses looking worn and jaded. There seemed
no way to avoid them, so Muir moved boldly forward, and after
walking a hundred yards or so beyond them he glanced back and
saw that all ten had turned their horses in his direction and were
apparently debating whether it would be worth their while to
rob him. They did nothing, however, perhaps because the leaves

protruding from Muir's plant press gave them the impression that he was only "a poor herb doctor," not worth holding up.

On September 12 Muir started down the eastern slope of the Cumberlands. He reached Kingston in the upper Tennessee Valley before dark, and from there, in order to lighten his load, he shipped to his brother Dan all the plants he had collected so far. Two days later he caught his first full view of the Great Smokies, the highest mountains he had yet seen. Before the next nightfall he reached the cabin of an elderly hunter, who said in answer to his request for lodgings: "Well, you're welcome to stop if you think you can live till morning on what I have to live on all the time." The old man proved to be a lively raconteur, with tales of deer hunts, "b'ar" hunts, gold mines, and other curiosities of the Smokies. He invited John to stay "a spell" with him, and so Muir remained for two days, botanizing and scrambling about the mountains.

When John made ready to leave, the old man cautioned him as the blacksmith had of dangers ahead, but Muir was not deterred from resuming his tour. On September 19 his path followed the winding bank of the Hiwassee River, whose "forest walls" he described as "vine-draped and flowery as Eden." He crossed the southwest corner of North Carolina into Georgia, finding that "his known flower companions" were deserting him not merely one by one as in Kentucky and Tennessee, but in entire genera, while at the same time he met countless companies of "shining strangers." He headed for Savannah, which he reached on October 8. He had instructed Dan to send a hundred dollars to him there, money he had left in his brother's keeping, but found no word from home. So as he was nearly out of funds, Muir spent that night at the "meanest-looking lodging-house" that he could find.

The next morning he went to the express office again, but still no funds had come from Dan. Then Muir walked down a white shell road to the Bonaventure Cemetery, half-enclosed by the tidal salt marshes of the Savannah River and bordered by live oaks draped with Spanish moss. As he could no longer afford even the cheapest lodging, he decided to camp among the tombs.

That decided, he returned to the city and spent his last dollar there on a supply of crackers. That night he pillowed his head on a grave, but mosquitoes and the beetles that crawled across his face kept his sleep from being as "sound as that of the person below."

The following day he constructed a bower of sparkleberry bushes in which to sleep. He went to the city every day for six days before Dan's draft arrived. Meanwhile, his crackers ran out, and hunger made him so lightheaded that all the trees seemed to run around in circles and all the roadside streams seemed to run uphill. In this curious state of mind it appeared to him that, for a place of death, the cemetery was remarkably full of life, and he noted the living creatures in his journal, beginning with the bald eagles that screamed over the salt marshes. "Bonaventure is called a graveyard," he wrote, " . . . but the few graves are powerless in such a depth of life."

The more closely one looked at nature, he decided, the clearer it appeared that the opposition of life and death dissolved and they seemed aspects of one fundamental unity, one beautiful cyclical process, life springing from death and death the goal of life. Thus, he now repudiated what seemed a customary Christian belief that death was something to be feared. "On no subject are our ideas more warped and pitiable than on death," he wrote. ". . . We are taught that [it] is an accident, a deplorable punishment for the oldest sin, the arch enemy of life, etc. Town children, especially, are steeped in this death orthodoxy, for the natural beauties of death are seldom seen or taught in towns." What he wrote on the subject had been a commonplace in English poetry since the Graveyard School, but it represented a breakthrough for Muir, another advance in his revolt against the religious doctrines of his boyhood and youth. In nature could be found balm for the fear of death, and he continued, "Let children walk with Nature, let them see the beautiful blendings and communions of death and life, their joyous inseparable unity, as taught in woods and meadows, plains and mountains and streams of our blessed star, and they will learn that death is stingless indeed."

In his meditations on death Muir had accepted his own death, so that his stay at Bonaventure had provided an important turning point in his life. But on receiving his draft from Dan, he was ready to move on, ready for Florida, once he had satisfied his gargantuan hunger.

In order to avoid the ubiquitous swamps of southern Georgia, he took passage on a coasting steamer to the "rickety town" of Fernandina at the northeastern tip of Florida. He found that state too "watery and vine-tied" to traverse in his usual pathless fashion, so he struck off along the roadbed of a railway that ran from Fernandina southwestward to Cedar Key, his destination on the Gulf Coast. On the way he frequently left the embankment to examine exotic plants and flowers, like the impressive *Magnolia grandiflora*. "But the grandest discovery of this great wild day," he wrote on October 15, "was the palmetto," which inspired him to philosophize: "They tell us that plants are perishable, soulless creatures, that only man is immortal, etc.; but this, I think, is something that we know very nearly nothing about. Anyhow, this palm was indescribably impressive and told me grander things than I ever got from human priest."

The next day he discussed alligators with a cracker who lived beside a stagnant pond. In crossing Florida John would see only one of these grotesque creatures, though his informant assured him they were common in the swamps. He had a dread of meeting them, but that did not keep him from assigning the alligator a respectable niche in his reordering of the human-centered Christian view of the world. In his journal he wrote, "Many good people believe the alligators were created by the Devil, thus accounting for their all-consuming appetite and ugliness." But this notion went against his grain in his zeal to prove the harmony of nature, and his contradiction of it was explicit. He argued that "doubtless these creatures are happy and fill the place assigned to them by the great Creator of us all. Fierce and cruel they appear to us, but [they are] beautiful in the eyes of God."

Later a deer hunt he witnessed gave him a peg on which to hang another antianthropocentric sentiment. When the deer escaped in an unpredicted direction, the hunter called it the "d———dest deer that ever ran unshot." "To me," Muir coun-

tered in his journal, "it appeared as 'd———dest' work to slaugh-
ter God's cattle for sport. 'They were made for us,' say these self-
approving preachers; 'for our food, our recreation, or other uses
not yet discovered.' As truthfully we might say on behalf of a
bear, when he deals successfully with an unfortunate hunter,
'Men and other bipeds were made for bears, and thanks be to
God for claws and teeth so long.'" He added that in case of war
between wild animals and "Lord Man," he would be inclined to
"sympathize with the bears."

At Cedar Key, which Muir found to be an empty port, he was
told on October 23 that a lumber schooner would soon sail from
there to Galveston, Texas, and that he could secure information
about it at the sawmill of Richard Hodgson. There would be no
ship for two weeks, Hodgson said, but meanwhile if Muir wished
to wait, he could be used at the mill. John accepted the job, but
three days later a fever that he had felt coming on for several days
broke "like a storm." In returning from Cedar Key he collapsed
and lay unconscious for several hours, and when he finally reached
the mill in the early hours of morning, the nightwatchman assumed he was drunk and refused to help him. Fortunately, Muir
reached his bunk under his own power and, on turning in, fell
into a deep coma. "I awoke at a strange hour on a strange day,"
he wrote. He heard Hodgson ask someone beside him whether
he had spoken yet, and when the answer was no, Hodgson added,
"Well, . . . keep pouring in quinine. That's all we can do."

Muir was not sure how long he had lain unconscious. The
Hodgsons had taken him from the bunkhouse into their home,
where Mrs. Hodgson could oversee his care. From near death he
had graduated to invalid status, suffering severe "dropsy," night
sweats, and such weakness that he found it easier to crawl than
walk. He remained an invalid for several weeks, often lying inert
under a moss-draped liveoak. But in time he regained strength
enough to wander feebly along the beach or to float leisurely in a
dinghy among the keys, where he studied the numerous water
birds.

He waited for health and—"like Crusoe"—for a ship, the
lumber schooner having come and gone during the period of his

coma. While he waited, he returned to his journal with new attacks on anthropocentrism. "The world, we are told, was made especially for man—a presumption not supported by all the facts. A numerous class of men are painfully astonished whenever they find anything, living or dead, in all God's universe, which they cannot eat or render in some way what they call useful to themselves." Such men, in Muir's opinion, were liable to have an unacceptable image of God. What was more, they were liable to have a "precise dogmatic insight" into his intentions, "and it is hardly possible to be guilty of irreverence in speaking of *their* God any more than of heathen idols." Muir went on to describe that deity in words that sound rather like those of Mark Twain at a later date.

"[God] is regarded as a civilized, law-abiding gentleman in favor either of a republican form of government or of a limited monarchy; believes in the literature and language of England; is a warm supporter of the English constitution and Sunday schools and missionary societies; and is as purely a manufactured article as any puppet of a half-penny theater." Muir then pointed out that along with such ideas of the Creator it was inevitable that there would be unacceptable ideas of creation. And what were some of those ideas? Well, sheep meant "food and clothing 'for us'"; whales were merely "storehouses of oil for us"; hemp's *raison d'être* was to serve mankind as "ship's rigging, wrapping packages, and hanging the wicked." "Cotton is another plain case of clothing. Iron was made for hammers and ploughs, and lead for bullets; all intended for us." At the same time all things inimical to people were dismissed as "unresolvable difficulties connected with Eden's apple and the Devil."

As a corrective to the Lord Man fallacy Muir suggested the proposition that "Nature's object in making animals and plants might possibly be first of all the happiness of each one of them, not the creation of all for the happiness of one." It was then but a step to his animistic corollary of the sentience of plants and minerals, a notion that smacked of an atavistic reversion on Muir's part, but it was an insight destined to take its place as a conspicuous tenet of his philosophy of nature. Thus, Muir conceded life not only to every creature but also to everything else in the world, a magnification of the extent of life that gave added point to certain questions he was prone to raise. "What creature of all that the Lord has taken the pains to make," he asked, "is not essential to the completeness of that unit—the cosmos?" He admitted that humanity was necessary for the universe to be complete, but he added that "it would also be incomplete without the smallest transmicroscopic creature that dwells beyond our conceitful eyes and knowledge." The shift from anthropocentric to the biocentric vision that such an insight inspired would remain the core development of Muir's thinking, to become likewise the central impulse of the preservation movement he would help to found.

One evening in early January 1868 Muir climbed onto the roof of the Hodgson house to watch the sunset, and there in the glitter of the Gulf he saw the white sails of a schooner putting into Cedar Key. In spite of his weakness, he hurried to the harbor and learned that the ship, the *Island Belle,* would sail for Cuba as soon as the winds were right. He engaged passage, for he still cherished his Humboldtian dream. Though the Hodgsons protested that he was still too weak to travel, he boarded the *Island Belle* the next morning.

A few days later the schooner sailed into Havana Harbor and dropped anchor in the lee of the Morro Castle. During the following month Muir passed his nights on board, while during the daylight hours he studied shells and flowers along the Havana beach or visited the botanical garden in the city. He also visited every shipping agency in Havana, but could not discover a single vessel bound for South America, so he decided to go to the cooler climate of New York City, where he knew he could find a ship for California, the next best destination after South America. Sometime in the middle of February the captain of the *Island Belle* pointed out a trim schooner loading oranges for New York, and with characteristic promptness Muir engaged passage.

CHAPTER 6

First Summer in the Sierra

MUIR did not tarry in New York City. On March 6, 1868, he boarded a small steamer for Panama. The ship was overcrowded and the voyage so unpleasant that he dismissed it with the contemptuous remark, "Never before had I seen such a barbarous mob, especially at meals." In pleasant contrast, however, he considered the trip by rail across the riotously wooded isthmus to Panama City as all too short. From the wharf at that city a small launch carried him out to the steamship *Nebraska,* riding in the bay, and by March 27 she brought him to San Francisco, a port that bustled with commerce and a glorified *laissez-faire,* or what Muir would later term "the gobble gobble school of economics." But he had no desire to remain and savor either the city's commercial atmosphere or its postvigilante law and order.

The next day he started for Yosemite with a young cockney named Joseph Chilwell, who called Muir "Scottie" and whom he had met aboard ship. On Market Street they encountered a man with a kit of carpenter's tools, and Muir asked him the best way out of town. "Where do you wish to go?" the carpenter asked. "Anywhere that's wild," Muir replied; whereupon the carpenter directed them to the Oakland ferry.

Since time was no problem, Muir rejected the regular route to Yosemite for one that took them to Gilroy and thence over Pacheco Pass, resounding with the calls of California quail. At the top of the pass they gained their first view of the San Joaquin plain and the Sierra Nevada, the mountains Muir would later call the Range of Light. "As far as I could see," he wrote, "lay a vast level flower garden [as] smooth [as] a lake of gold—the floweriest part of the world I had yet seen."

After making their way through "this greatest of flower gardens," Muir and Chilwell crossed the San Joaquin River, then followed the Merced River in an easterly direction. Their route took them through Coulterville, once a thriving mining town, and there an Italian storekeeper warned them of bears and deep snow ahead. They were not surprised, then, at having to flounder through snowfields six feet deep. But at last they reached the rim of Yosemite Valley, and into view came Bridalveil Fall. Not realizing that it was a wonder he had read about, Muir said, "See that dainty little fall over there. I should like to camp at the foot of it to see the ferns and lilies that may be there. It looks small from here, only about fifteen or twenty feet, but it may be sixty or seventy." In reality Bridalveil Fall had a drop of over six hundred feet.

They met other surprises in the valley, but Muir left no record of their experiences, except that they visited the various falls and highpoints about the walls and sketched and botanized among the ferns and flowers. Evidently, he was not prepared for the valley's stupendous dimensions. "Oh, no, not for me," was how he would remember his first reaction, and he later informed Jeanne Carr that "the magnitudes of the mountains are so great that unless seen and submitted to a good long time they are not seen [or] felt at all."

Meanwhile, after eight or ten days in the valley, Muir and Chilwell left by way of Wawona and the Mariposa Grove of Big Trees. The *Sequoia gigantea* there (now reclassified as *Sequoia-dendron giganteum*) far surpassed their expectations. "The longer we gazed," Muir wrote, "the more we admired." They camped in the grove for "long uncounted days," then moved down to Snelling on the now torrid San Joaquin plain.

"This Yosemite trip," Muir later wrote, "only made me hungry for another far longer and farther reaching, and I determined to set out again as soon as I had earned a little money." To that end he and Chilwell took temporary jobs on the ranch of Thomas Eagleson. Now free of malaria, Muir could manage well the rigorous work in the fields and so remained in the area after Chilwell bade him goodbye. It was true that he still yearned to emulate Humboldt in the rain forests of South America or even to explore "the palmy islands of the Pacific [or] the plains of

Mexico, . . . but," he concluded, "the attractions of California were yet stronger than all others, and I decided to stay another year or so." Whereupon followed stints then of breaking mustangs, shearing sheep, and running a ferry; and when autumn arrived, he became a ranch hand for Pat Delaney, a tall, rawboned Irishman with "a sharply hacked profile like Don Quixote's." This work lasted until late November, when Muir began to herd sheep for another Irishman named John Connel, alias "Smoky Jack" for what Muir called his "opaque" complexion.

After an inauspicious introduction to the job Muir entered the most agreeable period of his life since his first summer in Wisconsin. He did not find the work as demanding as he had anticipated, especially after the winter rains had come and the grass had sprouted, so that the sheep were no longer starved and hard to manage. The days passed serene and carefree, and on January 31, 1869, he confided to his journal that the past month was "the most enjoyed of all the Januarys of my life." During the following months he read Shakespeare and described in his journal the flora and fauna of the region, especially the delightful dell known as Twenty Hill Hollow. Then during the blazing days of May he realized that Smoky Jack's sheep would soon be famished again and ready for their summer trek to Sierra pastures.

But instead of herding Connel's sheep into the mountains, Muir again took work with Pat Delaney, who wished him to go with sheep of his own into the Sierra, not as a shepherd but as the overseer of Billy, the regular shepherd. The principal object, according to Delaney, was to have someone he could trust to see that the shepherd kept to business. "The Don," as Muir had dubbed Delaney from his fancied resemblance to Don Quixote, promised that Billy "would do all the herding," allowing Muir ample time to botanize, sketch, and study the geology of the mountains. Furthermore, Delaney said, he would himself go with them to the first base camp and return with supplies at intervals thereafter.

Muir took the job not only as a means of getting back into the Sierra, but also out of respect for Delaney as a kindred spirit and as his intellectual peer. The Irishman was well educated, having trained for the priesthood. He had worked as a placer miner during the gold rush years and then had turned to ranching. He sympathized with Muir's preoccupations with natural history and wished to encourage them.

The flock of more than two thousand sheep started for the Sierra on June 3, followed by "Don Quixote," Muir, Billy the shepherd, one Chinese, and a Digger Indian. There were also two dogs and packhorses loaded with camp equipment, including Muir's plant press. The sheep ambled along in a triangular wedge, their pace of one mile an hour setting the company's pace, so that it required two days for them to reach the first bench of the foothills. Muir now opened a detailed journal, which he would keep throughout the summer, noting the flora they encountered, and recording the events involved in their "following the sheep"—a narrative that on being revised, would be published in 1911 as *My First Summer in the Sierra*. Its faithful observations and its glowing sense of immediacy would make it one of Muir's most popular books and in some respects his finest work of art. Objective in approach, the journal would yet be interior in significance, spiritual autobiography of a high order; and like *A Thousand-Mile Walk* it would represent a flowering of Muir's personality and philosophy. In a day-by-day account of ecstatic prose, it would detail the beginning of his lifelong love affair with the Range of Light. Before book publication, *My First Summer* would run as a serial in the *Atlantic Monthly,* and on reading the manuscript the editor Ellery Sedgwick was moved to write to Muir: "I felt almost as if I had found religion."

Sedgwick's response was a natural reaction to passages like that of June 6, when the flock had reached the edge of a forest of yellow pine interspersed with magnificent sugar pines. "We are now in the mountains," Muir wrote, "and they are in us, kindling enthusiasm, making every nerve quiver, filling every pore and cell of us." He suggested that his body seemed as "transparent as glass to the beauty about us, as if truly an inseparable part of it, thrilling with the air and trees, streams and rocks, in the waves of the sun,—a part of all nature, neither old nor young, sick nor well, but immortal. Just now I can hardly conceive of any bodily condition dependent on food or breath any more than the ground or the sky." The feeling that inspired him was of a profound religious experience, the unitive transport of a mystic,* so that he continued rapturously, "How glorious a conversion, so complete and wholesome it is, scarce memory enough of old bondage days left as a standpoint to view it from! In this newness of life we seem to have been so always."

There seemed never to have been the grim dogmatism of Daniel Muir—the Christianity that exalted a "wrathful Father," who from his throne in the sky had decreed a hell burning everlastingly for sinners. Muir luxuriated in the presence of a loving God who interfused every whit of nature. The mountains radiated Him, the trees radiated Him, even the stones radiated Him. This was what Muir had meant when he confessed to Jeanne Carr, "I take more intense delight from reading the power and *goodness* of God from 'the things which are made' than from the Bible." This was what he had exchanged his father's crypto-Calvinism for—a mystical pantheism, though often expressed in theistic terms. In worshipping nature, Muir was worshipping an immanent God, present in every particle of nature, and in this way he would remain intensely religious to the end of his life.

Meanwhile, the flock reached the first base camp, which Delaney had selected on the North Fork of the Merced. There the Don left them, taking the Chinese and the Digger. He was delayed in his return with supplies, and Muir and Billy were sorely tried in the famine that developed. Their larder was reduced to tea and sugar, supplemented with mutton, which neither could abide. But their fast came to an end on July 7 when Delaney reached camp again with provisions. He also brought men to help drive the sheep to fresh pastures. Setting out the

---

*Muir also wrote of another unitive experience that he had felt earlier in the year in Twenty Hill Hollow, induced by the spiritual influence of the Sierra to the east. "[The mountains] rise as a portion of the hilled walls of the Hollow. You cannot feel yourself out of doors; plain, sky and mountains ray beauty which you feel. You bathe in these spirit beams, turning round and round, as if warming at a camp-fire. Presently you lose consciousness of your own separate existence; you blend with the landscape, and become part and parcel of Nature."

next morning, the procession moved in easy stages, and three days later, from their bivouac on Tamarack Creek, the Don rode out ahead in search of a new base camp.

At the same time Muir began to examine some large boulders that sat isolated on a granite pavement so smooth that it gleamed in the sun. The boulders differed in color and texture from the rock on which they sat, and from his grounding in glaciology he knew they were "erratics" brought from a distance. That their bearer had been a glacier he soon established by the parallel striae he found on the surface of the pavement. The glacier had swept down "from the northeastward," he wrote in his journal, "grinding down the general mass of the mountains, scoring and polishing . . . and dropping whatever boulders it chanced to be carrying at the time it was melted at the close of the Glacial Period." Muir capped this entry with the exclamation, "A fine discovery this!" And so for him opened a matter that would absorb his energies for years to come.

When the Don returned, he brought good news—that the Yosemite Creek country was "not half so lean as it looked." He announced that they would go there and stay until the snow had melted in the higher country. The decision delighted Muir, and he exulted in his journal, "What fine times I shall have, sketching, studying plants and rocks, and scrambling about the brink of the great valley."

On July 17 the party settled into their second base camp in a grove of firs on a small branch that flowed down through Indian Canyon into Yosemite Valley. To arrive there they had to drive the sheep across Yosemite Creek, a job that took a full day of yelling and cursing and the barking of dogs. The sheep could swim well enough, but they were as averse as cats to water. After the "noisy battle" Muir reflected, as he would often do, on the sheer stupidity of domestic sheep. "A sheep can hardly be called an animal," he wrote; "an entire flock is required to make one foolish individual."

But he could leave the witless creatures to Billy's care while he explored the heights around Yosemite Valley. He moved cautiously along the rim to the point where Yosemite Creek plunged into the valley below. He removed his shoes and stockings and crept down to the edge of the rushing stream. He had expected to be able to observe the fall's entire descent, but a small brow of rock obstructed his view, and the rock "appeared to be too steep for mortal feet." On observing it more closely, however, he saw a ledge that projected a few inches from the brink. Reason told him to go no further. At the same time some inner urge impelled him to slip down the cliff till he could stand on the narrow ledge. Then he shuffled sideways for eight or ten yards. "Here," he wrote, "I obtained a perfectly free view down into the heart of the snowy, chanting throng of comet-like streamers." He sensed no danger, nor was he aware of how long he remained there, nor how he made his way back. He knew only that this was a day long to be remembered.

But the highlight of Muir's exploration of the valley rim occurred on the afternoon of August 2—the experience of a flash of certainty that Professor Butler had come to the valley below. Since it was too late to reach the valley floor before dark and since he felt his clothes were too soiled and ragged to be presentable, he delayed investigating the hunch until the following morning when, clad in clean overalls and a cashmere shirt, he climbed down through Indian Canyon. At Hutchings Hotel he found the professor's signature on the register and learned that the Butler party had gone to visit Vernal and Nevada falls, and at Vernal Fall Muir found them. They made much of his psychic experience, the professor calling it "the most wonderful example of pure telepathy that I have ever heard of." The phenomenon impressed Muir himself; he called it "the one strange marvel of my life." But he ascribed nothing supernatural to it. It was only an instance of a mental occurrence that waited on science for an explanation. Interestingly enough, however, the future would hold for him at least two similar psychic experiences.

Several days after Muir had located Professor Butler, the Don arrived in the wake of an attack by bears on the sheep corral, and assuming that the bears would give no end of trouble once they had tasted mutton, Delaney decided that the flock should be herded to the Upper Tuolumne region. They started on August 7,

drifting northeast along the Mono Trail. They stopped at Lake
Tenaya, where Muir examined the pavement of glistening granite at the north end of the lake. He also climbed the rock that
overlooked the eastern shore and noted that it gleamed like glass
in the afternoon light. On finding similar phenomena astride
the Merced–Tuolumne divide the following day, he wrote: "This
entire region must have been overswept by ice." He would keep
alert through the summer for the evidence of glaciers, and his
observations enabled him to formulate as early as 1869 the core of
his later published theory that glacial sculpturing had given the
Sierra its characteristic contours.

The sheep grazed their way toward the Big Tuolumne Meadows, leaving havoc in their wake and causing Muir to write, "The
harm they do goes to the heart." He had thus begun to develop
not only his theory about the glacial erosion of the Sierra but also
his attitude toward domestic sheep that would eventually cast
him as the foremost opponent of flocks in the mountains—
flocks that he would anathematize as "hoofed locusts."

As with Yosemite Creek, there was a problem in driving the
flock across the Tuolumne River. The sheep had to be crowded
off the bank, and Muir observed, "They seemed willing to suffer
death rather than risk getting wet." They were then herded toward the third base camp, which the Don had located in a luxuriant meadow north of Soda Springs on the northern bank of the
Tuolumne River.

While there, Delaney encouraged Muir to explore Mono Pass
and Bloody Canyon down to Mono Lake east of the Sierra. Muir
allowed a week for the trip, observing glacial phenomena galore,
including parallel and crosscutting lateral moraines that gave
plentiful evidence of periodic glaciation; he unfortunately missed
grasping their significance, as he would do throughout his glacial
studies except for one hesitant instance in Nevada in 1878. Muir
remained a faithful adherent of Louis Agassiz's concept of
a single great ice age. Along the way he met Mono Indians, who
inspired him with profound ambivalence. "To prefer the society
of squirrels and woodchucks to that of our own species must
surely seem unnatural," he admitted, only to add, "Perhaps if

I knew them better I should like them better. The worst thing about them is their uncleanliness." No Indian he would observe in the West, however, would cause him to respect the Native American. That would come only after he had met the Indians of Alaska.

Having crossed Mono Pass, Muir found Bloody Canyon a wild, deep chasm, its walls "savagely hacked and scarred." Their metamorphic slates were red enough to have given the canyon its name, as some believed, though others thought it derived from the blood of horses whose legs had been gashed by jagged rocks during the mining rush to Mono Lake in 1858. Muir leaned toward the latter explanation of the name, but he really seemed more interested in the stands of wild rye that grew at the canyon mouth between great terminal moraines. The stalks were six to eight feet tall, and he watched intently as Mono women bent them down and beat the grain into enormous baskets.

By August 21 he was back at the camp near Soda Springs. Frost occurred shortly thereafter, and the Don remarked on the inadvisability of remaining much longer at so high an elevation, where an early storm might mean disaster. So Muir hastened in the remaining days to climb Mounts Dana and Lyell and one or two other peaks at the head of the Tuolumne River. Then on September 9, while reviewing the experience of the summer, he concluded that "the most telling thing" he had learned in his mountain excursions was "the influence of cleavage joints on the features sculptured from the general mass of the range"—an important factor in the glacial hypothesis that was taking shape in his mind and a fact that he would diligently pursue in his future studies. Also on September 9 the Don ordered their camp gear loaded onto the packhorses, and by herding the flock toward the home ranch, the company reached the plain on the twenty-second of the month. "I have crossed the Range of Light," Muir ended his journal, "surely the brightest and best of all the Lord has built; and rejoicing in its glory, I gladly, gratefully, hopefully pray I may see it again."

CHAPTER 7

Incomparable Valley

THE Sierra's call was so strong that Muir worked only eight more weeks for Pat Delaney before starting out for Yosemite Valley with a "partner" named Harry Randall. They walked at a leisurely pace and reached Yosemite in a week. Another week passed while they sketched and climbed around the valley. Then James M. Hutchings, proprietor of the Hutchings Hotel and probably the author of the brochure on Yosemite that Muir had read in 1866, approached their campfire. The tall, lean Englishman had recognized the tourist potential of the valley shortly after its "discovery" by the Mariposa Battalion in their move to round up the Ahwahneechee or Grizzly Bear Indians in 1851* and had begun to publicize it as early as 1856 in *Hutchings' Illustrated California Magazine,* which he had edited in San Francisco. Then in 1864 he had bought the Upper Hotel on the south bank of the Merced, facing Yosemite Fall. For lumber to improve the hotel and to build several tourist cottages around it, he had recently constructed a small sawmill, which had failed to run.

"Mr. Hutchings . . . asked whether I knew anything about mills," Muir wrote. "I told him I was a millwright"—at which he asked Muir to examine the mill to see if he could make it run. After the inspection Muir indicated that the water wheel and most of the machinery would have to be replaced. Hutchings then talked him into taking the job for 90 dollars a month and board.

Randall was also hired, or as Muir tartly put it, "We sold our-

*The first white men to see Yosemite Valley were a band of mountain men under the leadership of Joseph Reddefern Walker, who skirted the rim of the valley in 1833, but they did not make Yosemite known to the world at that time.

selves to J. M. H. to feed sows and turkeys, build henroosts, laying boxes, etc. Also to take charge of the ladies and [re]build a sawmill." The ladies were Hutchings's wife Elvira and his mother-in-law Florantha Sproat, both of whom he was about to leave behind while he went to Washington, D.C. On buying the hotel he had taken up 160 acres of surrounding land. But Congress had ignored such claims in its legislation to grant Yosemite Valley to California as a state park and so had the state legislature on accepting the cession in 1866. Since then Hutchings had sought the recognition of his claim, and to lobby for it was his object now in going to Washington. During his absence he would need someone to work about his establishment, so Muir and Randall could not have appeared at a more propitious time.

Hutchings outlined their duties. The sawmill was Muir's responsibility, first to put it into working order and then to saw lumber from the many yellow pines uprooted by a high wind two winters before. Considerable lumber would be needed to replace with wood the bedsheet partitions in the hotel and to build the various tourist cottages that Hutchings had planned. Randall's assignment included chores like milking Buttercup the cow and driving the oxen Duke and Paddy to haul logs to the sawmill. But the partners' initial work involved building quarters for themselves; for though they would board with the Hutchings family, they agreed to furnish their own lodgings.

They set to work at once splitting sugar pine shakes to build a one-room cabin not far from Yosemite Fall. Though it cost them only three dollars, Muir thought it about "the handsomest building in the Valley." A special feature of the dwelling was a stream brought into it by means of a ditch heading at the foot of Yosemite Fall. The water flowed into one end of the cabin and out the other "with just current enough to allow it to sing and warble in low, sweet tones," to lull them to sleep at night as they lay in hammocks suspended from the rafters. After completing the cabin Muir turned to rebuilding the sawmill and installing "new machinery of the simplest kind." The mill, located near the new cabin, was powered by a millrace that ran from a westerly branch of Yosemite Creek.

Since their second week in the Yosemite Valley, Muir and Randall had seen much of the Hutchings family, mostly at meals, for which the staunch and able Floranda Sproat served as cook. There was also Mrs. Sproat's daughter, Elvira Hutchings, twenty-eight and two decades younger than her husband. She would soon be described in a Yosemite-based novel as "a slight semi-girlish, semi-matronly figure, with a Madonna cast of countenance, deep, pensive hazel eyes, a blush-rose complexion, and brown hair." She was interested in both botany and art, having come from a family that included several successful painters. She herself was a creditable watercolorist, often painting flowers.

Elvira had three children. The oldest was five-year-old Florence or "Floy," the first white child born in the valley, with movements so quick that Muir soon dubbed her "Squirrel." His favorite child, however, was the cheery two-year-old Gertrude, known as "Cosie"; but he also felt a deep sympathy for the baby Charley, who suffered a deformed spine.

The Hutchings family were not the only residents of Yosemite. Other hotelkeepers included the Leidig family and the A. G. Blacks. The original white settler was James C. Lamon, whose house and orchard were located in the upper end of the valley, opposite the Royal Arches. There was also a small settlement of shingle shanties known as Yosemite Village, with a motley handful of mule skinners, packers, horse wranglers, hunters, trappers and other similar characters, whose social center was the Cosmopolitan Saloon, with its "seven whiskey soirées a week." A remnant group of the once warlike tribe of Yosemite or Grizzly Bear Indians also made the valley its home.

Mrs. Sproat had studied the weather lore of these Indians and had become a canny weather prophet. In mid-December she predicted the season's first snowstorm, much to Muir's satisfaction, for he had looked forward to a Sierra storm. Snow fell all night, covering the landscape with "winter jewelry." Christmas brought another storm, but by New Year's day the snow had melted, so Muir celebrated the holiday by climbing to the crown of El Capitan.

It became his custom to climb about the valley on Sundays

and any time he could spare from the sawmill, and later he would snatch whole blocks of days for tramps into the backcountry, his object not only to botanize but especially to seek information about the long-extinct glaciers to confirm his theory of how the Sierra had been shaped and, in particular, how Yosemite had come into being. On occasion he would ride a wiry dun-colored mustang, which carried blankets and eight or ten pounds of bread and oatmeal; but more often he went on foot, without blankets no matter how cold the weather.

The pattern he set on his early trips into the backcountry, those on foot without blankets, would persist throughout his mountaineering career, prompting a scientist friend, C. Hart Merriam, to remark after Muir's death: "As a woodsman, he was peculiar, combining an unusual knowledge of forest and mountain with a remarkably slender fund of what is commonly called woodcraft." Merriam considered him "as innocent as a child" of the art of camping as generally understood, no matter how astute Muir was at finding protected spots in which to sleep or to build small, safe fires for warmth or for brewing cups of tea or coffee.

Muir once acknowledged that his dependence on small fires instead of blankets for warmth allowed him to sleep for no more than half an hour before the cold would rouse him. "I would [then] start up the fire and get a little warmed, and then try it again, and so wear the night out." While asleep, he would toast on one side and freeze on the other. "In the morning I was naturally stiff and cold, but soon from the effect of tea and sunshine I felt 'lifted up.'" Concerning his reliance on bread alone for food, Muir once told a physician friend that bread was about the only food he couldn't do without "through some temperamental quality."

Meanwhile, by March 1870 Muir had the mill in operation and "it works extremely well," he wrote. Randall and Lamon cut the uprooted trees into ten-foot logs, and the oxen dragged them to the mill, where Muir sawed them into lumber. When a sufficient quantity of it had accumulated, he started to build new partitions for the hotel with the help of two carpenters. With their aid he also built an extention to the hotel, the "Tree Room" around the trunk of an incense cedar twenty-four feet in girth. This room would become Mrs. Sproat's kitchen and a warm, intimate social center when the preparations of meals was not too hectic.

In April, however, came the vanguard of the season's tourists, and in the absence of Hutchings Muir had to interrupt his regular work to serve as guide, a job he did not care for because of the blasé insensitivity of most sightseerers to nature's beauty. "They climb sprawling to their saddles," he wrote to Jeanne Carr, "like overgrown frogs pulling themselves up a stream bank through the bent rushes, [and] ride up the valley with about as much emotion as the horses they ride on." Of the finishing school girls in the parties he was equally scornful.

He much preferred to walk with Elvira Hutchings, with whom he had developed a sympathetic friendship. They studied ferns and flowers, shrubs and trees together. Something appears to have happened between them, though it seems unlikely that it was anything improper. Deeply religious, Elvira was the soul of rectitude, and solid Mrs. Sproat, a missionary's wife, would never have stood for any kind of dalliance. Besides, Muir's heart was filled with sublimated love for Jeanne Carr. Yet his long walks with Elvira, unchaperoned, raised several eyebrows in the small community of the valley, and for a long time thereafter (indeed until the present day) innuendo would brand their relationship as not entirely platonic.

Hutchings returned from Washington about May 22 and found to his deep chagrin that Muir was supplanting him in the favor of the tourists. He had long considered himself *the* authority on the valley, not without justification, and his vanity was piqued by Muir's popularity. At the same time he may have heard gossip about his wife and Muir and their long walks. At any rate he conceived an implacable dislike for Muir that would become mutual and grow with time. To worsen matters, Jeanne Carr, who had lately settled in Oakland, where the doctor had been named professor of agriculture in the youthful University of California, sent a stream of notables, beginning with J. B. McChesney, superintendent of schools in Oakland, and Gilbert W. Colby, a judge at Benicia. She told them to see John Muir on the assumption that meeting him would benefit them and that his association with "kindred minds" would give him a degree of polish. It graveled Hutchings that the notables approached him only to inquire the whereabouts of his sawyer.

One of the celebrities who came to the Yosemite Valley in the summer of 1870 was Thérèse Yelverton, "Countess" of Avenmore. With a heart-shaped face, red-brown hair, and a voice described as "bewitching," she was one of the most discussed women of the day. She had begun her career as a lady-in-waiting to Empress Eugénie of France. Then after serving as a nurse in the Crimean War, she had married Captain William Yelverton, heir to the insolvent Viscount of Avonmore. After the birth of their son, Yelverton had left her for a richer woman, and to escape bigamy charges he had sought to have their marriage annulled. Thérèse had fought back valiantly, and the case had dragged on for nine years until the Irish civil court had vindicated her. But Yelverton had then taken the case before the highest tribunal, the House of Lords; and there the peers had closed ranks behind a fellow aristocrat, annulling the marriage, and awarding the child to Yelverton. With her means all but exhausted by the litigation, Thérèse Yelverton had turned to a globe-trotting role and writing travel books.

While staying at the Hutchings Hotel, she fastened herself on Muir like a woodtick, and with Hutchings's grudging approval Muir guided her about the valley. She saw in its grandeur not material for a travelogue but the setting for a novel, with Muir, the Hutchingses, and Lamon serving as models for some of her characters. On Muir Mrs. Yelverton based her hero, whom she called Kenmuir. Little Floy, grown up, became the heroine, a tragic figure called Zanita, a name coined from *manzanita;* and when published, the novel would bear the title *Zanita: A Tale of the Yo-Semite.*

The countess entered the story as the narrator Mrs. Brown, wife of a college professor. On meeting Kenmuir, Mrs. Brown wrote that his "lithe figure approached, skipping over the rough boulders, poising with the balance of an athelete." As he came nearer, she studied his "bright intelligent face . . . and his open blue eyes of honest questioning and glorious auburn hair. . . . His figure was about five feet nine, well knit, and bespoke the active grace which only trained muscles can assume." The best thing about the novel was the characterization of Kenmuir, written from the author's heart, but the story itself brimmed with senti-mental melodrama. It would thus fare poorly with the critics, and one reviewer would even call Kenmuir's characterization "bosh."

Yet Thérèse Yelverton did her groundwork conscientiously. She studied Muir, took notes on his speech, and transcribed nature notes from his journal to weave into the narrative; and all the while she grew more infatuated with him. Between his mill-work and her attentions and demands he grew increasingly frus-trated in his pursuit of glacier data. He therefore felt a sense of relief when another dignitary arrived in August with a note from Jeanne Carr. The visitor was Joseph Le Conte, professor of geol-ogy at the University of California, and with him came nine students, organized into a military-like unit by the professor's West Point assistant. They found Muir at work in the sawmill, and the professor described him as "a man in rough miller's garb, whose intelligent face and earnest clear blue eyes excited my interest." Le Conte claimed to be astonished to discover "a man of so much intelligence tending a sawmill—not for himself, but for Mr. Hutchings."

He invited Muir on a field trip to Mono Lake. Muir accepted the invitation and spent ten days with Le Conte and his party. He led them to places where the glacial evidence was unmistakable, and on Eagle Point they enjoyed a comprehensive view of Yosem-ite and its backcountry. They could plainly trace the mighty high-ways down which the rivers of ice had flowed, finally fusing as the trunk glacier that had filled Yosemite Valley. Le Conte was impressed with Muir's hypothesis of the valley's glacial origin. "I have talked much with [John] to-day about the probable manner in which Yosemite was formed. He fully agrees with me that the peculiar cleavage of the rock is a most important point, which must not be left out of account."

Le Conte was not ready to accept glaciation as the exclusive creator of Yosemite; he correctly thought that much of the work had been done by preglacial fluvial erosion. But when Muir left the party at Mono Lake, Le Conte was a firm believer that the Yosemite glacier had actually existed, and he would return to the University of California as an enthusiastic advocate of Muir's "discovery."

When serving as guide, Muir explained his glacier theory to all who would listen, especially if the audience was inclined to cite Professor Josiah D. Whitney, chief of the California Geological Survey, on the "subsidence origin" of the valley. Whitney, a foremost geologist of the day, had led the California Survey since 1860. He had proceeded in proper scientific spirit, devoting his first report to paleontology, thus alienating California's mining interests. He had financed the survey from his own resources when legislators withheld appropriations, and the only chinks in his armor were obstinacy and intellectual arrogance.

When Clarence King, his young assistant, reported evidence of an ancient glacier in Yosemite, Whitney had published the details of King's discovery, only to retract them later and deny any importance to glaciers in explaining the valley's origin. A catastrophist of the first order, he had published in 1865 a cataclysmic hypothesis, to which he would doggedly adhere through years of controversy. In the first volume of *Geology*, the principal report of his survey, he advocated the probability that the same geological forces that had elevated and molded the surface of the Sierra had "roughly hewn" Yosemite Valley into its present shape. He could find nothing about the domes "and such masses as Mount Broderick" to suggest that they were the result of common denudation, and so he attributed their origin to the process of upheaval. Half Dome, he concluded, had been "split asunder in the middle, the lost half having gone down in what may truly be said to have been 'the wreck of matter and the crush of worlds.'"

When he came to publish *The Yosemite Book* in 1868, he stated flatly that King's report of glacial relics in Yosemite was "an error" and that it was an even greater error to attribute "the peculiar form of the Yosemite" to glacial erosion. "A more absurd theory," he went so far as to claim, "was never advanced than that by which it was sought to ascribe to glaciers the sawing out of those vertical walls and the rounding of the domes." Besides, he insisted, no proof existed that glaciers had ever filled any part of Yosemite Valley, "so that this theory, based on entire ignorance of the whole subject, may be dropped without wasting any more time upon it."

At such an early date Muir and his beliefs could not have been the objects of Whitney's scorn, nor was Clarence King a likely object, for King did not assign to glaciers the degree of erosive power that Muir did. Probably Whitney was clashing with William Phipps Blake, the geologist who had claimed in 1867 that subglacial erosion by water from the ice above had shaped Yosemite Valley. But in addition to denying glacial erosion as the creator of the valley, Whitney had again advanced his subsidence theory. "In simple language," he had written, "the bottom of the Valley sank down to an unknown depth, owing to its support being withdrawn from underneath during some of the convulsive movements of so extensive and elevated a chain." He had reprinted his opinion the following year in *The Yosemite Guide-Book*, which became the bible of many visitors to the park.

Muir continued to expound his theory of glacial erosion to tourists and to refute Whitney's hypothesis, and some of his audience were convinced. At the same time Le Conte continued to espouse his "discovery," so that Whitney became aware of Muir's opposition to his views. But their controversy would come to a climax only after Muir had discredited the subsidence theory in "Studies in the Sierra," seven papers that would run in the *Overland Monthly* in 1874 and 1875. Galled, Whitney would dismiss Muir as "Ignoramus" and "that shepherd." Clarence King, as head of the Fortieth Parallel Survey, might publicly have found some virtue in Muir's position, but he would remain loyal to his former chief, perhaps in part because of Muir's treading on his toes concerning his mountaineering; and before the controversy could run its course, he would belabor Muir with as much sharp irony as had Whitney himself. He would hope, in a brusque footnote in *Systematic Geology*, the crowning report of his survey, "that Mr. Muir's vagaries will not deceive geologists who are personally unaquainted with California, and that the ambitious amateur himself may divert his evident enthusiastic love of nature into a channel, if there is one, in which his attainments would save him from hopeless floundering."*

Meanwhile, Muir had returned from Mono Lake to the attentions of Thérèse Yelverton and found them hard to tolerate. At last, when she pressed him to go to the Orient with her as her secretary, he felt it necessary to escape from her importunities. In the fall, therefore, when Harry Randall announced that he was sick of doing chores for Hutchings and that he aimed to leave the valley for the plain, Muir decided to join him. He resigned his job at the sawmill, and the two suddenly left Yosemite. They hiked down the entire tortuous course of Merced Canyon, perhaps the first white men to do so, and on reaching the San Joaquin plain Muir again went to work for Pat Delaney.

*On December 24, 1901, the day Clarence King died, Muir wrote to his close friend Robert Underwood Johnson, who was also a friend of King's, "Sorry to hear of brilliant King's illness"—suggesting that he bore no grudge for their differences. Henry Adams would call King "the most remarkable man of our time" and cite him as the representative symbol of nineteenth-century America. King helped found the U.S. Geological Survey in 1879 and served as its first director.

CHAPTER 8

The Sage of Concord

JAMES Hutchings did not detest Muir so much as to bar asking him back to the sawmill when another competent sawyer could not be found. He sent his invitation to Muir in the early winter of 1870–71, and Muir accepted it, his plans for South America having receded and longing as he did to return to the Sierra now that Mrs. Yelverton had left Yosemite. But on reaching the valley he found that Hutchings had preempted for his sister the cabin Muir and Randall had built, so Muir set about constructing new living quarters. At one end of the mill he built a room that jutted out like a closed-in balcony and covered it with an extension of the mill-roof. This he called his "hang-nest." It was reached by a "chicken-ladder" of planks across which he had nailed strips of wood. There Muir kept his journals and sketches, herbarium and geological specimens, and the hang-nest became his study. But he elected to sleep in the sawmill in order to enjoy the murmur of the millrace at night and to watch the stars through the window in the roof.

The snow was heavy that winter, but by March it had melted from the valley floor. Meltwater swelled Yosemite Fall, and the flood came down in a sonorous roar. A full moon shone the evening of April 3, 1871, and from Fern Ledge beside the fall, to which Muir had climbed to spend the night, he could see a lunar rainbow in the spray five hundred feet below. Suddenly he felt the urge to creep behind the "down-rushing waters" and enjoy the glory of the moonlight shining through them. Fern Ledge on which he stood ran behind the fall. He edged along it, though it narrowed to only six inches wide at one place, and in a moment he was behind the hurtling water. "I was in fairyland," he wrote, but not for long. In a moment all grew dark, the wind having

blown the fall inward, and down crashed a deluge of "spent com-
ets," savagely hard and rocklike against his head and shoulders.

At that moment, as Muir would later inform his sister Sarah,
he feared being swept from the ledge and dashed to the rocks
below. He instinctively grasped a projecting knob of rock and,
curling up "like a young fern frond," submitted to his pounding
ablution as best he could. Then the moonlight returned, indicating that the fall had again swayed outward, and he scurried to the
safety of the open ledge, where he built a fire to warm himself. At
midnight, though still wet from his frigid drenching, he wrote
buoyantly to Jeanne Carr about the experience.

She responded by the end of the month, at which time she
notified him of the startling news that Ralph Waldo Emerson
would come to the valley in a few days. Emerson and his party
reached Yosemite on May 5, 1871, and put up at Leidig's Hotel. In
the afternoon of life, he was the most venerated literary man in
America, and his entourage guarded him like royalty. Muir went
to the hotel, but was too shy to approach Emerson, although he
knew that Jeanne Carr had informed her friend about him. "I
was excited," Muir later told a group at Harvard, "as I had never
been excited before." And when he heard that Emerson planned
to leave the valley in three or four days, the news compelled him
to request a meeting with the poet in a note that he delivered to
Leidig's in person. In response, without waiting for Muir to
come to him the next day, Emerson rode a pied mustang to the
mill, and after Muir had identified himself the great man enquired why he had not made himself known the previous evening. "I should have been very glad to [see] you," Emerson said.

Emerson entered the mill and climbed the chicken ladder to
the hang-nest, where Muir showed him his sketches, geological specimens, and herbarium. The sage drew Muir out with numerous questions and found him of such singular interest that he
returned to the mill every day he remained in the valley. "Muir is
more wonderful than Thoreau," he would say later. They talked,
among other things, of the Sierra's ancient glaciers; and Emerson
concluded that Muir was "the right man in the right place—in
[his] mountain tabernacle." At the same time Muir found Emer-

son equal to his towering reputation. Years afterward Muir would
identify the two supreme moments of his life—his finding *Calypso* in a Canadian swamp and his meeting with Emerson. All his
shyness melted in the warming company of the older man, and
he dared to extend to him an audacious invitation. "I proposed
an immeasurable camping trip back in the heart of the mountains," Muir would recall long afterward. "'We'll go up a cañon
singing your own song, "Goodby, proud world! I'm going home"
in divine earnest.' . . . But alas, it was too late,—too near the
sundown of his life."

Yet when Emerson prepared to leave the valley, he invited
Muir to ride with him as far as the Mariposa Grove of Big Trees.
"I'll go, Mr. Emerson," Muir replied, "if you will promise to
camp with me in the Grove." Emerson agreed, as enthusiastic as
a boy. But the camping out was not to be. When the party
reached Clark's Station, after Muir had amused them with the
uncertainty of his literary grounding but had taught them the
name of every new variety of tree they had passed, he was surprised to see everybody dismount. On his inquiring whether they
intended to camp in the Big Tree grove, the guardians of the
great man said, "No; it would never do to lie in the night air. Mr.
Emerson might take cold." In his disappointment Muir thought
at first of camping alone among the sequoias and waiting for
everyone to appear there the next morning; but since Emerson
was to leave so soon, he changed his mind and spent the night at
Clark's. "[Emerson] hardly spoke a word all the evening," Muir
recalled years later, "yet it was a great pleasure simply to be near
him, warming in the light of his face as at a fire."

The following morning they rode to the grove, where Galen
Clark, the guardian of Yosemite and the Mariposa Big Trees,
asked Emerson to give a name to a yet unchristened sequoia, and
Emerson selected that of Samoset, the Pemaquid Indian of Pil-
grim days. At lunch Muir pleaded with his hero, "You must not
go away so soon. It is as if a photographer should remove his
plate before the impression was fully made." But Emerson merely
shook his head a little sadly. The party tarried in the grove for an
hour or so. Then as they prepared to leave, Muir once again

urged the poet to remain: "You are yourself a Sequoia," he said. "Stop and get acquainted with your big brethren." But the appeal was futile.

When the party got under way, Muir followed them to the edge of the grove. Emerson brought up the rear, and when the others had disappeared behind a ridge, he turned his horse and waved to Muir in a last farewell. Then he also rode behind the ridge, to rejoin his companions and say, "There is a young man from whom we shall hear." Muir gazed a moment at the spot where Emerson had passed from view, then retreated into the grove, where he made a bed of ferns and sequoia plumes, and at sunset he lit a fire. He later wrote that "as I sat by the fire, Emerson was still with me in spirit, though I never again saw him in the flesh."

They would correspond, however. Muir sent Emerson a package of Libocedrus flowers and received in turn a two-volume set of Emerson's collected essays, which he would read and reread, underscore, and annotate, sometimes dissenting, so that Emerson probably influenced him as much as any other writer, giving him literary direction and confirming him in his rejection of materialism. Emerson's influence on Muir would be reinforced by that of Thoreau to such a degree that certain literary critics would call Muir a full-blown Transcendentalist, a characterization that certain present-day reassessments of Muir's thinking tend to reject. For one thing, like Thoreau, Muir immersed himself more deeply and totally in nature (his alpha and omega) than Emerson had ever done; and Muir could not accept all the tenets of Emerson's *Nature,* however much he admired the essay in general. Nature could not confirm for him, as it did for Emerson, a belief in a transcendent God; rather for Muir God and nature were synonymous.

But none of Muir's reservations could affect the sympathy that flourished between the two friends. Emerson hoped that Muir would come east, and to that end he cautioned him that "Solitude was a sublime mistress, but an intolerable wife." He advised Muir to bring to an early close his business with the glaciers and pack up his sketches and his herbarium and come to

Concord. In nearby Cambridge the botanist Asa Gray would be at home, and so would Louis Agassiz on his return from Tierra del Fuego. Emerson even imagined a suitable job for Muir; in his opinion Muir would make the ideal editor for the works of Thoreau.

But Muir had planted his feet securely on his instincts, à la Emerson's advice in "Self Reliance." "I will follow my instincts," he wrote, "be myself for good or ill, and see what will be the upshot." His instincts told him to hold fast to the Sierra Nevada, and he continued, "As long as I live, I'll hear waterfalls and birds and winds sing. I'll interpret the rocks, learn the language of flood, storm, and avalanche. I'll acquaint myself with the glaciers and wild gardens, and get as near the heart of the world as I can." Thus, planted on his instincts, Muir could be called a confirmed Emersonian; but apparently he would never know that Emerson had added his name to a list he called "My Men"— a list that included the names of Carlyle, Agassiz, Thoreau, Holmes, Lowell, and a dozen others. Muir held Emerson in equal esteem, and in old age he would write, "Emerson was the most serene, majestic, sequoia-like soul I ever met"—ample justification for naming a mountain in the Sierra Nevada for the Sage of Concord, as would occur in time.

CHAPTER 9

Mountaineer-Glaciologist
of the Sierra

AFTER Emerson's departure Muir returned to the sawmill on weekdays and to the enigmas of the ancient glaciers on Sundays. About this time he solved the mystery of the origin of the Yosemite Creek basin north of the valley, a conundrum that had preoccupied him for the past year. He could account for the basin only by assuming that a glacier had gouged it out, but could find no evidence for such an assumption. Now one Sunday morning a breakthrough came when he found deep grooves in the granite of "a narrow hollow where the ice had been compelled to wedge through under great pressure," the sort of clue he had long sought. Thus encouraged, Muir traced the course of the indicated glacier backward to its sources on the flanks of Mount Hoffmann, a discovery that assured him of what he had long suspected—that ice had flowed into Yosemite Valley from all of its side canyons, carving the walls and slicing off Half Dome in the process. In one inspired day he traced the path of the Yosemite Creek Glacier and determined that the expanse of ice had measured some fourteen miles long and five miles wide, the direction of its flow nearly due north and south.

He then went down into the valley for bread. But before he could return to measure the glacier's height, he was interrupted by the appearance of another notable with an introduction from Jeanne Carr—Dr. Clinton L. Merriam of the Smithsonian Institution. Dr. Merriam took an instant interest in Muir's revelations about glaciers and thought he might be about to add a significant page to earth history. He urged Muir to write up his findings, and when Muir had finally described the Yosemite Creek

Glacier, along with several others, Dr. Merriam helped to get the
article published in Horace Greeley's *Daily Tribune,* no doubt
the most influential American newspaper of the day. "Yosemite
Glaciers," for which Muir received two hundred dollars, would
appear on December 5, 1871, not only to inaugurate his career as a
writer but also to intensify his controversy with Professor Whitney.

The work at the sawmill had become a bothersome distrac-
tion to his concentration on the problems of glaciation, so on
about July 10 Muir sawed his final log of yellow pine and settled
his accounts with Hutchings. "By working in the mill," according to John Swett, a future intimate, "Muir [had] earned a few
hundred dollars, enough to buy his bread for several years"; for
he lived frugally, preferring poverty like Thoreau to any loss of
freedom. He was now at liberty to make increasingly systematic
surveys of the mountains, and his first trip in his newfound
independence was a month-long packtrip to the high country
around Mount Dana and to "the lavas and volcanoes" beyond
Mono Pass.

On his return he found John Daniel Runkle, president of the
Massachusetts Institute of Technology, waiting for him. Muir
conducted Runkle on a five-day tour of upland *névé* fields and
showed him age-old glacier paths strewn with moraines and alpine meadows. He convinced Runkle of the truth of his glacial
theory, and Runkle encouraged him to write it up for the *Proceedings* of the Boston Academy of Sciences. Runkle, moreover,
offered Muir a job at M.I.T. As Muir explained to Emerson, "He
thinks that if the damp mosses and lichens were scraped off I
might make a teacher—a professor faggot to burn beneath their
Technological furnaces. All in kindness but I'd rather grow green
in the sky." Thus, Muir let Runkle know that he was bound too
fast to the mountains to accept the invitation. But Runkle's urg-
ing him to write, without doubt, helped to propel his pen toward
serious publication in the future.

On September 8, 1871, a few days after the visit of M.I.T.'s
president, Muir informed Jeanne Carr of his decision to write a
book on glaciation, and in the same letter he described the course
thus far of his studies on glacial erosion. "You know that for the

last three years I have been . . . making observations about this valley and the high mountain region to the east of it, drifting broodingly about and taking in every natural lesson that I was fitted to absorb." He told her that all his questions and all his study had brought him little light until he had said to himself, "You are attempting what is not possible for you to accomplish. Yosemite is the *end* of a grand chapter. If you would learn to read it, go commence at the beginning." Thereupon he had changed his strategy and gone "to the alphabet valleys of the summits, comparing cañon with cañon, with all their varieties of rock structure and cleavage." Only then had come the light he had sought. "I soon had a key to every Yosemite rock and [every] perpendicular and sloping wall."

In the wake of that gratifying achievement, and during the same September that he had written Jeanne Carr, Muir intensified his exploration of the various basins that drained into Yosemite Valley. One day after crossing the Yosemite Creek basin, he climbed the Merced-Tuolumne divide to where it became a smooth, sedgy tableland. After pitching camp, he explored the plateau as far as the brink of an awesome precipice, down which he could see the Tuolumne River where it "shimmered and spangled" and wound through groves of pines and incense cedars four thousand feet below. At first the precipice, forming part of the south rim of the Great Tuolumne Canyon about midway between the canyon's head and foot, appeared completely impassable. But soon Muir discovered a steep side canyon that promised to provide a practicable way into the chasm, and so he made his decision to climb down into the canyon the following day.

He set out after breakfast the next morning, and after a hard climb of several hours, in which the side canyon proved a false start, he found himself on the river bank in the middle of a trunk canyon just half as wide at one point as its walls were tall. To Muir the place was a wonderland. He saw features that reminded him of Yosemite, including "royal arches" and a shattered dome that bore a striking resemblance to Tissiack. He followed the river for about three miles, shouting at intervals to warn the bears whose wallows he had seen among the ferns and shrubbery. He consid-

ered lingering there for several days, but he was in his shirt-
sleeves and had no bread. So at last he began his retreat, climbing
the first three thousand feet of the canyon wall without trouble,
but "the last thousand feet seemed long indeed." Though he had
walked no more than fifteen miles that day, nearly two miles of
them had been virtually straight up and down, and much of the
rest had been as probably the first white person to tread the
unexplored heart of the Great Tuolumne Canyon. He was so
smitten with its beauty that he would return in November to
explore, in a "last raid of the season," that part of the canyon
which opened into the valley called Hetch Hetchy by the Indians
because of its luxuriant meadows. Muir had heard that a hunter
named Joseph Screech had discovered Hetch Hetchy in 1850, a
year before the Mariposa Battalion had revealed the existence of
Yosemite. Muir noted so many correspondences between the two
valleys that forever afterward he would refer to Hetch Hetchy as
"the Tuolumne Yosemite."

Meanwhile, October 6 found him studying the *névé* amphitheaters of the Merced group, later known as the Clark Range.
Below a cirque between Red Mountain and Black Mountain, the
latter subsequently called Merced Peak, he noticed on the bottom of a stream a deposit of silt as fine as flour. "Glacial mud,
mountain meal!" he exclaimed, kneeling down to scoop some
into his hands.

Then on climbing to the top of a nearby moraine, he was
delighted to recognize "a small but well characterized glacier
swooping down from the gloomy precipices of Black Mountain."
He moved along the ice until he came to a crevasse that yawned
for twelve feet between the glacier and the mountain-side—the
bergschrund. "A series of rugged zigzags enabled me to make my
way down into the underworld of the crevasse," he wrote. There
he found a host of "clustered icicles" draping the "chambered
hollows," all glimmering "with indescribable loveliness" in the
subdued light. He could hear the tinkling of overhead drippings,
and from deep below sounded the murmur of water making its
way "through veins and fissures in the dark." Without a coat, he
soon began to shiver from cold, while at the same time he felt

threatened by a leaning wall of ice; nevertheless he found it "hard to leave the delicious music and the lovely light."

Muir climbed back into the open air, exulting in his discovery of a living glacier, the first to be recognized in the Sierra Nevada, but not the first in California. The previous year Clarence King had found three live glaciers on the flanks of Mount Shasta and had announced their presence before the date of Muir's Black Mountain find.

Muir later wrote that, after the Black Mountain discovery, he had tramped throughout the High Sierra and found that what looked like great snowfields in the distance—exactly what Whitney and King persisted in calling them—were in reality often glaciers. He quickly followed the find on Black Mountain with the discovery of glaciers crawling from cirques on Mount Lyell and Mount Maclure; and before the end of his long search, he would locate no fewer than sixty-five residual glaciers in the Sierra. But finding them and convincing skeptics that they were really glaciers were two different matters.

Meanwhile, beginning on December 16, Muir witnessed a storm that dropped ten inches of snow on Yosemite Valley before it changed to torrential rain. A multitude of cataracts began to stream down the valley walls, and Yosemite Fall swelled to ten times its normal volume. Muir looked on in delight, and the ecstatic description he wrote to Jeanne Carr of this "jubilee of water" so impressed her that she copied it out, with minimal editing, and had Dr. Carr take it to Benjamin Avery, Bret Harte's successor as editor of the *Overland Monthly*. Avery soon published the piece under the title "Yosemite in Flood," and he accepted Muir's essay "Twenty Hill Hollow" two months later. Meanwhile, Muir continued to send articles to the New York *Daily Tribune*, and though he was too much a perfectionist for salable writing to come easily, he began to think he might make his living by reporting his experiences with nature for magazines and newspapers.

He spent the winter writing and roaming about the snowbound valley. He was housed in a cabin at Black's Hotel, where he served as caretaker; and there at half-past two on the moonlit morning of March 26, 1872, a tremendous jolt nearly threw him out of bed. The cabin reeled like a bough buffeted by the wind. He had never experienced an earthquake, but recognized instinctively that this was one, and concerning it he wrote, "I ran out of my cabin, both glad and frightened, shouting, 'A noble earthquake! A noble earthquake!'"* The shocks were so savage and convulsive and came so close upon each other that Muir found it hard to walk and had to balance himself against a tree. Suddenly Eagle Rock on the south wall toppled in an immense arc of green, friction-caused fire. The arc impressed him "as true in form and as serene in beauty as a rainbow in the midst of the stupendous, roaring rock-storm." Instantly Muir understood what had created the taluses that heretofore had puzzled him both in the valley and elsewhere in the range.

Hardly had the fragments of Eagle Rock come to rest than he was climbing the new-made talus and noting the grating noises caused by the rocks settling into place. The brand-new boulders were still warm as he clambered over them, and the air was aromatic with the scent of the Douglas fir trees crushed by the falling rocks. Curiosity about the birth of talus quelled his fears, and the inhabitants of the valley, gathering before the Hutchings Hotel, thought him a little daft to be so fascinated by the quake. All of them had been converted in a twinkling to Whitney's cataclysmic theory and feared that the valley's bottom might collapse. Muir tried to joke away their dread. But far from feeling any amusement, they commandeered every mule and mustang in the valley and fled posthaste.

Shortly after the quake Muir began building a new cedar-log cabin in a clump of dogwood bushes close by Lamon's orchard and near the Merced. He planned it in anticipation of the arrival of Merrill Moores for an extended visit in the valley, and it held a

---

*Muir's "noble earthquake" would be called the Inyo earthquake, since its epicenter was located in Inyo County, east and south of Yosemite Valley. It completely demolished the town of Lone Pine in Owens Valley, killing many of its townsfolk. The Inyo temblor may even have been more severe than the earthquake that razed San Francisco in 1906, said to be 8.5 on the Richter scale. Both Professor Whitney and Clarence King studied the effects of the Inyo quake in Owens Valley.

special "Carr corner" for Muir's dearest friends, a sort of gallery under the rafters. Before April had passed, it was finished enough for him to move inside.

For the rest of the spring and summer of 1872, he continued to study the riddles of the Sierra glaciers, making trip after trip into the high country as the snow receded from the "alphabet canyons." Again he spent several days with Professor Le Conte and his students, showing them glaciers he had discovered, and then in July Merrill Moores arrived, now a youth of sixteen years. Their first trip together took them to Mount Lyell to plant stakes in its glacier to measure its flow in the manner prescribed by Agassiz and John Tyndall. On the trip Muir taught Merrill how to use the "aneroid barometer presented to him by Professor Tyndall," who had visited the valley earlier in the season. Muir had read with a critical eye, yet with great interest and profit, Tyndall's *Hours of Exercise in the Alps* and had accepted his ideas on the viscous property of glacial ice, and soon the Irish scientist would send him a package of additional instruments for his Sierra studies. Muir would later describe Tyndall as a "man with eyes that can see far down into the fountain truths of Nature."

That summer Muir met the Harvard botanist Asa Gray, to whom he had sent botanical specimens. With Gray came his former teacher, the noted plant specialist John Torrey, and now Muir took them on a week-long tour of alpine gardens and found that, of all his aquaintances, only Galen Clark had better "traveling legs" than Gray. At night beside their campfire Muir listened rapt to the two men's talk. "They told the stories of their lives," he later recalled, "Torrey fondly telling all about Gray, Gray about Torrey." This outing consolidated Muir's friendship with Gray, which would be long and rewarding (Torrey would unfortunately die the following March). Soon Gray would send to Muir his four botanical works, all standard texts, and Muir continued to ship him specimens of Sierra flora. "What a splendid *plant-finder* you are!" Gray wrote back on one occasion. On another a specimen turned out to be of a species new to science, and so he named it *Ivesia muirii*. Then he urged, "Get a new Alpine genus, that I may make a Muiria glacialis."

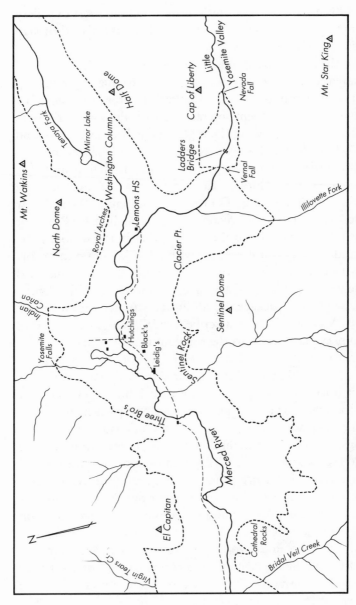

Yosemite Valley in 1872, Muir's home between 1870 and 1873, based on map published in Samuel Kneeland, *Wonders of Yosemite* (Boston, 1873). Muir first visited the valley in 1868.

The scientist whom Muir did not have the good fortune to meet was Louis Agassiz, for on reaching San Francisco that August, the glacialist was too ill from his journey to Tierra del Fuego to make his anticipated visit to Yosemite. At the same time Muir himself was too absorbed in observing stakes on several glaciers to go down to the bay. But he wrote the ailing celebrity "a long icy letter," which Elizabeth Agassiz answered for her husband. In her reply she said that Agassiz had exclaimed on reading Muir's letter, "Here is the first man who has any adequate conception of glacial action!" And when Professor Le Conte suggested that Muir knew more about the glaciation of the Sierra than any other person, Agassiz exclaimed, "He knows *all* about it!" Muir was gratified but not overwhelmed by such praise given in private and off the record. He knew as well as anyone how much more massing of evidence was necessary before the scientific establishment would accept the truth of his hypothesis, so he continued to range the mountains on his single-minded quest.

While he was thus engaged, a ten-day jaunt among the peaks of the Sierra Crown brought him to a scene that excited his admiration. Mounts Lyell and Maclure towered against a cobalt sky, their glaciers gleaming white, while in the foreground a valley flamed with gold and red and purple, and through its luxuriant meadows sluiced the Upper Tuolumne. "I turned again and again to gaze on the glorious picture," Muir wrote, "throwing up my arms to enclose it as in a frame." The scene, he sensed, awaited some special painter; but it did not have to wait long, for the following day the landscape artist William Keith arrived at Yosemite with two artist companions.

No sooner had Muir reached his cabin on returning from the Sierra Crown than Floy Hutchings brought the trio to him. Keith, a muscular man with unruly hair and deepset, piercing eyes, pulled from his pocket a letter from Jeanne Carr and asked in a rumbling voice and Scots burr, "Do you know any piece of Alps that would make a picture?"

"Yes," Muir answered. "I saw it only yesterday . . . and mind you, it needs none of your selection, or 'composition.' I'll take you there tomorrow."

That evening Muir and Keith, the latter a Swedenborgian nature-lover who had come west in 1858 to paint scenes for *Harper's Weekly*, began to call each other "Willie" and "Johnnie," and the friendship of a lifetime was under way, to be cemented by loud but amicable wrangling. "Muir is Scotch, and I'm Scotch," Keith would later explain, "and so we always quarrel." It pleased Muir to learn that Keith was born not only in Scotland but also in the same year as himself. But that was only a suggestion of all that time would demonstrate they had in common. Meanwhile, when morning came, Muir led his new friend, along with Keith's two companions, to a scene in the Sierra Crown that would send Keith rushing forward in excitement, shouting and waving his arms.

Muir then left the painters to their sketching, for he meant to climb Mount Ritter a few miles away. The peak, soaring over thirteen thousand feet and bearing several glaciers in its steep, rugged canyons, had remained unscaled after defeating Clarence King six years before. As Muir left camp, he told the artists that he planned to be gone for three days.

He reached Mount Ritter on the second day and began to climb its flank of metamorphic slate. Eventually he reached a position from which he could not retreat without great peril, yet he was faced by an almost vertical cliff. Up the cliff he went, each advance made with deliberate caution. He later wrote that, after reaching a spot halfway to the top of the precipice, "I was suddenly brought to a dead stop, with arms outspread, clinging close to the face of the rock, unable to move hand or foot either up or down." He seemed doomed to fall to his death on a glacier below, and in the face of such danger he panicked for the first time in his mountaineering career. "A stifling smoke" seemed to invade his mind, but only for a moment, and then his alertness returned like a blaze. "I seemed suddenly to become possessed of a new sense," he later wrote, and what he termed his "other self" ("bygone experiences, Instinct, Guardian Angel,—call it what you will") appeared to take control, firming his trembling muscles and clarifying every "rift and flaw in the rock." The preciseness and certainty with which his arms and legs then moved seemed other than by his own will, and the result appeared miraculous. "Had I been borne aloft upon wings," he concluded, "my deliverance could not have been more complete."*

His remarkable escape, however, did not relieve him of further difficulties. The way was still savagely forbidding. But the strength he had received seemed to have no limits; he made his way over "beetling crags" with apparent effortlessness and soon gained the highest pinnacle, for a view that would provide an extraordinary description for *The Mountains of California*.

When he rejoined the artists the next day, his look of mingled exaltation and utter weariness reminded them, they said, of Jesus descending from the mountain after his round with Satan. The artists then hatched a plot to bring Muir down to the bay, and two months later found him in Oakland. A two-week exposure to civilization followed, with the Carrs, Keiths, Le Contes, and McChesneys all competing in the attentions they paid to him. They took turns in drawing him out, not a difficult thing to do, for as a professor friend from Stanford University would later write, "He always appeared eager to put everything aside for the sake of a long talk."

As a conversationalist, consensus would assign Muir to the same league as Theodore Roosevelt and Clarence King—that is, to the league of the best talkers of their generation. Muir's memory was blessed with almost total recall. At the same time he enjoyed the faculty of utterly spontaneous speech in which to express his recollections. His descriptions were so vivid, his choice of words so picturesque that his audience (according to another admiring friend) could feel the wind on their foreheads, the rain on their necks, and fairly see the colors of the trees and the lakes and the flowers that he conjured up. Muir could talk in monologues of remarkable range and cogency, volunteering meticulous information; even later when he came to relish French cook-

---

*Muir's experience on Mount Ritter was paralleled by an adventure of Major John Wesley Powell, leader of the U.S. Geographical and Geological Survey of the Rocky Mountain Region. In *The Exploration of the Colorado River* he narrated how he had become stranded on the edge of a precipice and managed to save himself only by a strange impersonal resurgence of strength.

ing, he would often let his meals grow cold while holding forth in exuberant conversation.

All in all, his loquacity was a definite social asset, encouraging Jeanne Carr to make him acquainted with the most distinguished poets of California—Edward Rowland Sill, Ina Coolbrith, and Charles Warren Stoddard—to whom he was introduced as "the wild man of the woods." Stoddard gave him the sobriquet "the Faun" and called him that forever after. In the course of his socializing he was ferried back and forth across the bay; in San Francisco he met and dined with Benjamin Avery of the *Overland* and had his picture taken by a fashionable photographer before rebelling at the "smother" of society.

Muir's reaction against the overdose of social fellowship that he had met in the bay area was triggered not only by a paradoxical shyness heightened by years of isolation in the wilderness but also by a certain antisocial streak that had developed in his makeup and caused him to distrust the vaunted blessings of civilization. He suspected that such blessings were largely a delusion and that urban culture was shot through with sickness, or as he would declare in a defensively exaggerated way after a later and longer sojourn in the cities, "There is not a perfectly sane man in San Francisco." With such an attitude, small wonder that he should feel profound relief on escaping back to the Sierra.

On reaching Yosemite Valley, Muir decided to explore Tenaya Canyon, the most difficult stretches of which were all but inaccessible, but for his glacier studies he needed to obtain altitudes and sections there with his barometer and clinometer. While climbing a steep rock face on a shoulder of Mount Watkins towering above the sheer-walled gorge that formed the depths of Tenaya Canyon, he made one of the few serious missteps in his climbing career. He fell and struck his head, and the blow knocked him unconscious. On coming to, he found himself wedged among stiff shrubs of spiraea and dwarfed live oaks. A few more feet of rolling and he would have gone over a cliff into the Tenaya Gorge; and in his words, "My mountain-climbing would have been finished." Muir's fall was as close a brush with death as his impasse on Mount Ritter and even more so than his subsequent involvement with a snowslide that he would describe in *The Yosemite* ("In all my mountaineering I have enjoyed only one avalanche ride, and the start was so sudden and the end came so soon I had but little time to think of the danger that attends this sort of travel").

To the accident in Tenaya Canyon he reacted much as he had done, only more so, on nearly drowning in Fountain Lake. He felt humiliated and upbraided his feet for having lost their cunning from contact with the "dead pavements of civilization." A countermeasure was in order, and he wrote, "I determined to guide my humbled body over the highest practicable precipices, in the most nerve-trying places I could find." A long letter to Jeanne Carr detailed the prodigious effort that followed during his exploration of the entire length of Tenaya Canyon, a feat no one had managed before him. He did not intend the letter for publication, but she sent it to Benjamin Avery, who ran it in the *Overland* for April 1873 under the subdued title "A Geologist's Winter Walk."

During the winter of 1872–73 Muir continued with his writing. It gave him a great deal of trouble, for his usual nimbleness of speech and the verbal spontaneity that characterized his letters to family and friends would desert him and cause him to freeze whenever he sat down to write for publication. It was a block that tended to make him a compulsive reviser and to fill him with myriad misgivings.

But having kept his expenses to a minimum, Muir found that he could live on what he earned as a writer. He was also able to save a little money, even accumulating enough in time to send funds home to help Dan and Mary with their college expenses. He also promised his mother that she would never want for bread, now that she and Daniel had separated, with him going to a group of Disciples in Hamilton, Canada, where he preached in the streets and solaced the sick and dying in the local hospital. The prospect of possibly having to support his mother pressed Muir to apply his quill as never before.

His cabin near Lamon's orchard made an excellent study, and there he did his writing, but he also read a varied assortment of

books there. His favorite genre remained travel literature, and he
returned to the works of Humboldt. But he read and reread the
books of Emerson and Thoreau. Among the volumes that Jeanne
Carr sent to him was one by Sir Charles Lyell, which he claimed
to be "just what I wanted"; and very likely it was during these
Yosemite years that Muir made his intensive study of Darwin. He
continued to read geological reports and freely sampled mountaineering literature, more books by Tyndall, *Scrambles in the
Alps* by Edward Whymper, and *Mountaineering in the Sierra
Nevada* by Clarence King. J. B. McChesney sent him a set of
John Ruskin's *Modern Painters*, which he read intently for its
impressions of the Alps, but he reacted against Ruskin's concept
of "Mountain Gloom" and dismissed it as "bogle humbug."
Even worse, he rejected Ruskin's "lack of faith in the Scriptures
of Nature" and decided that Ruskin knew little about them.
Muir found more value in such works as the botanical books sent
by Asa Gray, who seemed intent on weaning him away from
geology and bringing him back to his first love, botany. Muir
would continue to read extensively throughout his life, but he
would never trust book learning as much as the direct study of
nature, and so his writing would never become "bookish."

No doubt, the books that Jeanne Carr sent him intensified his
vicarious sense of her presence. "You are so fully in my life," he
had written her on July 6, 1872, "that I cannot realize that I have
not yet seen you here." She finally visited him at Yosemite in June
1873. Her party of eight or ten people included Keith, botanist
Dr. Albert Kellogg, and Emily Pelton, who had recently moved
to California. The company camped for nine days at the mouth
of Tenaya Canyon, and when most of them had returned home,
Muir accompanied Jeanne Carr, Keith, and Albert Kellogg to
Hetch Hetchy, where Mrs. Carr (Victorian gentlewoman though
she was) announced herself ready to brave the Great Tuolumne
Canyon that had balked Professor Whitney and Clarence King.
Muir found it a pleasure to be with her again. He retained his
warm regard for her, but it seems that after these few weeks with
her he would begin to disentangle himself from her emotionally

and to look on her less and less as his "spiritual mother." At least, not long thereafter, he began to write her fewer long, full letters.

Shortly after the camping trip to Hetch Hetchy and the Great Tuolumne Canyon, Muir made a trip down to Mount Whitney, the highest point in the United States, exclusive of Alaska. His companions were Galen Clark, Albert Kellogg, and Billy Simms, a youthful artist. They made their first camp at Clark's Station, where Muir entered into his journal a note that portended his future stance as a conservationist. "It is almost impossible," he wrote, "to conceive of a devastation more universal than is produced among the plants of the Sierra by sheep." Then, after describing the havoc sheep had wrought at Clark's Meadows, he added, "Nine-tenths of the whole surface of the Sierra has been swept by the scourge. It demands legislative interference."

Clark accompanied the party only as far as the San Joaquin–Kings Canyon divide, where he turned back, pleading lack of time and the call of official duties. Muir forged ahead with Simms and Kellogg, crossing the North and Middle forks of the Kings, and on October 6 they made camp at Thomas's Mill. The General Grant Tree and its grove were located close by, and they paid a visit there the next day, finding that visitors had disfigured the tree "barbarously" by "hacking off chips and engraving their names in all styles." Soon Simms and Kellogg crossed the Kearsarge Pass for the town of Independence in Owens Valley, while Muir pressed on for Mount Whitney, or rather for the peak that had passed for Mount Whitney during the past two years.

"The bogus Mount Whitney" was so easy to climb that its summit could be reached by muleback (it was locally known as Sheep Rock, but would later be renamed Mount Langley). In a storm in 1871 Clarence King had climbed it by apparently the only difficult route and had, in an error caused by the storm, identified it as Mount Whitney. Muir at once detected a higher peak not far away, the true Mount Whitney, and set out for it, only to be caught himself in a freezing storm that blew up by nightfall. He pushed on, however, until he reached a summit that would later bear his name, and there in minus 22-degree weather

John Muir in 1873, a portrait by Billy Simms, who accompanied him to the Mount Whitney area that same year. Courtesy of the Bancroft Library, University of California, Berkeley.

he spent one of the worst nights of his life. To keep from freezing, he had to dance the Highland fling, thrashing his arms for hours and jumping high into the air. Dawn came at last, and he started on for Mount Whitney until that "other self" which had saved him on Mount Ritter turned him back, and he retreated to lower ground.

He rested for two days, then again advanced on Mount Whitney, ascending the east face to timberline, where he camped for the night. On gaining the summit the next morning, October 21, he found a statement left by Clarence King in a powdered yeast can. It told how King had learned of his error in New York and had come west to climb the true Mount Whitney on September 19, a month previously. "Clouds and storms prevented me from recognizing [my mistake] in 1871," King had written, "or I should have come here then. All honor to those who came here before me." The first to climb Mount Whitney had been three trout lovers from Owens Valley, and by right of first ascent they had fixed "Fisherman's Peak" upon the helmet-shaped summit, a name that would endure for yet a while, but in the end "Mount Whitney" would prevail.

CHAPTER 10

"Studies in the Sierra"

AFTER his descent from Mount Whitney, Muir rejoined his friends at Independence and together they made "a simple saunter" along the eastern face of the Sierra as far north as Lake Tahoe. Then he went to Oakland for a ten-month stay with the J. B. McChesneys to write his long-projected series on glaciation and mountain sculpture for the *Overland Monthly*. The series would include seven papers under the general title "Studies in the Sierra."

Muir had sketched his plans for an extended presentation of his glacial hypothesis in his letter to Mrs. Carr of September 8, 1871; but having decided not to hold his "wheest" (the Scottish term for "silence") in the interest of a conclusive, book-length statement, he had made piecemeal publication in newspapers and magazines of his observations on glaciers and their action. Yet continued study of the glacial record had matured his thesis, and he was now ready to frame a definitive statement. To accomplish this, he had organized his data on glacial geomorphology into comprehensive and systematic order, conducive to cogent argument. He was well-read in the glaciology of the day and had studied the works on glaciers and their action by Agassiz, Tyndall, and James David Forbes. But as so much of his subject related uniquely to the Sierra Nevada, with little treatment of it to be found in books, the main source of Muir's facts remained his own patient study of the glacial effects he had found throughout the range.

Muir's observations of nature in most of his writing would not prove systematic enough to qualify as science, but "Studies in the Sierra" amply justified his penchant for thinking of himself as a scientist. However, the *Overland Monthly*, in which the series was to run, was a literary journal, with a predominantly lay readership. Still, Muir was keen on impressing scientists, so he fol-

John Muir in a photograph taken in 1873 by Carleton E. Watkins of San Francisco, perhaps while Muir lived with the McChesney family in Oakland. Watkins rivaled Eadward Muybridge in photographing Yosemite Valley. Courtesy of the State Historical Society of Wisconsin, neg. no. WHi(X3)5766.

lowed the advice of Jeanne Carr and deliberately curbed his usual
exuberance of style in favor of lean, direct prose, yet with occasional quaint word choices like "mountainet" and "peaklet," as
well as such odd constructions as "past flowed rock" to indicate
rock past which a glacier had moved. Altogether the series cost
him more anguish than any other writing he would ever do. He
strove for meticulous correctness, and John Swett, a new crony,
would later write, "So careful were his observations, so accurate
his notes and sections, that when he [wrote] on geological subjects his statements and conclusions [had] the force of mathemati-
cal demonstrations."

In Study No. I, called "Mountain Structure," Muir established that all categories of relics from glacial times existed in the
present Sierra Nevada and that multitudinous surface features of
the range qualified as residual glacial phenomena. From this he
argued that at the outset of the Great Ice Age postulated by
Louis Agassiz (Muir was not aware that four shorter stages of
glaciation had occurred in the Sierra instead of one long winter)*
the range had formed a comparatively featureless massif under-

---

*Muir believed the sixty-five glaciers he had discovered in the Sierra were relics of
the universal ice sheet hypothesized by Agassiz. "Toward the close of the glacial
period," he wrote in *The Mountains of California*, ". . . the lower folds of the ice-
sheet in California . . . began to shallow and recede from the lowlands, and then
move slowly up the flanks of the Sierra in compliance with the changes of climate."
He postulated further that the vast mantle of ice on the mountains divided into a
train of enormous glaciers, which in turn melted into smaller ones, "until now only a
few of the smallest residual topmost branches of the grand system exist on the cool
slopes of the summit peaks." Subsequent geologists, however, have determined that
modern Sierra glaciers do not extend back to the Pleistocene. They contend that
since the end of that epoch about 10,000 years ago the climate has fluctuated,
warming slowly during the millennia after about 8,000 years ago to a climatic optimum
that lasted for about 3,000 years, during which all glaciers disappeared from the
Sierra. Then between about 4,000 and 3,000 years ago, beginning with the cool
cycles that François Matthes lumped together under the collective designation of
"little ice age," the climate cooled enough to allow glaciers to return to the range. It
is of this interval only that Muir's sixty-five glaciers are relics. They represent only a
fraction of the glaciers now known to exist in the Sierra, a number claimed by
N. King Huber to total nearly 500, as of 1980, most of them so small that their motion
is hard to detect. But glaciers come and go, as demonstrated by the fact that Muir's
"first living glacier" (that of Black Mountain or Merced Peak) has entirely disappeared.

John Muir, again as a young man, in a daguerreotype published as the frontispiece of volume I of *The Life and Letters of John Muir*, by William Frederic Badè. Copyright 1923 by Houghton Mifflin Company, copyright renewed 1951 by John Muir Hanna. Reprinted by permission of Houghton Mifflin Company. All rights reserved.

lying the universal ice sheet that Agassiz had envisioned. Muir assumed too much, of course, in designating this ice sheet (not unlike those that currently overspread Greenland and Antarctica), and the many separate glaciers into which it had presumably divided upon the warming of the climate, as virtually the sole agents for imparting to the range its present contours.

Close observation, brilliant inference, and equally brilliant induction, however, underlay his decisive insight that the factor controlling the outcome of ice action on the native rock was the principle of cleavage, as he called it, known to most geologists as jointing. It was at any rate the fundamental on which Muir and Joseph Le Conte had agreed in 1870 and which Muir now specified: "The whole mass of the Sierra . . . is built up of brick-like blocks whose forms and dimensions are determined chiefly by the degree of development of the elected *planes of cleavage*, which individualize them, and make them separable from one another while yet forming undisturbed parts of the mountain."

Muir's researches had established five different planes of cleavage or jointing, each responding so distinctively and individually to the stress generated by glacial ice as to lead him to generalize that "*glaciers do not so much mold and shape, as disinter forms already conceived and ripe* [his italics]"—forms predetermined by the special character of the jointing in the given rock. He argued further that, compared with the disinterring power of a glacier, the degree of a rock's capacity to control its own form ranged in direct proportion to its hardness and the quality of the development of its specialized cleavage planes. Softer rock with less specifically developed cleavage planes would have correspondingly less capacity to resist the action of the ice and retain its inherent shape. "In general," he summed the matter up, "the *grain of a rock determines its surface form.*" Thus Muir established a systematic rationale to account for the varied glacial sculpture found throughout the Sierra Nevada.

His second Sierra study continued the subject of "Mountain Structure," and to it he added the subtitle "Origin of Yosemite Valleys." It began by classifying *every* canyon and *every* valley of the Sierra as the product of erosion and by confirming Yosemite as another valley of erosion with ice as the erosive agent. Muir proceeded by defining four valley subtypes, two of slate and two of granite. He characterized the second granite subcategory as "branching at the head, with beveled and heavily abraded lips at foot," with very high walls in the main, frequently interrupted by side canyons, and with a level floor on which lakes and meadows abounded. It was to this type of granite valley that he assigned Yosemite, and in so doing he adopted the name *yosemite* as a generic term in addition to its specific use. "Nature," he stressed, "is not so poor as to possess only one of anything," and by that token Yosemite Valley was not unique in either its groundplan or its cross sections.

Muir then outlined his concept of the origin of all yosemite valleys. He pointed out that the Merced yosemite lay at the confluence of five ancient glaciers that had coalesced into the prodigious trunk of ice which had gouged out Yosemite Valley and which he called the Merced Glacier after the name of the

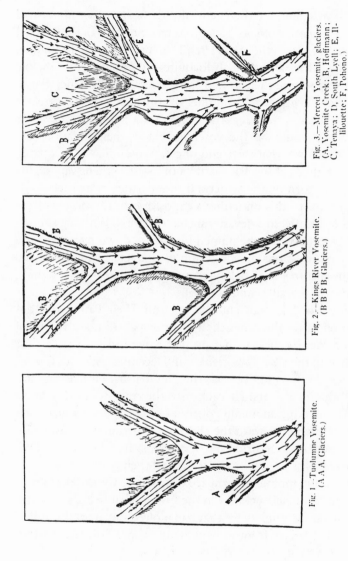

Fig. 1.—Tuolumne Yosemite.
(A A A, Glaciers.)

Fig. 2.—Kings River Yosemite.
(B B B, Glaciers.)

Fig. 3.—Merced Yosemite glaciers.
(A, Yosemite Creek; B, Hoffmann;
C, Tenaya; D, South Lyell; E, Il-
lilouette; F, Pohono.)

Diagrams by John Muir to illustrate his theory of yosemite creation, as published in "Studies in the Sierra" in the *Overland Monthly* for 1874–75. Photograph by Caroline Lawson Hinkley.

river. All yosemites, he then generalized, "*occur at the junction of two or more glacial cañons.*" Such was true not only of the Merced yosemite but also of those of Hetch Hetchy, the Upper Tuolumne, the Kings River, and the San Joaquin—all found directly below the convergence of their primordial glaciers. Muir further generalized that the greater the number of confluents and the greater their magnitudes, as well as the steeper their gradients, the wider and deeper would be the yosemite below their junction. He added, moreover, that the trend of every yosemite was invariably the direct effect of specific features of its convergent valleys, influenced in turn by the structural singularities of its rocks.

By means of this punctilious exposition of the origin of yosemites Muir offered a devastating alternative to Whitney's subsidence hypothesis, and he pinned his theory down by marshaling copious observations on the common characteristics of glacially wrought features that belonged to all yosemites—half domes, capitans, royal arches, and so forth.

Study No. III, "Ancient Glaciers and Their Pathways," described one after the other the five principal tributary floods of so-called Pleistocene ice that he had named in his first article published in the *New York Tribune* in December 1871: the Yosemite Creek, Hoffmann, Tenaya, the Nevada or South Lyell, and the Illi-louette glaciers. He cautioned the reader to bear in mind that each description would concern only that phase which each glacier "presented toward the close of the period when Yosemite and its branches were works nearly accomplished." He proceeded, then, to reconstruct the five glaciers and their pathways in clockwise order, beginning with the ice of Yosemite Creek. His imposing account reached a climax in the fusing of all five glaciers into the tremendous trunk of ice that had plowed out Yosemite Valley, with the help of ice from Indian, Sentinel, and Pohono canyons, as well as canyons on either side of El Capitan.

Muir had touched on the topic of glacial erosion while describing the principal glaciers of the Merced system, but for the full development of this theme he waited until Study No. IV, entitled "Glacial Denudation." First, he discussed the three main kinds of evidence for glacial action, one of which comprised "polished, striated, scratched, and grooved surfaces" brought about by glaciers moving over or past rocks lying in their way, with the striae and grooves produced by rocks imbedded in the base of the ice. Moraines of all types constituted the second category of evidence, while the third included all sculptured rock throughout the range. Attention to such evidence led to an appreciation not only of the various methods of glacial action but also of the massive quantity of glacial denudation produced.

An assessment of that quantity could be reached, Muir thought, from the fact that (no matter how many different kinds of rock could be found throughout the Sierra) only two kinds predominated on the surface of the range—slate and granite. Slate, he pointed out, covered the bathylithic granite along the axis of that section of the range under special consideration as well as several peaks in outlying spurs, while slate generally covered the base of the range, with granite predominating everywhere else. Muir argued that circumstances associated with the occurrence of the slates in their several localities and their absence in others all but demonstrated that long ago they mantled the granite of the entire range. Their "known thickness" in the present places of their occurrence made possible an approximate estimate of the quantity displaced in the various localities where they were either less abundant or entirely lacking. Close and analytical study of the problem had led Muir to conclude that the entire amount of glacial denudation in the middle stretches of the western flank of the range averaged more than a mile in depth, an overestimate in the opinion of later authorities.

Muir had also studied the problem of postglacial erosion, which he addressed in Study No. V, "Post-Glacial Denudation." He had observed that present-day rock surfaces lay only a little below the plane that he was able to demonstrate as the level left by the ice. After discussing the various means of postglacial degradation—rock avalanches, snow avalanches of at least three different sorts, land-slips, running water, frost, and finally atmospheric weathering, he stated as his studied opinion that the postglacial denudation had been entirely negligible. The polished pavements that abounded in the upper and middle reaches of the range, where they arrested the puzzled attention not only of the Indians and mountaineers but even of dogs and horses, "have not been denuded the one-hundredth part of an inch." In summing up, Muir declared that in upland areas other than the unaltered polished surfaces, the postglacial denudation averaged less than three inches and in the middle elevations not quite a foot.

Having considered in the two papers dealing with glacial and postglacial denudation how masses of rock particles had been dislodged from their bases, Muir devoted Study No. VI, called "Formation of Soils," to the treatment of how such detached particles had been transformed into soil suited to the support of vegetation. Predictably, he postulated the vanished glaciers as having been the most important of the soil-building agents, especially in the case of the various moraines, which now supported lush forests. The morainal deposits had, of course, been modified by atmospheric decomposition and by the wear of rain and melting snow. Snow avalanches, resembling glaciers in their method of soil production and distribution, were second to rock avalanches and earthquake avalanches in the transport of the soil for the use of trees, shrubs, ferns, and other Sierra plants. But glaciers remained the supreme soil makers and movers, and Muir argued that if the glaciers had melted suddenly, without an opportunity to build up soil on the western flank of the range, the magnificent forests there would never have come into being.

"Studies in the Sierra" ended with a seventh paper called "Mountain Building," dealing with formative processes within a strip of the range two hundred miles long—a paper that had already appeared in the *Proceedings of the American Association for the Advancement of Science*. Early in the discussion Muir deliberately but incorrectly disposed of preglacial erosion by water as a factor for serious consideration and settled on glacial ice as practically the sole formative agent in the Sierra. In exploring the origin of the distinctive features of the Sierra crest—the pinnacles, the grand summit peaks, and the "peaklets" that protruded from the sides of more massive mountains—he found, quite predictably, that erosion by ice had "disinterred" such forms in accordance with the nature of cleavage planes or combinations of planes (or jointing) in the summit rock and that such pinnacles, peaks, and peaklets must be considered the residual leavings "of the once solid wave of the whole range." Thereafter he individualized the development of the study by describing "the formation of a few specifically illustrative groups and peaks"—the Lyell group, the Merced group, Mount Ritter, Mount Whitney, and so forth.

It would appear, as he concluded the seventh paper and the series as well, that regardless of how the preglacial body of the range had come into being, all the individual mountains occurring between latitude 36° 30' and 39°, "whether the lofty alps of the summit, or richly sculptured dome-clusters of the flanks, or the burnished bosses and mountainets projecting from the sides of the valleys"—all had resulted from the action of that general ice sheet of the presumed great winter and the separate glaciers into which later it had supposedly divided. He denied that there had been any upbuilding throughout that awe-inspiring process, only "a universal razing and dismantling, and of this," he declared, "every mountain and valley is the record and monument." Muir's view of the shaping of the Sierra as razing and dismantling illustrated a principle that had become a fundamental tenet of his philosophy of nature—that destruction was, in fact, creation.

"Studies in the Sierra" was a most original effort, a pioneer venture in most respects. Muir had trod in no one's footsteps, for none had explored the glacial history of the Sierra as earnestly as had he. At the same time this series would remain his only really scientific treatise. It was true that in later years he would return to the subject of glaciers, not only in chapter two of *The Mountains of California* and chapter eleven of *The Yosemite,* but especially in connection with his seven trips to Alaska in order, among other things, to see ice at work as it had worked in Ice Age Yosemite. Noteworthy were the two reports on glaciation he would render after his participation in the cruise of the *Corwin* and the Harriman-Alaska Expedition, and the last years of his life would be concerned with ice in *Travels in Alaska.* But all Muir's subsequent preoccupation with glaciation in the North, circum-

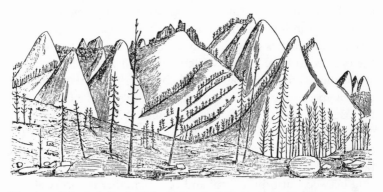

"Portion of the Left Bank of the Channel of the South Lyell Glacier, near the Mouth of Cathedral Tributary." Illustration drawn by John Muir for "Studies in the Sierra," *Overland Monthly* for 1874–75. Photograph by Caroline Lawson Hinkley.

scribed as it was by preconceptions from his Sierra researches, would in the main merely confirm the concepts he had formulated in "Studies in the Sierra." It would not materially add to the seminal contribution of his Yosemite years.

Unfortunately, the "Studies" did not immediately establish Muir as a responsible scientist. The prestige of adversaries like J. D. Whitney and Clarence King was too great within the scientific establishment, and the *Overland* was too provincial a magazine, with a circulation of only three thousand copies. Muir would have done better to send the "Studies" to *Scribner's* or *Harper's* or the *Atlantic Monthly*. For scientific consideration the best press of all would have been the *American Journal of Science and Arts,* which did indeed run a portion of his first study, though the credit went to Dr. Carr.

Muir aimed to republish the series as a book, but never got around to doing so; and not till thirty-six years after his death would the Sierra Club bring it out in book form. "It was unfortunate for his fame," wrote William E. Colby in the preface, "that Muir did not . . . do this himself. With the passing of years these studies have become increasingly unavailable and, on this account, have not been as widely read as they merit."

In the meantime, however, Muir's glaciation studies slowly came into their own. In 1885 the glacier expert Israel C. Russell, of the U.S. Geological Survey, published his findings on glacial action in the United States, with an approving nod in Muir's direction. In 1901 Henry Gannett, also of the U.S. Geological Survey and a personal friend of Muir's, produced a paper entitled "Origin of Yosemite Valley," which promoted the idea that hanging side canyons like that of Yosemite Creek were typical of heavily glaciated terrain. In his low-keyed conclusion Gannett characterized Yosemite Valley as "quite an ordinary product of glacial erosion."

But the crowning affirmation of Muir's theory would come only years later when the U.S. Geological Survey assigned the expert glaciologist François E. Matthes to study the Yosemite region. Matthes's survey, initiated in 1913, would lead by 1930 to the classic monograph *Geologic History of the Yosemite Valley* and a posthumous successor called *The Incomparable Valley: A Geologic Interpretation of the Yosemite,* edited for lay readers in 1950 by Fritiof Fryxell. "Systematically and in detail," Matthes wrote in 1938, the centennial year of Muir's birth, "I covered the very ground that Muir studied with such zest." Matthes concluded that while Muir had erred in extending glaciation down to the foothills, in hewing to Agassiz's concept of a single Great Ice Age, and in excluding preglacial fluvial erosion as a significant factor in shaping the Sierra, he was yet "more immediately familiar with the facts on the ground and was more nearly right in their interpretation than any professional geologist of the time. . . . Muir was probably as nearly right in his glacial theory of the Yosemite as any scientist in the early [eighteen] seventies could have been."

As late as 1987 Matthes's texts on the geology of Yosemite would remain, according to the subsequent authority N. King Huber, "the best source of descriptive material on the glaciation of Yosemite." Like Muir, Matthes presented an "imaginary traverse" of the Sierra Nevada as a basis for considering the Yosemite as an integral part of the range, even during the Ice Age. By 1913, when Matthes began his survey, the concept of an Ice Age of multiple stages interspersed by warmer intervals had come to stay, a scenario that his work would further confirm. He found evidence for at least three stages of glaciation in the Yosemite area during the Ice Age and gave them suitable names. But simultaneous investigations by Eliot Blackwelder on the eastern side of the Sierra established four major glaciations for the range. Blackwelder named these stages Tioga, Tahoe, Sherwin, and McGee, in a sequence from most recent to the oldest—names that became entrenched with the passing of time, eclipsing those laid down by Matthes.

In like fashion, in reviewing Muir's glacial theory on the origin of Yosemite, Matthes found that much confusion could be avoided by readjusting the names Muir had given to several of the glaciers he had described. First, it was only logical, Matthes reasoned, to designate the trunk glacier that had shaped the Yosemite Valley not as the Merced Glacier, as Muir had done, but as the Yosemite Glacier,* and in consequence to shift the name "Merced" to the ice flood that had come down Merced Canyon, but which Muir had called the Nevada or South Lyell Glacier. Such redesignation of the trunk glacier required, as a matter of course, a name change for Muir's Yosemite Creek Glacier. This Matthes renamed the Hoffmann Glacier, thus necessitating a new name for Muir's Hoffmann Glacier—specifically the Snow Creek Glacier. But in the case of those ice rivers that Muir had called the Tenaya and the Illilouette respectively, there was no reason to change their names, and they remained the same.

In reevaluating Muir's contention that five principal tributaries had fused to form the enormous ice trunk that had shaped Yosemite Valley, Matthes allowed that during the stages of the Ice Age that Blackwelder called the Sherwin and Tahoe, such fusion had occurred in the case of merely four of Muir's main tributaries of ice; but he said that the Illilouette Glacier had never advanced as far as Yosemite Valley, and that during the

*When compiling *The Yosemite* three years before his death, even Muir began to substitute "the Yosemite Glacier" for "the Merced Glacier" as his designation for the main trunk of ice that had plowed out Yosemite Valley. He retained, however, all the original names of the five principal tributaries.

final glacial stage (Blackwelder's Tioga) only two of Muir's principal tributaries had converged on the valley—the Tenaya Glacier
and the one that Matthes had renamed the Merced. The comprehensive scope of Matthes's survey would, of course, lead to the
correction of other details in Muir's glaciological analysis, but
Matthes would generously chalk such shortcomings up "primarily to the limitations of the science of [Muir's] day."

Meanwhile, Muir had found the grind of writing the "Studies"
relieved by the company of friends. The McChesneys were en-
dearingly warmhearted, their small daughter Alice a delight. At
the same time Muir enjoyed friendly but contentious banter at
weekly intervals with Keith, who cajoled him fruitlessly to loosen
up his illustrations for the "Studies," some sixty-five rigid pen-
and-ink line drawings. There were also evenings of scientific talk
with the Le Conte brothers, Joseph and John, the latter having
just been named president of the University of California. And on
visits to the Oakland Public Library to consult reference works
Muir would linger to chat with the librarian, Ina Coolbrith, a
niece of Joseph Smith, the founder of Mormonism. Muir also
found a wise friend in John Swett, a fellow Emersonian and a
former state superintendent of public instruction who had developed a model school system for California. Like Keith, Swett
visited every week and listened critically as Muir read his papers
in a cloud of smoke, much of it from his own pipe, for he had
lately taken up tobacco. "Write as you talk," Swett urged. "Stop
revising so much. You make your style so slippery a man can't
stand on it."

Muir saw much of the Carrs, and once at their house he met
three people who would figure large in his future—Dr. John
Theophile Strentzel, his wife Louisiana, and their daughter Louie
Wanda. Dr. Strentzel, a Polish exile who had enjoyed European
training in medicine and horticulture, now raised fruit on a ranch
in Contra Costa County. Louie Wanda had graduated from the
Benicia forerunner of Mills College and was a pianist accomplished enough to receive encouragement to try the concert stage.
She had remained at home, however, and helped with the accounts of her father's ranch.

Dark-haired and gray-eyed, she had received a number of marriage proposals, but had turned them down in her shy, retiring way. She was twenty-seven in 1874, the summer she and Muir met, and now approached the age of spinsterhood by the accepted standards of the day. But Jeanne Carr had designs on Louie for her protégé and had written to her two years before: "I want you to meet my John Muir. I wish I could give him to some noble young woman 'for keeps' and so take him out of the wilderness into the society of his peers." Sensing perhaps a matchmaking scheme on Jeanne Carr's part, Muir was noncommital when Dr. Strentzel and his wife invited him to visit their ranch-house near Martinez. In a sense, however, the potentials inherent in the meeting with the Strentzels made it the unspoken climax of Muir's Oakland sojourn.

The stay ended in September 1874. After taking the last installment of "Studies in the Sierra" to the *Overland* office, Muir walked along a plank sidewalk in San Francisco and suddenly met a spray of goldenrod crisping in the end-of-summer heat. In the uncongenial atmosphere of the city he felt as alien and withered as the flower, and all at once he knew that he had had enough. He rushed home, gathered up his few belongings, said goodbye to the McChesneys and the Carrs, and fled to the mountains in what he described as "a dreamy, exhausted daze."

CHAPTER II

King Sequoia

ON reaching Yosemite, Muir sensed that his relationship with the valley had changed, now that he had completed "Studies in the Sierra." "No one of the rocks seems to call me now," he informed Jeanne Carr, "nor any of the distant mountains. Surely this Merced and Tuolumne chapter of my life is done." Yet he remained there until October, taking stock and dedicating his life anew. What he next wrote to her was of special significance in view of the future course of his career. "I care to live only to entice people to look at Natures's loveliness." This was an admission that he wished to live for a cause, to become an apostle of nature. On another occasion he described the newfound mission as "preach[ing] Nature like an apostle"; and on still another occasion he described it with even fuller religious overtones: "Heaven knows that John [the] Baptist was not more eager to get all his fellow sinners into the Jordan than I to baptize all of mine in the beauty of God's mountains."

But until his preparation was complete, there were other things to do, other things to see. One thing he longed to behold was Mount Shasta with the three glaciers Clarence King had discovered there in 1870. So in late October 1874 he headed "Shastaward" over the stage road to Oregon. When fifty miles from the mountain, he could see its white cone rising eight thousand feet above the "braided folds" of the Sacramento Valley, and he wrote that the sight had turned his blood to wine and that he had not been weary since. He stopped at Sisson's Station, site of the future city of Mount Shasta, and there on November 1 Justin Sisson fitted him out with blankets and a week's provisions and added the stern warning that it was much too late in the season to climb the peak. "But I like snow," Muir replied.

A guide named Jerome Fay accompanied him the first day. They camped at timberline, rising at one thirty in the morning, Fay heading back to Sisson's with the horses, while Muir climbed on alone through drifts of deep snow. By half-past ten he reached the highest pinnacle, only to be forced back by a dense storm cloud that engulfed the mountain. He regained his timberline camp an hour before dark, with only time enough to prepare a "nest" for himself by hollowing out a stretch of sand on the leeside of a mass of maroon lava, where plentiful firewood lay at hand.

For three days Muir remained snug in his "nest" while the storm raged. He occupied himself with such diversions as listening to the modulations of the wind, watching the "gestures" of a white-bark pine, studying snow crystals through his pocket lens, and observing a Douglas squirrel dig unerringly into the snow for grains of barley left by the horses. On the fourth day Sisson sent Jerome Fay back with two mustangs, and reluctantly Muir agreed to return to the hotel, where everyone welcomed him effusively, having given him up for dead.

From Sisson's he made excursions to such places as the foot of the Whitney Glacier. He also made a hundred-mile traverse around the base of the mountain to Rhett and Klamath lakes and to the Modoc Lava Beds, scene of the recent Modoc War, the hostilities of which he heard much about from wandering hunters and vaqueros. He reported what occurred in the Shasta area in five letters to the *San Francisco Evening Bulletin*, thus beginning a long association with that influential newspaper. As for the *Overland*, it would continue long enough to complete the serialization of "Studies in the Sierra" and to run four additional essays by Muir, including "By-Ways of Yosemite Travel: Bloody Cañon," "Wild Sheep of California," and "Wild Wool," the latter two pieces based to a large degree on his study of the bighorns in the Shasta area.

Muir left Sisson's near the end of December 1874 and drifted south to the region of the Feather and Yuba rivers. At Brownsville he visited Emily Pelton, who lived with relatives there. The highlight of this visit he later recounted in "A Windstorm in the Forests of the Yuba," an essay that *Scribner's Monthly* would publish in November 1878, and which, upon revision, would serve as a chapter in *The Mountains of California*. When a violent gale blew up, Muir stepped outdoors with his customary rejoicing in storms and pushed through the forest to realize the full excitement of the occasion. "I heard trees falling for hours at the rate of one every two or three minutes," he noted.

Suddenly the urge seized him to climb a wind-tossed tree to bring his ear "close to the Æolian music of its topmost needles." The right tree must be selected, one that would stand fast in the gale; and after a careful examination, he chose the tallest stalwart in a dense clump of Douglas firs. It would not topple, he reasoned, unless its companions went down with it, not a likely eventuality. Muir had no trouble climbing it, reaching a perch to which he clung like "a bobolink on a reed."

The wildest sweep of his tree-top seat registered an arc of some twenty or thirty degrees, but he felt sure of the tree's elastic defiance of the wind. He reveled in the splendid view it gave him of the agitated forest. The fascination afforded by the multicolored play of light was equalled only by what he felt at the play of sound, in which he could distinguish the individual chanting of every species of tree. He also savored the fragrance that streamed past, caused by the chafing together of resiny branches. He clung to his perch for hours, exhilarated by the spectacle, and climbed down only after the gale had begun to wane.

Muir was still in Brownsville on January 19, 1875, when another storm broke—a hard, warm rain with summery winds that melted the mountain snows, causing the rivers to flood. Muir braved the rain, as he had braved the gale, and enjoyed the downpour immensely, calling it "one of the grandest flood-storms" he had ever seen. He described it in "Flood-Storm in the Sierra," his final contribution to the *Overland*. It appeared in June 1875, and later a revised portion of it became a chapter in *The Mountains of California*. In it he assumed a rather supercilious attitude toward the havoc wrought. "True, some goods were destroyed," he wrote, "and a few rats and people were drowned, and some took cold on the rooftops and died, but the total loss was less than the gain."

Before the end of January 1875 he was back in Oakland, where he worked at his writing until April. Then he again turned Shasta-ward, having agreed to make barometrical readings there and locate a position for a geodetic monument for the U.S. Coast Survey. Jerome Fay climbed the peak with him, and they were caught in an unexpected storm. It proved so violent that they could not make a safe descent to their camp at timberline, so they prepared to spend the night among the hissing fumeroles near the summit.

By talking to one another they managed to keep awake—they dared not fall asleep, lest the noxious fumes overcome them. They parboiled on one side and froze on the other and thus managed to wait out the night. With morning they began the struggle down to camp, finding it difficult to walk, since the legs of their frozen trousers refused to bend at the knee. But they reached camp by 10:00 A.M., half an hour before they heard Sisson call from a stand of firs. He had brought horses as far as possible and come the rest of the way on foot.

"Our feet were frozen," Muir wrote, "and thawing them was painful, and had to be done slowly by keeping them buried in soft snow for several hours." Muir remained so lame that Sisson had to drag him on a canvas to the waiting horses. The frostbite would leave him affected for the rest of his life, though not to the point of preventing him from doing further spectacular mountain-climbing.

On returning to San Francisco, Muir took up lodgings at John Swett's three-story house on Taylor Street. There he settled down again to his writing, but it came as hard as ever, much of his trouble stemming from the tyranny of an overweening criti-cal faculty. Now that the *Overland* was about to fold, not to resume publication until 1883, Keith suggested that he aim his work at journals in the East. In response to that advice Muir revised "Living Glaciers of California," an *Overland* article of 1872 that had been reprinted in Silliman's Journal, and sent it off to *Harper's New Monthly Magazine,* whose editor not only ac-cepted it, but also requested more, so that, with the *Bulletin* in San Francisco, Muir had a double market now for his work.

Meanwhile, in July 1875, Muir agreed to guide George Bayley, a wealthy San Franciscan, down to Mount Whitney. The first part of their itinerary corresponded roughly with Muir's route in 1873, even to their visiting the General Grant Grove. There they heard the sound of axes and, on investigating, found a gang of men at work preparing a section of a sequoia twenty-five feet in diameter for display at the Centennial Exposition, then impending in Philadelphia. "The section cut for exhibition," Muir reported, "is 16 feet long, split into eight immense staves, the heartwood being removed by splitting and hewing until the staves measure about eight inches in thickness inside the bark." These were to be transported by wagon to the railroad station at Visalia for shipment to the East. Muir added, "Many a poor, defrauded town dweller will pay his dollar and peep, and gain some dead arithmetical notion of the bigness of our Big Trees, but a true and living knowledge of these tree gods is not to be had at so cheap a rate. As well try to send a section of the storms on which they feed."

Muir and Bayley pushed on to the yosemite of the South Fork of the Kings, following an old Indian trail. It led them over Kearsarge Pass and down into Owens Valley, where they outfitted themselves at Independence for their proposed ascent of Mount Whitney. They climbed the peak by the route Muir had taken two years before, with certain variations in the interest of safety.

Afterward Muir returned to Yosemite, from where he set out again at the end of August 1875 to explore the southern groves of giant sequoias. He anticipated much hardship on the trip, but as he predicted, his "love of King Sequoia will make all the labor light." He traveled alone, except for a tough, rust-colored mule called Brownie. His first camp was at the Mariposa Grove, where he spent a week seeking clues on whether the grove had ever been larger, but he found no sign of that possibility. Then he headed southeast, finding neither sequoias nor evidence of their former existence until he scaled a towering rock called Wah-Mello by the Indians but now named Fresno Dome. This vantage point gave him a view of the heavily wooded basin of the upper Fresno, and amid the forest there he could see "the majestic

John Muir, in his customary slovenly clothes, standing next to a young specimen of his beloved Sequoia gigantea, the southern groves of which he toured
in 1875. The photo was doubtless taken at a later date. Courtesy of the Bancroft Library, University of California, Berkeley.

dome-like crowns of Big Trees." He hastened back to camp, packed Brownie, and struck out at once for the Fresno Grove.

On arriving there, he found that the grove occupied an area of some four square miles; and on wandering through it, he came upon a handsome new cabin, with a gray-haired old man reading a book beside the door. He seemed surprised that his hermitage had been discovered, but he welcomed Muir on learning that he was a tree enthusiast out to study the giant sequoias. The hermit's name was John A. Nelder; he had been a forty-niner and had endured many ups and downs before retiring to the grove. Muir found that he was "a fine kind man, who in going into the woods has at last gone home." During the following week Nelder showed Muir many features of the Fresno Grove, which would in time undergo a name change—to that of Nelder.

The next Big Trees that Muir located were a small stand on the northern tributary of the Kings called Dinky Creek—a grove that would later bear the name of McKinley. From there Muir descended into the main canyon of the Kings, finding it fully a mile deep. He had to lead Brownie, and sometimes even shove and drag him through chaparral and over talus, the long-enduring mule having become more of a liability than a help. They made their way through deep gorges until they came to the stands of sequoias along the South Fork of the Kings.

Shortly thereafter Muir reached the Converse basin, which nourished a luxuriant forest nearly six miles long and two miles wide, composed mostly of Big Trees. He spent almost a week studying these giants, most of which would eventually be felled quite wastefully. Here Muir found that young sequoias were more numerous than in either the Fresno or the Dinky Creek groves. Here he also found the largest tree of all, a stump one hundred and forty feet tall. It was over thirty-five feet in diameter inside the bark at four feet above ground, and Muir estimated that before the bark had been burned away the stump had measured forty feet across. It was burned half through, and on chopping away the charred surface, he counted the annual rings with his pocket lens. He learned that the tree had reached an age of over four thousand years before it died.

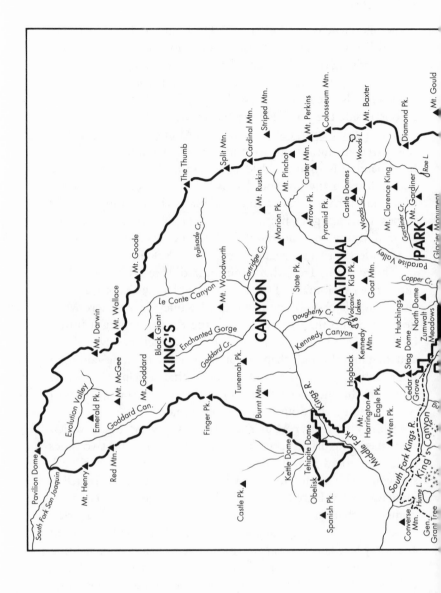

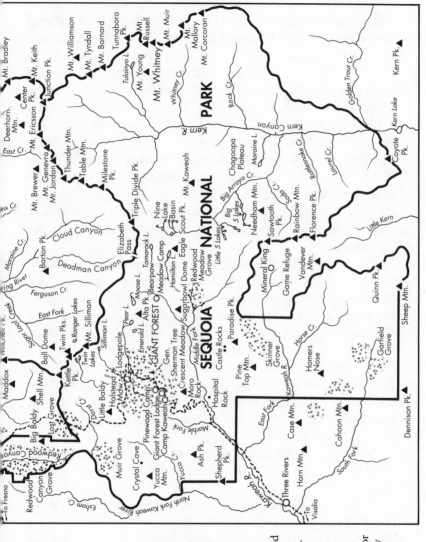

Map of Kings
Canyon and
Sequoia national
parks. Muir worked
hard to establish
Kings Canyon Na-
tional Park, and
there was an un-
successful move-
ment to have it
named in his honor
when it was finally
created in 1940.

Next Muir found scattered sequoias on the Kings-Kaweah divide, extending almost as far as Hyde's Mill, "a sore, sad center of destruction" on a tributary of Dry Creek. Long strings of oxen dragged logs up to twelve feet in diameter and rolled them into a chute, down which they slid to the mill. There the largest of them were blasted into sizes suitable for the saws. "And as the timber is very brash," Muir wrote, "by this blasting and careless felling on uneven ground, half or three-fourths of the timber was wasted"—squandering that appalled him. At the outset of his Big Tree survey he had posed a question in his journal: "What is the human part of the mountains' destiny?" To see the Hyde Mill in operation suggested a distressing answer—that "the human part" was to extract the mountains' wealth as speedily as possible, as wastefully as necessary, without a single concern for the future.

For several days he studied the sequoias along the Kings-Kaweah divide and counted annual rings on the stumps of felled trees. Then he secured fresh provisions and headed south again. Eventually after an exploration of the Kaweah basin, he decided that the splendid forest on the Marble and Middle Fork divide was the finest he had yet met, and he called it the Giant Forest, a name that would endure. One afternoon, while admiring a lush Kaweah meadow, he heard the drum of a horse's hoofs, and suddenly a single horseman burst into view. The rider seemed surprised to see Muir and abruptly asked, "What are you doing? How did you get here?"

Muir replied that he had come from Yosemite to study trees.

"Oh then, I know," the stranger said. "You must be John Muir."

At the horseman's shift from suspicion to civility, Muir wondered if he might replenish his all but empty breadsack. He asked the stranger if he could spare some flour. "Oh yes," said the man, who introduced himself as Hale Tharp. "Just take my track, and it will lead you to my camp in a big hollow log on the side of a meadow two or three miles from here." Tharp said he had to round up some strayed horses, but that he would return before night. "In the meantime make yourself at home."

Muir found the hollow sequoia without trouble—"a spacious loghouse of one log, carbon-lined [for fire had consumed its heart], centuries old yet sweet and fresh, weather proof, earth-quake proof, likely to outlast the most durable stone castle." When Tharp came in, he gave Muir many particulars about the forest, on whose meadows his many horses grazed. He said the Big Trees extended far to the south—just how far he wasn't sure. Under his guidance Muir examined the Giant Forest for several days thereafter, then moved on, lest an early storm end his survey prematurely.

He had not gone far when he met a forest fire that blazed between the Middle and East forks of the Kaweah; "and as fire is the master scourge and controller of the distribution of trees," he wrote, "I stopped to watch it and learn what I could of its works and ways with the giants." He tied Brownie a safe distance away, then selected for himself a strong hollow trunk, which he considered safe from being shattered by the fall of burning trees. Inside, he made a bed of ferns and sequoia foliage. He got little sleep, however, for he spent most of each night in watching the spectacle of the flames as they swept through the trees.

After his study of the fire, Muir again struck southward. In the Tule basin he found magnificent forests, and the one on the North Fork of the Tule River seemed the finest of all, surpassing, he suspected, even the Giant Forest of the Kaweah. However, sheep had mercilessly grazed the entire basin, consuming every sprig of grass and every edible shrub, so that Brownie began to starve. One evening he approached Muir with "a pitiful mixture of bray and neigh." "It was a mighty touching prayer," Muir wrote, and he gave the mule half a loaf that he had baked from his last flour.

"Yes, poor fellow, I know, but soon you'll have plenty," he said. "Tomorrow down we go to alfalfa and barley."

Muir kept his word, heading west the next morning toward the Tulare lowlands. There Brownie received grain and was put to pasture. Two days later Muir returned to the mountains with-out him and searched out the southerly extremity of the Big Tree belt on the South Fork of Deer Creek. By the close of his explora-

tion he had visited fully two-thirds of the seventy-five sequoia
groves finally located in the Sierra Nevada. He had found that the
Big Tree belt extended about 260 miles in length, but that the majority of the trees were concentrated in the section that stretched
for about seventy miles south of the Kings River. The size of the
trees averaged about the same throughout the belt, a diameter of
twenty feet and a height of 275 feet being the norm. Trees twenty-
five feet across were not uncommon, some rising nearly three
hundred feet in the air. Now and then one encountered a specimen thirty feet in diameter, but almost never any that were
larger. Nowhere had he found any indication that the sequoia
had ever grown beyond its present limits. "On the contrary," he
pointed out, "it seems to be slightly extending its boundaries; for
the outstanding stragglers, occasionally met a mile or two from
the main bodies, are young instead of old monumental trees."

Muir described his exploration of the Big Tree belt in two
letters for the *Bulletin;* a third letter on the later stages of the
trip, if ever sent to the newspaper, was never published. But he
would later revise the material of all three letters in an article
called "The New Sequoia Forests of California," which *Harper's*
would publish in 1878. A later version, further revised and entitled "Hunting Big Redwoods," would appear in the *Atlantic* in
1901 and be incorporated under the title of "The Sequoia and
General Grant National Parks" that same year in *Our National
Parks.*

On retrieving Brownie, Muir returned to Yosemite, where he
learned that a hardy Scotsman named George Anderson had
climbed Half Dome by drilling holes in the granite and inserting
eyebolts, to which he had attached ropes. Muir resolved to climb
the dome himself, regardless of how late the season. Both the
rock and Anderson's ropes proved perilously slippery, but he
succeeded in gaining the top. "The first view was perfectly glorious," he would remember in *The Yosemite*. "A massive cloud of
pure pearl luster . . . was arched across the Valley from wall to
wall." As he gazed, he saw the rare optical illusion the Scots

called the Specter of the Brocken. "My shadow, clearly outlined, about half a mile long, lay upon this glorious white surface with startling effect. I walked back and forth, waved my arms and struck all sorts of attitudes, to see every slightest movement enormously exaggerated."

CHAPTER 12

New Directions

ON coming down from the Sierra in the fall of 1875, Muir felt more dedicated than ever to his mission of "entic[ing] people to look at Nature's loveliness." He was convinced of humanity's need for the healing power of nature, and he wrote on November 12, "I . . . think of the thousands needing rest—the weary in soul and limb, toilers in town and plain, dying for want of what those grand old woods can give. And though . . . it may be of no avail, I yet shout: 'Ho, come to the Sierra forests. The King is waiting for you— King Sequoia!' There is health and life in his very looks."

He recognized, of course, that bringing people to the forests and mountains would entail liabilities. The slovenly appearance of the floor of Yosemite Valley amply demonstrated the cost of tourism and "improvement." At the same time sawmills and sheep had hurt the Sierra forests even more. On his recent survey of the Big Tree groves south of Yosemite Muir had encountered no fewer than five sawmills, where wastefulness had made him sick at heart; while of the sheep he had written that no recurrence of a universal volcanic outpouring or return of a glacial winter could destroy the shrubs and flowers of the Sierra more completely than did the sheep. But even greater menaces were the sheepmen and the fires they set when leaving the mountains at the end of the summer's grazing in order to "improve" the pastures for the coming year. Sawmills, sheep, and sheepmen put the forests in mortal jeopardy, and if their combined onslaughts should destroy the watershed, the lowlands would become desert wastes, with floods in the spring and minimal water in the summer.

Muir mulled these matters over in San Francisco during the early winter of 1875–76. And when he agreed to speak about glaciers before the Literary Institute of Sacramento on January 25, he decided to inject something about Sierra forests into his talk. In spite of his suffering stagefright to the point of nausea and cold sweat, the speech pressed its forest gospel so effectively that a local newspaper reported, "Mr. Muir was at once the most un-artistic and refreshing, the most unconventional and positive lec-turer we have yet had in Sacramento."

John Swett wondered if any legislators had heard the lecture, and it may have been his remark that prompted Muir to fall at once to writing an article that advocated government oversight of forests on public lands. The *Sacramento Record-Union* pub-lished it on February 5, under a headline inspired by a poem by William Cullen Bryant: "'GOD'S FIRST TEMPLES:' How Shall We Preserve Our Forests?" Since Muir was appealing to "practical legislators," he stressed the economic necessity of forest protec-tion. In doing so, he indicted the sawmills as destroyers of the watershed. But the "deadliest enemies," he argued, were the sheepmen and their fires.

That something should be done about the situation seemed self-evident, and Muir indicated that much could be learned from the measures taken by several European governments to study the economics of forestry and to protect their trees. "Whether our loose-jointed Government is really able or willing to do anything in the matter," he speculated, "remains to be seen. If our law-makers were to discover and enforce any method tending to lessen even in a small degree the destruction that is going on, they would thus cover a multitude of legislative sins." Predict-ably, the article had little impact on the legislators at whom it was aimed, but as William Frederic Badè later pointed out, "It made Muir the center around which conservation sentiment began to crystallize."

Muir's debut as a forest advocate coincided with the emer-gence of the American Forestry Association, organized the pre-vious year under the leadership of John A. Warder, said to have first used the term "conservation" in the sense that it now gener-ally conveys. Like Warder, who helped to establish Arbor Day, Muir drew on a philosophical fountainhead that had, since 1864, prepared the way for the conservation movement—George Per-

kins Marsh's *Man and Nature*. Muir mined Marsh's seminal statement for data and direction, even though its thesis did not exactly
square with his demotion of Lord Man. Nevertheless, Marsh's
ideas informed still another case that Muir now made on behalf of
trees—a paper "On the Post-Glacial History of Sequoia Gigantea."

In it he advanced his conclusion that the area inhabited by
the Big Trees had probably not shrunk during postglacial times.
But now relentless forces worked against the giant sequoia, and
Muir closed his long, scholarly paper with a statement reminiscent of "'God's First Temples'": "It appears . . . that notwithstanding our forest king might live on gloriously in Nature's
keeping, it is rapidly vanishing before the fire and steel of man;
and unless protective measures be speedily invented and applied
in a few decades at the farthest, all that will be left of Sequoia
gigantea will be a few hacked and scarred monuments." The
paper, read at Asa Gray's request at a meeting of the Association
for the Advancement of Science, appeared in the *Proceedings* of
that society in May of the following year, shortly after Muir's
departure for the territory of Utah.

In that Mormon land he studied glacial evidence in the Wa-
satch Mountains, bathed in the Great Salt Lake, heard Brigham
Young exhort the Saints in the Mormon tabernacle, and closely
observed Salt Lake City and its people—men, women, and children. On watching the children, whom he called "Little Latter
Days," he found it "hard to believe the dark, bloody passages of
Mormon history." To him the women seemed more married to
one another than to their shared husbands, and he judged that
polygamy exerted "a more degrading influence upon husbands
than upon wives." From Salt Lake City he sent four letters to the
Bulletin, and they were posthumously included in *Steep Trails,*
which Professor Badè would assemble and publish in 1918. *Steep
Trails* would open with "Wild Wool," one of the most penetrat-
ing essays Muir ever wrote, ostensibly a comparison of the fine-
ness of the wool of the wild mountain sheep with that of its
domestic relative, but in reality a polemic on the question of wild
nature versus culture or civilization. The rest of the book, however, other than its chapters on Mount Shasta and the Grand

Canyon as well as the letter to Mrs. Carr called "A Geologist's Winter Walk," would seldom rise above the ordinary, even though it stressed description, Muir's literary forte.

After Utah, Muir went to southern California, where he visited the San Gabriel Mountains and the San Gabriel Valley, reporting his experiences in two letters to the *Bulletin;* and they, too, would reappear in *Steep Trails.* While returning to San Francisco he made plans to explore the forests of Oregon and Washington, but had to defer them when he found Asa Gray and his wife awaiting him, along with the English botanist Sir Joseph Hooker, director of Kew Gardens. They asked him to be their guide to Mount Shasta, and he gladly agreed to do so. On the way to the peak they stopped at Rancho Chico near the Sacramento River, and General John Bidwell and his wife and her sister joined the party.

They made their camp near timberline on Shasta, and from there the four men went forth every day in search of plants. A highlight of their botanizing was their finding *Linnaea borealis,* a plant named for Carl Linnaeus, the pioneer botanist of whom Muir would write an appreciation in 1896. At the day's end they would talk around their campfire until far into the night, and in *Our National Parks* Muir would reminisce about one of their conversations. Knowing that Gray and Hooker were familiar with all the great forests of the earth, he inquired if they were aware of any coniferous forest that matched those of the Sierra. "No," they said without hesitation. "In the beauty and grandeur of individual trees, and in number and variety of species, the Sierra forests surpass all others."

After Sir Joseph and the Grays had started back to San Francisco, the Bidwells invited Muir to go with them to Mount Lassen, then spend a week at their Italianate mansion at Rancho Chico. This he did, and when ready to depart, he confessed an urge to float down the Sacramento in a skiff. No sooner said than Bidwell ordered his carpenter to build a boat, which the general pronounced "a poor thing" when it was finished. "A poor thing," Muir agreed, "but mine own!" He named it the *Spoonbill.*

He bade his hosts goodbye on October 3 and rowed out into

the river. He had plenty of food, a warm quilt from Mrs. Bidwell, and two American flags, one flying at the bow, the other at the stern. He floated with the current, rowing only when necessary, and kept alert for river life, especially water birds; and all the while the *Spoonbill* eased over algae-covered snags so handily that he soon changed its name to *Snagjumper*. Five days of floating, paddling, and rowing brought him to Sacramento, where he abandoned the boat; for river water was at such a low stage that he now gave up a plan to row up the San Joaquin. Instead, he decided to explore the Middle Fork of the Kings Canyon, which contained a gorge termed "inaccessible," one that he had glimpsed but never entered.

He went by rail to Visalia and from there he headed by an indirect route to the Middle Fork of the Kings, down whose entire length he forged, exploding the reputation for inaccessibility that its lower reaches had heretofore enjoyed, though in doing so he ran out of food and had to starve for the last four days of his excursion. Then on emerging from the mountains, he went by rail and stagecoach to Hopeton on the Merced. "Here," he wrote, "I built a little unpretentious successor to *Snag* out of some gnarled, sun-twisted fencing, launched it in the Merced . . . and rowed down into the San Joaquin—thence . . . past Stockton and through the tule region into the bay near Martinez"—a voyage of 250 miles, requiring two weeks. *Snagjumper II* leaked badly, and Muir found it necessary to drag it over many sandbars in the shrunken San Joaquin.

At Martinez he decided to accept the three-year-old invitation of the Strentzels to visit their ranch in the Alhambra Valley with its 2,600 acres of orchards and vineyards. The Strentzels welcomed him warmly. "They pitied my weary look," he wrote to Sarah. Not only was he gaunt, but his beard was unkempt, his red-brown hair reached nearly to his shoulders, and his faded greenish coat was ragged at the wrists and elbows. The Strentzels pressed him to stay a month, so he rested there for two days. "[They] made me eat and sleep," he wrote, "stuffing me with turkey, chicken, beef, fruits, and jellies in the most extravagant manner." And he and Dr. Strentzel talked earnestly about scientific matters.

On leaving the Alhambra Valley Muir walked to Oakland by way of Mount Diablo, then crossed San Francisco Bay by ferry, and finished his wandering at the house of John Swett. To Mary Swett he spoke of his visit with the Strentzels and made much of the doctor's scientific knowledge. "Did you by any chance observe a young lady about the house?" Mary asked with a twinkle in her eye.

"Well, yes," he conceded, "there was a young lady there."

In his third-story room at the Swett house Muir again went at his writing, which he interrupted to give public lectures about glaciers, the Big Trees, and even the Mormons in Utah; at the same time there was much lively talk at home. The Swett children refused to go to bed until "Uncle John" had told his nightly bedtime story, and he loved to relate his adventures to John and Mary Swett, who would then say, "Now, John, go upstairs and write that down just as you have told it to us." This he sometimes did, and some of his best writing came that way.

This period saw the production of popular essays like "The Douglas Squirrel of California," a character sketch of the species Muir considered the "master-forester," and "The Humming-Bird of the California Water-Falls," about the small gray water ouzel, of which he said, "Among all the the mountain birds, none has cheered me so much in my lonely wandering." The articles of this period, mostly destined for collection in *The Mountains of California,* gave Muir a national reputation when published in such eastern magazines as *Harper's* and *Scribner's.*

Along with the articles of John Burroughs, they brought the nature essay in America to a high surpassed only by the work of Thoreau. Their effect on the reading public exceeded that made by the work of such nature writers as Wilson Flagg and Thomas Wentworth Higginson, the latter of whom had taken time off from leading a black regiment during the Civil War to write evocative essays like "Water Lilies" for the *Atlantic Monthly.* But beguiling as Flagg's and Higginson's nature essays were to postwar readers, it was first Burroughs and then Muir who emerged as the chief contributors to the flowering of the nature writing genre in the 1870s.

In the winter and spring of 1878 Muir laid down his quill to pay several visits to the Strentzels. He not only talked science with the doctor again, but he also walked through the orchards and over the nearby hills with Louie Strentzel as his sole companion. He had confessed to Sarah how restless he had grown in the loneliness of bachelorhood. But if romance was budding, it did not keep Muir at home beside the bay. In the summer of 1878 he accepted the invitation of Captain A. F. Rodgers to join a geodetic survey across Nevada, an expedition of the U.S. Coast Survey (soon to add "Geodetic" to its name) to make a primary triangulation along the thirty-ninth parallel. The Strentzels advised him not to go because of the Bannock War, which they feared would make Nevada unsafe. "The war country," Muir explained to Mrs. Strentzel, "lies to the north of our line of work some two or three hundred miles."

He joined the survey party at Sacramento, and on July 11 they reached the Walker River, from where Muir informed the Strentzels that all was well: "All the Indians we meet are harmless as sagebushes, though perhaps about as bitter at heart." Assigned work led the survey party by August 17 to the Toquima Range, where on a peak called Mount Jefferson Muir found fine glacial monuments—"moraines, cañons with U-shaped cross sections, wide névé amphitheaters, moutonéed rocks, glacier meadows, and one glacier lake, all as fresh and telling as if the glaciers to which they belonged had scarcely vanished." Otherwise the general sparsity of glacial signs in Nevada tended to attenuate his adherence to Agassiz's axiom of the universal ice sheet.*

Having traveled south from Austin through the Big Smoky

---

*"There probably was," he noted in his journal, "a period of general glaciation of the whole continent by a general flow from the north southward, sweeping like a mighty wind over this and all the other plateaus, but of this action I have as yet found no monuments that I am capable of reading." In his letter to the *Bulletin* on Nevada glaciation he suggested more than one glacial stage, but evidently did not settle down to that new belief.

Valley, between the Toquima and the Toyabe ranges, the survey party came at last to Lone Mountain, which Captain Rodgers decided their work required them to climb. Muir counseled against the ascent, since the only known water was forty miles away, but his advice went unheeded. Near disaster followed, with his two companions almost dying when their water gave out. "I suffered least," Muir wrote the Strentzels, "and was the only one strong enough to ascend a sandy cañon to find and fetch the animals after descending the mountain." Next he had to locate his two companions, who had wandered away. He discovered one of them lying "deathlike" in the baking sand, barely conscious and able to speak only in a ghastly whisper. Muir found the other in the sagebrush, stupefied and delirious. Their ordeal was far from over, however, for they did not reach water until daybreak of the second day.

Muir returned to San Francisco late in the fall of 1878, having sent the *Bulletin* six letters, five of which were later gathered in *Steep Trails*. His personal correspondence to the Strentzels had been addressed to the doctor and Mrs. Strentzel, but beyond all doubt the letters were meant for Louie as well. He found her charming, with her prim-looking face, high cheekbones, firm mouth, and clear, gray eyes. In many ways their liking for one another was a case of the attraction of opposites, for she was as diffident as he was outgoing, and as careful and correct in her dress as he was slovenly and farmerish. Muir had not gone to church for years, but she was a staunch churchgoing Methodist.

But they had things in common too, like their mutual love of botany. Louie cultivated a flower garden, and she paid close attention to the wild plants she met in her walks through the hills. "Whenever in my wanderings," she wrote to Jeanne Carr, "I look upon rare and perfect trees or flowers . . . the thought of their loveliness helps and comforts me all the day." Muir and Louie also had a mutual interest in astronomy. But she knew about a number of subjects that were strange to him, and she had a greater interest than he in politics and current affairs. She read with care everything he published, and he knew from her comments what a perceptive critic she was. A friend called her "old-

fashioned," but if she was, she would prove herself to be up to the
minute in resourcefulness.

More and more Muir felt he had found in her the right woman.
But his courtship was restrained, and not until a day in April 1879
did he summon courage to write to her directly, addressing her
formally and making only awkward progress until a box arrived
from the Alhambra Valley. Instantly, the floral contents broke his
inhibitions down. "Aren't they lovely!" he wrote. ". . . An orchard
in a bandbox!" Muir continued to visit the Strentzel ranch, and
there were still more walks through the orchards and on the hills.

But in the summer of 1879 he would have interrupted his
courtship for his long-deferred examination of the forests of Oregon and Washington, except that something caused that trip to
be postponed yet once again. The sponsors of a Sunday-school
convention in Yosemite Valley offered him a hundred dollars to
speak on glaciers and to lead some easy field trips about the
valley. Muir's appearance was a great success. Both the *San Francisco Chronicle* and the *Bulletin* gave it enthusiastic coverage, the
reporter for the *Chronicle* writing: "John Muir's living rehearsal
of the testimony of the rocks would charm an audience on the
sands of the Sahara—how infinitely more delightful in the very
theater of its well-studied facts." On going to the Alhambra
Valley afterward Muir found the Strentzels delighted with the
newspaper reports. Later that night he revealed the chief motive
for his visit, and the next day, June 17, 1879, Mrs. Strentzel recorded in her diary:

"Yesterday evening Louie and Mr. Muir became engaged for
life. Papa and I had retired, when about 1 o'clock Louie came
to me, overcome with emotion, threw her arms around me and
said, O, Mother, all is well, all is well. . . . This morning we all
arose with thankful hearts. I wondered if there ever were four
happier people than we." Then she added, "Mr. Muir is the only
man that the Dr. and I have ever felt we could take into our
family as one of us and he is the only one that Louie has ever
loved."

Muir had proposed on his own terms, and Louie had accepted them. The first condition was that, before the wedding,

he must go north, possibly as far as Alaska to see the glaciers that
Dr. Sheldon Jackson, Alaska missionary, had described at the
Yosemite convention. Muir had wanted to see the glaciers of
Alaska for a long time—to study in actual operation the processes
by which Yosemite Valley had been formed. The engagement
could be announced upon his return.

CHAPTER 13

First Trip to Alaska

ON June 19, 1879, Muir wrote to Jeanne Carr, with no mention of Louie or their engagement, that he intended to leave the next day for the North. He sailed first to Puget Sound for delightful views of the Olympic Mountains, then doubled back to Portland, where he caught the mail ship *California* for southeastern Alaska via the inland passage. On board were three eminent divines, including Dr. Sheldon Jackson. They did not encourage Muir's company, calling him "that wild Muir," but he was just as aloof as they. That was not so with the young missionary who met the doctors of divinity when the ship docked at Fort Wrangell, Alaska. Muir, in a Scots cap and a long tweed ulster, was introduced to the missionary as "Professor Muir, the Naturalist" and learned that the young man's name was S. Hall Young. "A hearty grip of the hand," Young would write, "and we seemed to coalesce at once in a friendship which . . . has been one of the very best things I have known in a life full of blessings."

At first sight Fort Wrangell struck Muir as the most inhospitable town he had ever encountered, without a single tavern or lodging house to be found. He spent the first night on the shavings-covered floor of a carpentry shop connected with the Presbyterian mission located inside the stockade of the old abandoned fort. The next day a merchant named John Vanderbilt heard of his plight and invited Muir to stay with his family at "the best house in the fort." Muir's impression of the two-street town—later known merely as Wrangell—did not improve with time, and he described it as "a lawless draggle of wooden huts and houses, built in crooked lines." In general the whites lived in the middle of the town, with Stikine Indians (regularly spelled "Stickeen" in Muir's day) inhabiting either end.

S. Hall Young, missionary
friend of Muir's and his
companion on excursions
in Alaska. After Muir's
death Young published
the engaging book *Alaska
Days with John Muir.*
Courtesy of the Bancroft
Library, University of
California, Berkeley.

Shortly after his arrival there Muir made an interesting short
trip from the town up the Stikine River on the small steamer
Cassiar. The visiting divines had chartered the vessel for missionary purposes, and along with Hall Young they invited Muir to
accompany them. The *Cassiar* steamed as far as the head of
navigation, passing more than a hundred glaciers. On their return the captain tied up at Glenora, British Columbia, a post of
the Hudson's Bay Company at the foot of Glenora Peak, and announced that he would not get under way again until the next
morning. Therefore, although it was already three in the afternoon, Muir decided to climb the peak, which towered seven
thousand feet above the river. Young begged to accompany him,
insisting that he was a good climber. What he did not reveal was
that, in his adolescence, he had dislocated both shoulders while
breaking colts in West Virginia, and that the joints had never
regained their original strength. Unaware of this disability, Muir
accepted the missionary as his climbing companion.

In the first stages of the ascent Young proved himself a sturdy

climber, hard put though he was to keep up with Muir, who
impressed him as the finest mountaineer he had ever seen, seeming to slide up the mountain. At one point they crossed an imposing glacier, and then they were faced by a slate precipice one
thousand feet high. It struck Young as inaccessible, but on examining it, Muir's experienced eye detected a route by which it
could be climbed. Up he started, and to follow him Young had to
press himself so hard that he could feel his left humerus begin to
slip from its socket. Then as Muir climbed around a shoulder of
the cliff about fifty feet from the summit, he came upon a place
of disintegrating rock that was in danger of sliding. "Be careful
here," he shouted to Young. "This is dangerous."

The missionary was only a dozen yards behind, but failed to
understand the warning. Soon Muir heard him cry for help, and
on hastening back, he found Young lying face down, with arms
stretched out and fingers clutching at crumbling projections on
the edge of a gulley that plunged to the glacier a thousand feet
below.

"My God!" Muir said. "Grab that rock, man, back by your
right hand."

"My arms are out," Young gasped in reply.

"I'm going to get you out of this," Muir assured him. He
then explained how he would have to come down from the other
side, then moved away, whistling "The Bluebells of Scotland" as
though to hearten Young. It took him ten minutes to work himself around to a narrow ledge below where the missionary's legs
dangled over the brink. "I'm below you," he encouraged Young.
"You're in no danger. You can't slip past me." Muir then reached
up and grabbed Young's trousers at the waist, cautioning him to
hold steady, then swung him over the perilous edge and slowly
tipped him upright until the disabled man could touch the cliff
with his shoes. Muir directed him to work downward with his
feet. Then as Young's feet found the narrow shelf that supported
Muir, Muir seized his collar with his teeth, necessary as it was to
free his hands in order to climb.

In his later account Hall Young confessed that he could never
understand how Muir succeeded in saving him, and Muir himself

would write that he was at his wit's end as to how to roll or drag Young to some spot where he could determine how badly hurt he was, not to mention how to find a way down the mountainside. "I hastily examined the ground," he wrote, "and saw no way of getting him down except by the steep glacier gulley. . . . Accordingly, I cheered him up, telling him I had found a way, but that it would require lots of time and patience."

Muir then dug a foothold in the crumbling rock five or six feet below the missionary, and reaching up, he took hold of one of Young's feet and, sliding him carefully downward, settled his heels in the excavated step. Then Muir repeated the process, going down another five or six feet and digging another notch for Young's heels and sliding him down to it on his back. "Thus," Muir summed the operation up, "the whole distance was made by a succession of narrow steps at very short intervals, and the glacier was reached . . . about midnight." There, with his heel in the missionary's armpit, Muir succeeded in pulling one humerus into its socket, but all his strength was not great enough to correct the dislocation of the other. Muir lashed the arm securely to Young's side by means of the missionary's suspenders and his own handkerchiefs. Then he asked if Young had strength to walk.

"Yes," Young answered, resolutely.

By slow stages, building fires at intervals to keep Young warm, Muir brought him to the boat landing by 7:30 in the morning.

Hall Young would tell of the Glenora adventure in many later lectures, and after Muir's death he would publish an account of it in *Alaska Days with John Muir*. But Muir mentioned the adventure neither in his journal nor in any of his letters to the *Bulletin*. He never intended to publish anything about the matter until the minister George Wharton James published in the *Craftsman* what in Muir's opinion was "a miserable sensational caricature of the story." Then to set the record straight he decided to include a strictly factual version in his final book, *Travels in Alaska*.

Meanwhile, of the several trips Muir made from Fort Wrangell, that which he considered the high point of his first Alaska sojourn was a canoe voyage northward to visit the Chilcats, the fiercest, richest, and most influential Indians on the Alaska coast, and to search for a mysterious place of ice the Indians called Sitadaka. On October 16 came the time for departure. There were six in the party that Young had organized—Young "the Sky Chief"; Muir "the Ice Chief"; Toyatte, a senior Stikine chief who owned the party's transportation (a thirty-six foot canoe, hewn from a large log of red cedar); Kadachan, son of a Chilcat chief and a Stikine mother and a Stikine chief in his own right; Stickeen John, the interpreter; and Sitka Charley, a seal hunter who had visited Sitadaka in his boyhood. Toyatte became captain because the canoe was his and because of his wisdom in matters of seamanship and woodcraft.

The trip took them through the northern part of the Alexander Archipelago. As a rule, they camped in sheltered nooks abounding in firewood, their canoe pulled up on shore beyond the contact of the waves. An unexpected bonus of the trip was the improved opinion of Indians that it gave to Muir, prompting him to feel much more respect for Native Americans than his meetings with Indians in the lower American West had done. "After supper we sat long around the fire," he wrote, "listening to the Indians' stories about the wild animals, their hunting-adventures, wars, traditions, religion, and customs." Most of what he heard he found excellent, especially the Indians' belief in the immortality of animals. His approval was reinforced by the behavior of his native companions, which remained above reproach throughout the trip. Nor did any of the natives they encountered along the way undercut Muir's improved opinion of Indians. "Every Indian party we met we interviewed," he wrote, "and visited every village we came to."

The first village was of the Kake tribe on Kupreanof Island. It was Young's custom on such occasions to present the village chief with a "potlach" of rice, sugar, and tobacco, then request him to call his people together, so that Young could preach to them. Toyatte and Kadachan would assist by praying in Tlingit; even Stickeen John and Sitka Charley would help by singing hymns. The Indians would ask the "Ice Chief" to speak, too; but Muir tried to avoid doing so by having Stickeen John explain that he was only a visitor, come to observe the glaciers, mountains, and forests. But that was what the Indians wanted to hear about most of all, so they would press him further. It became his routine therefore to say that all men were brothers and that God loved the red man as much as the white, the proof being "the beautiful and foodful country" He had given to the Indians.

After an agreeable session with the Kakes, Muir's party moved on to Admiralty Island, where the Hootzenoos lived. They had a gratifying reception at the first Hootzenoo village; but at the main village, Killisnoo, they encountered the "whiskey howl," indicating pervasive drunkenness; and judging the situation quite unpromising, they did not tarry. They crossed Chatham Strait and proceeded in the general direction of Sitadaka until they came to the main village of the Hoonahs beside an attractive bay on the south side of Icy Strait. Here all went well, with another successful palaver, in the course of which the Hoonahs confirmed rumors that the Chilcats were drinking whiskey freely and fighting among themselves, news that persuaded Young and Muir to defer their visit to that tribe. Instead, they would go at once in search of Sitadaka, and the Hoonahs gave them directions that seemingly agreed with Sitka Charley's memories.

But when they reached Sitadaka two days later, Sitka Charley seemed confused, declaring that the scene had changed so much since his boyhood that he scarcely recognized it. Therefore, on coming upon a camp of Hoonah seal hunters, Muir hired a Hoonah guide. The next day they followed a northwest course up the edge of the bay, passing the snout of the large glacier that Muir afterward named for the Scottish geologist, Archibald Geikie. The next day was Sunday, and as Hall Young refused to budge on the sabbath, Muir set out alone, glad to stretch his legs, cramped as they had been for days in the canoe. He climbed the ridge that bordered a second large glacier.

At first clouds obscured the landscape, but later they lifted; and Muir could see the bay, filled with bergs discharged from five huge glaciers, the nearest of which lay almost underneath him. This was Muir's first comprehensive view of Sitadaka, a scene that he would later describe as "a solitude of ice and snow and newborn rocks, dim, dreary, mysterious." It was later named

Glacier Bay and was destined to become a national monument in 1925 and a national park in 1980. Muir would often be credited with its discovery, but he was not the first white man to see it. According to the Indians, Russians had been there long before; and two years prior to Muir's visit, Colonel Charles Erskine Scott Wood, flamboyant poet, writer, painter, lawyer, and soldier, had pitched his camp there with a party of seal hunters.

On returning to the bivouac, Muir found that Toyatte and his crew wished to discontinue the trip because of the lateness of the season. "They had been asking [Young] what possible motive I could have in climbing mountains when storms were blowing; and when he replied that I was only seeking knowledge, Toyatte said, 'Muir must be a witch to seek knowledge in such a place as this and in such miserable weather.'" That was an ominous turn, since Alaska Indians regularly killed those they considered witches. But addressing the crew with unruffled confidence, Muir claimed that he had sought knowledge for ten years in perilous places and that God had always protected him. He assured them that the best of luck was always his lot, so that in his company they need fear nothing. His knack of inspiring confidence proved successful, and the Indians quickly regained heart.

The party spent five more days exploring Sitadaka, catching a fleeting glimpse of the majestic glacier that would later bear Muir's name. Then they took their Hoonah guide back to his camp, and at still another Hoonah camp they learned that peace had returned to the Chilcats. Therefore, on October 31 they headed up the Lynn Canal toward their original destination. At the first Chilcat village ceremonies were a great success, lasting three days, with the resident chief decked out in his best calico shirt. Also, Muir succeeded in saving a Chilcat baby's life. He heard wailing on the first night and was told that a baby was starving, since the mother had died and the Indians had no milk for the infant. He therefore took eight cans of Eagle brand milk from the party's stores (they had to drink their coffee black thereafter), and, mixing some of the condensed milk with warm water, he fed it to the baby. He left the remaining milk with the attending women, and the baby survived, as Young would report in his autobiography.

The lateness of the season forced Muir's party to cut short their visit to the Chilcats and abandon plans to visit others of their villages. Forerunners of winter were closing in as they headed south along the east bank of the Lynn Canal; ice made the way dangerous, especially with Muir compulsively seeking a glacier in every inlet. Toyatte lost patience when they entered Sum Dum Bay, a large, crooked, two-armed fiord filled with charging bergs, and refused to honor Muir's request that they proceed along the west branch to seek out whatever glacier might lie hidden there. Muir accepted the old chief's ultimatum, but resolved to return the following year to locate the "lost glacier of Sum Dum Bay." They reached Fort Wrangell on November 21, 1879, having completed a round trip of nearly eight hundred miles. Unfortunately, the mail ship had sailed eight days before, and Muir had to wait until late December to return to California.

CHAPTER 14

Stickeen

THE interest aroused by the eleven letters Muir sent to the *Bulletin* from Alaska led to his being "kuffed"—his word—into lecture engagements in Portland and San Francisco. He was therefore delayed in reaching the Alhambra Valley until the middle of February 1880, at which time Louie and he set April 14 for their wedding date. On that day, a week before Muir's forty-second birthday, the heavens burst in a gray downpour, but in contrast the walls of the Strentzel house glowed with sprays of red astrakhan apple blossoms. In the midst of such vibrant color the couple were married by a minister from Sacramento. "I could not have been more pleased," wrote Jeanne Carr, "if I had mixed the cup myself."

The wedding surprised a number of Muir's friends and relatives, who had come to think of him as the perennial bachelor. Sometimes, unfortunately, on breaking the news to others, he would forget to mention Louie, as when he told Asa Gray that his marriage had provided him with "a fixed camp" for storing burrs and grass. "You have mentioned the name of one party, John Muir," Gray fired back, "but you say not a word about the other. Now, who is she?" Such oversights on Muir's part might suggest that his love for Louie was hardly more than tepid at the time of their wedding—that his main motive for marrying seemed not so much love as security, "bairns," and a settled place to hang his hat. Nevertheless, in his own eccentric way he would make Louie an excellent husband over the years.

As a wedding present, Dr. Strentzel gave the newlyweds the Dutch Colonial ranchhouse and twenty acres of orchards surrounding it. Muir promptly leased additional land and compulsively went to work in the orchards and the vineyards the day

Louie Strentzel Muir, John Muir's wife, whom he married in 1880 and who lived with him at the Muir-Strentzel ranch until her death in 1905. *From The Life and Letters of John Muir,* Volume 2, edited by William F. Badè. Copyright 1924 by Houghton Mifflin Company, Copyright renewed 1952 by John Muir Hanna. Reprinted by permission of Houghton Mifflin Company. All rights reserved.

after the wedding. He toiled there until late July when, during the ripening of the grapes and until the principal harvest in October, he was free to go to the wilderness with Louie's blessing, even though she was now pregnant. With plans to return to Alaska to search for the "lost glacier" of Sum Dum Bay, he sailed north on July 30, reaching Fort Wrangell nine days later. At the dock he met Hall Young, who had come to meet the ship.

"When will you be ready?" Muir inquired. At Young's puzzled expression, he added, "Man, have you forgotten? Don't you know we lost a glacier last fall?"

Young instantly agreed to secure a canoe and a crew of Indians. Old Toyatte was dead, he said, shot in the forehead by whiskey-crazed Hootzenoos when he tried to make peace between them and the Stikines. As for Kadachan, he had taken to drink and was no longer reliable. But there were others, the missionary said, and he soon had a crew ready. Muir set out with him on August 16 in a twenty-five foot canoe, manned by two Stikine Indians—Captain Lot Tyeen and Hunter Joe—along with an interpreter known as "Smart Billy" Dickinson. Young also brought his dog, whom the Fort Wrangell Indians had honored with their name. "His markings were very much like those of an American Shepherd dog," Young wrote, "black, white and tan; although he was not half the size of one." At first Muir protested that Stickeen would be a nuisance, but soon the dog won him over and became a passenger for the duration of the trip.

The voyagers reached Sum Dum (later Holkham) Bay in four or five days. Muir requested that they first explore the eastern fiord, later known as the Endicott Arm, where they found a massive glacier that Muir named for Young. A later chartmaker changed the name to Dawes, however—"stole my glacier," as Young would complain in his autobiography. "I mourned the loss silently, and not until the visit of President Harding in 1923, when one of the officials of the Department of Topography learned of my loss, . . . did I get my glacier back."

Meanwhile, on August 21 the party paddled up the fiord later called the Tracy Arm, and at nine o'clock that evening, they came upon Muir's "lost glacier." "There is your lost friend," Tyeen declared, with a hearty laugh. "He says, 'Sagh-a-ya?' [How do you do?]"; for it was calving berg after berg with peals like thunder.

After the exploration of Sum Dum Bay, the voyagers investigated Taku Inlet, then moved on to Cross Sound, into which opened an inlet later known as Taylor Bay. At 5:00 P.M. on August 29 they made camp at the head of the bay near an immense flood of ice later known as the Brady Glacier, and while the Indians prepared supper, Muir and Young began to examine its terminus of ice. Muir noticed that it was not receding like all the other glaciers they had observed thus far, but was advancing like a titanic plowshare.

He informed Young of his aim to explore it the next morning. "I wish you could come along," he added. The unstable condition of Young's shoulders prevented him from going with Muir on his more strenuous climbs, but Muir had another companion.

Stickeen had adopted him as his master and followed him everywhere. That was so the next morning when Muir rose before
dawn and set out for the glacier of Taylor Bay after "bread and
rain for breakfast." At first he had thought Stickeen was asleep,
but as Young observed, "The little dog . . . always slept with one
eye and ear alert for Muir's movements."

"Go back," Muir ordered, "and get your breakfast." But
there was no turning Stickeen aside, and at last Muir accepted
him as his comrade for the day and gave him a piece of the bread
he carried in his pocket. They explored the glacier until five
o'clock in the afternoon, at which time they found themselves
about fifteen miles from camp. "I had to make haste," Muir
wrote, "to recross the glacier before dark." He then set his course
by compass and the structure lines of the ice; whereupon two
difficult hours followed, during which Stickeen trailed bravely
after him, "never hesitating," Muir wrote, "on the brink of any
crevasse I had jumped. But now that it was becoming dark and
the crevasses became more troublesome, he followed close at my
heels instead of scampering far and wide."

Finally they found themselves in a genuine predicament. In
the case of the last crevasse they had leaped, the edge on which
they had landed lay at a lower level than the side from which they
had jumped, and Muir doubted that he could make a successful
leap back. He had, thus, violated the "rule of mountaineers who
live long" by taking a course he couldn't retrace. It was necessary
to proceed forward, except that before them yawned a crevasse
forty feet wide, and on exploring its edge for a mile, they found
that it widened to not less than seventy-five feet. In dismay Muir
perceived that both ends of it joined the crevasse across which
they had only lately jumped. They were thus marooned on an
island of ice, and their only escape appeared to be by way of a
sliver-like bridge of ice that "hung diagonally from side to side
like a loose rope" some ten feet lower down. This sliver was apparently ancient, Muir decided, for it had been weathered to a
knife-edge and into "the worst bridge I ever saw." Getting down
to it and then up again on the other side looked like an im-
possibility.

But stooping, he cut a step with his ice ax in the blue wall of the ice; then standing on that, he chopped another. Successive chopping brought him at last to the wasted sliver-bridge. This he straddled, and hitching himself forward, he shaved the weathered knife edge of ice before him to produce a path four inches wide for Stickeen to walk along. And then when Muir himself had crossed the bridge, he chopped steps in the opposite wall and so regained the surface of the glacier. Now it was Stickeen's turn to make the crossing.

The little dog held back and tried to find some other way across, but always came back to the steps Muir had chopped. Muir reasoned with him as if he were a small boy, encouraging him to cross. At last Stickeen ventured down the hacked steps and advanced cautiously along the bridge. It was at the other wall that Muir feared he might fail, for as he wrote, "Dogs are poor climbers." While Muir considered the feasibility of fashioning a rope from his clothing to loop around Stickeen's neck, the little dog studied the ice stairs. "Then suddenly up he came," Muir wrote, "with a nervy, springy rush . . . and whizzed past my head, safe at last!"

Thereupon Stickeen darted hither and yon, as if a little daft, swirling around "like a leaf in a whirlwind," lying down and rolling over, all the while barking loudly, as if to say, "Saved! Saved! Saved!" Muir was convinced that he had spied into Stickeen's heart and that what he had seen there was of no essential difference from the human heart. "Stickeen's homely clay," he declared, ". . . had in it a little of everything that is in man; he was a horizontal manchild."

The two reached camp by ten o'clock that evening. A supper of mulligan stew and wild strawberries awaited Muir, but he was too worn out to eat at once. So was Stickeen, who spurned the wild goat meat Hunter Joe held out and quietly crept to his blanket in the tent. Only after Muir had stripped off his sodden clothing and dressed again in dry garments and warmed himself by the fire did he sit down to eat and drink hot coffee. After his third cup he broke his silence: "Yon's a brave doggie," he remarked; and as if Stickeen understood what Muir had said, he

thumped his tail against his blanket. When refreshed and restored, Muir gave an account of their day on the ice that held
Hall Young spellbound till midnight. It was "a succession of vivid
descriptions," the missionary would claim, "the like of which I
have never heard before or since."

On leaving Taylor Bay they doubled back through Cross Sound
and Icy Strait to Sitadaka, where they remained a week, with
Muir concerning himself principally with the extraordinary glacier that was soon to bear his name. One day he and Stickeen
crossed it diagonally for a round trip of thirty miles and found
that the glacier was so immense that he estimated it contained
as much ice as all the eleven hundred glaciers of Switzerland put
together. On another occasion he and Young drove lines of stakes
into its surface to determine its rate of flow, about fifty or sixty
feet a day. "This trip of ours to the Muir Glacier," Hall Young
subsequently wrote, "prepared the way for what was [later] considered the greatest scenic trip in the world."

From Sitadaka the voyagers went to Sitka by the most direct
route, lest Muir miss the monthly mail ship. "We traveled two
days and two nights without stopping," Young wrote, "and . . .
were rejoiced to find that the steamer had not yet arrived." They
were greeted warmly by the senior U.S. official in Alaska, Captain L. A. Beardslee of the gunboat *Jamestown*, who was extremely interested in their exploration of Sitadaka. At Beardslee's
request and from their notes and estimates of distances, Muir and
Young drew a rough map of the bay. This the captain sent to the
Navy Department with his annual report, and he would be credited with naming Glacier Bay, since he had penciled that designation on Muir and Young's map. It was also Beardslee who gave
Muir's name to the principal glacier of the bay.*

---

*The naming of the Muir Glacier continued a process that may have begun with
the naming of Muir Gorge in the Great Tuolumne Canyon. The esteem in which
Muir's name was held caused it to be given to a number of places in California. For
hiking pleasure there is the John Muir Trail paralleling the axis of the Sierra from
Yosemite to Mount Whitney. The trail crosses Muir Pass, nearly 12,000 feet in elevation, and near the trail's Mount Whitney's terminus stands Mount Muir, some 14,000
feet high, from which Muir Lake is visible. In Sequoia National Park one may visit the

Soon the hour arrived for Stickeen and the crew to depart for
Fort Wrangell, Hall Young having elected to stay behind on missionary business. "Muir explained the matter fully to [Stickeen],"
Young wrote, "talking to and reasoning with him as if he were
human. Billy led him aboard the canoe by a dog-chain, and the
last Muir saw of him he was standing on the stern of the canoe,
howling a sad farewell." Muir never saw Stickeen again. Young
later told him that in 1883 a tourist had stolen him and spirited
him away on a departing steamer.

But Stickeen had made an imperishable impression on Muir.
He would toy with the dog's story for seventeen years, retelling
it to a multitude of people and filling a notebook and the end
pages of several books with notes and drafts. Then in 1897 he
would send a manuscript to the *Century Magazine*, claiming that
it had cost him more time and effort than anything else he had
ever written. The magazine ran it in September under a title devised by the editor, "An Adventure with a Dog and a Glacier"—
a name that Muir did not particularly like, and when the story
was republished as a slim book in 1909, it would be called simply
Stickeen. Even in its second appearance the account would not
escape a touch of sentimentality, with Muir over-anthropomor-
phizing Stickeen, so that he would be charged with "nature-
faking" by certain of his opponents. But with the possible exception of "A Wind Storm in the Forests of the Yuba," it would

---

Muir Grove and the Muir Wilderness Area, and on the flank of Mount Tamalpais
near the Golden Gate one may wander through the Muir Woods National Monument. Muir's home near Martinez has been designated the John Muir National
Historic Site, and close to it runs the John Muir Parkway. The nearby stop on the
Santa Fe Railroad is called Muir Station. Muir Beach and Muir Crest both commem-
orate the naturalist, as does Muir Peak not far from Los Angeles. But Muir place-
names are not limited to California. In Washington State the Muir Snowfield lies
south-southeast of the crest of Mount Rainier, between the Cowlitz and Nisqually
glaciers, along with more than twenty other glaciers on the peak. In Alaska may be
found another Mount Muir, Muir Point, and Muir Inlet. Muir Knoll graces the
campus of the University of Wisconsin, and the John Muir County Park, 160 acres in
extent, surrounds Fountain or Ennis Lake, haunt of Muir's boyhood in Wisconsin.
Even Dunbar, Scotland, enjoys a 1,667-acre pleasure ground known as the John Muir
Country Park, which includes not only the ruins of Dunbar Castle but also eight
miles of coastline with cliffs where Muir once clambered as a boy.

bring him more fanmail than anything else he ever wrote; and
the statement by Hall Young is a good example of the praise it
would receive (or overpraise, as the case may be): "Muir's story
of 'Stickeen' ranks with 'Rab and his Friends,' 'Bob, Son of
Battle,' and far above 'The Call of the Wild.'" William F. Badè
would call it "one of the noblest dog stories in English literature." But the opinion of the *Century* editor Robert Underwood
Johnson was the most effusive of all: "It is one of the finest
stories of dogliness in all literature."

CHAPTER 15

The Cruise of the *Corwin*

JOHN Muir spent the fall of 1880 and the succeeding winter hard at work on the land he had leased from Dr. Strentzel and the acres that had come to him and Louie as a wedding gift. He plunged into every aspect of the ranch's operation. But his labors exacted a distressing toll—nervous indigestion and a racking bronchial cough, possibly aggravated by an allergy. He lost his appetite, so that it taxed the ingenuity of Louie and Mrs. Strentzel to devise dishes he cared to eat. He had not been so ill since the fever in Florida, and his weight fell to little more than a hundred pounds.

His spirits soared, however, when on March 25, 1881, Louie gave birth to a daughter, whom they named Annie Wanda for Muir's mother and Louie herself. "Our darling firstborn is a tiny, healthy happy daintily featured lassie," he wrote to his mother the day after. "She looks about her with her bright blue eyes as steadily as if she were a year old instead of only two days."

No doubt Muir's engrossment in Annie Wanda was one reason why he declined an invitation from Captain Calvin Hooper to sail as a scientific observer and the captain's cabinmate on the U.S. revenue cutter *Thomas Corwin* to search Arctic regions for the lost exploring ship *Jeannette* and two whalers, the *Vigilant* and *Mount Wollaston*. Hooper was not easily discouraged and urged Muir to discuss the matter with his wife. Louie thought the voyage would do both his health and his writing good, and Muir changed his mind and joined the cruise before the *Corwin* could steam through the Golden Gate on May 4, 1881. A run of thirteen days brought the cutter to Unalaska in the Aleutian Islands, where Muir sent five letters to Louie, with directions to forward some of them to the *Bulletin* after she had read them.

In a letter to his mother he sketched Captain Hooper's plans. "We mean to proceed from here past the seal islands St. Paul and St George [i.e., the Pribilofs]," he wrote, "then northward along the Siberian coast to about Cape Serdze [-kamen]." There a dog sled party would be put ashore to comb the north Siberian coast for any trace of the three lost ships, while at the same time the *Corwin* doubled back to the American shore and put into port at St. Michael, Kotzebue Sound, and other havens. It was also Captain Hooper's intention to steam north around Point Barrow as soon as the polar ice broke up and search for clues in that area before returning to the Siberian coast to retrieve the sledge party. Last of all, Muir added, Captain Hooper planned to push "through the ice to the mysterious unexplored Wrangel Land," and then if all went well, to steam back to San Francisco by October or November." The plans would be carried out substantially as Muir outlined them.

For the Siberian sled party Captain Hooper had difficulty buying dogs, managing to secure only six on initial stops in Siberia, so the *Corwin* steamed on north to the Diomede Islands, bleak rocks in the Bering Strait, where the resident Inuits (or Eskimos) parted with nineteen wolf-like dogs for a sack of flour each. The *Corwin* then rounded East Cape and headed on a northwesterly course along the edge of the shore ice that hedged the north Siberian coast. Progress slackened when on June 1 the polar ice pack moved down to join the shore ice. As the pack closed in, Captain Hooper ordered a retreat. Suddenly, however, the ice collided against the ship so violently that the oaken shaft of the rudder snapped. Fortunately, the seamen lost no time in constructing makeshift stearing gear, which would serve until more permanent repairs could be made.

Since the *Corwin* could no longer steam to the northwest, Captain Hooper decided to put the sled party ashore at this point. The group consisted of two officers, a seaman, and two Chukchi dog drivers, one of whom served as interpreter. "They have twenty-five dogs," Muir wrote, "four sleds, a light skin boat to cross rivers and any open water they might find in their way, and two months' provisions." Their orders were to scour the coast for the crews of the *Jeannette* and the two whalers or any clues of their fate. They were instructed to interview any natives they met and to examine all promontories along the coast for cairns, then to return to Tapkan, the Chukchi village selected for the rendezvous.

Captain Hooper then headed back around East Cape and south through the Bering Strait to Plover Bay (later known as Provideniya), where the Russian navy maintained a store of coal for its ships, a situation the *Corwin* took advantage of. The crew blasted a way through the shore ice and built a stopgap drydock. Then they dog-sledded coal and piled it on the ship's prow (the cutter was only 137 feet long) until the stern was raised enough for the repairs to be made.

The *Corwin* then steamed across the Bering Sea to St. Michael, a small old-fashioned post the Russians had established for the fur trade near the Yukon delta. There the crew took on provisions for the cruise back along the Siberian coast to meet the search party, which they learned at Tapkan had gained no news of the *Jeannette* or its crew, but had solved the mystery of the *Vigilant*. Near Cape Vankarem the sled party had met three Chukchi seal hunters, who had sighted and boarded a marooned whaler, finding four dead men in the cabin. The officers of the search party were satisfied that the ship was the *Vigilant*, for according to the Chukchi sealers, its jibboom was decorated with an enormous pair of antlers, and the *Vigilant* was the only vessel in the whaling fleet known to be so adorned.

Aside from its search for the lost vessels, the *Corwin* was obliged to continue its regular revenue duties, including the enforcement of federal regulations against trading alcohol and repeating rifles to native people. The need to keep alcohol from the Inuits was brought emphatically home when the *Corwin* stopped at St. Lawrence Island, where, drunk and carefree, the inhabitants had failed to lay in stores for the unusually hard winter of 1878–79. As a result, two-thirds of the people starved to death, so that in the company of E. W. Nelson, a collector for the Smithsonian Institution, Muir found two hundred skeletons at one village, "lying about like rubbish." Nelson stoically gathered up

about a hundred skulls for the Smithsonian, "throwing them together in heaps to take aboard," Muir wrote, "just as when a boy
in Wisconsin I used to gather pumpkins in the fall."

If the bleached skulls represented a condemnation of alcohol,
Muir had only to reach St. Michael again for testimony against
repeating rifles. There he found that all caribou had been exter-
minated in the surrounding country, repeating rifles having made
the people "kill crazy," so that when they came upon a herd, they
would fire away until their ammunition was exhausted. Then
they would leave the slaughtered animals for the wolves, a discovery that distressed Muir, for his brief encounter with Inuits had
given him a high regard for their character. "They are better behaved than white men," he thought, "not half so greedy, shame-
less, or dishonest."

On leaving St. Michael the *Corwin* steamed up the Alaska
coast toward Point Barrow. But on July 21 the polar ice pack
prevented further progress in a northeasterly direction. Point
Barrow had to be deferred to later in the season, and after refuel-
ing at a coal seam near Cape Lisburne, Captain Hooper set his
course for Herald Island. This was an important objective, for in
September 1879 a whaler had sighted the *Jeannette* trapped in the
ice off its shore.

According to Muir, Commander George De Long, skipper of
the *Jeannette,* had stated in a letter of August 17, 1879, that he
planned to touch first at Herald Island, where he would leave
records under a cairn, and then to go on to Wrangel Land and,
while proceeding up its east coast, leave records under a series of
cairns about twenty-five miles apart. At that time it was believed
that Wrangel Land, actually an island of modest size, might be of
continental dimensions, trending toward the North Pole, and De
Long hoped to reach the Pole by following its hypothetical east
coast. No one was known ever to have set foot there or on Herald
Island, whose discoverer had called it "an inaccessible rock."

On July 30 the crew of the *Corwin* sighted Herald Island
beyond a ten-mile pack of ice. The cutter's prow was sheathed
with boiler plate to serve as an icebreaker, and the ship rammed
through the barrier until it rode alongside the island. During the

approach Muir had studied the precipitous bluffs through a spy-glass and etched all features of the topography on his memory. He refrained from joining the impetuous scramble of eight sailors, who in their eagerness to gain the island jumped from the bow-sprit chains and dashed across the narrow belt of floes that bobbed between the cutter and the island. They began to clamber up a steep gulley, only to be thwarted by a thousand-foot cliff.

Followed by Nelson and two others, Muir set out with an ice ax and reached the island at a point north of the ravine that had swallowed the sailors. With his ax he hacked steps in a hundred-foot bank of ice and compacted snow and on reaching the top, he found that not a single difficulty blocked their way beyond that point. The four explored the entire length of the island, about six miles in all, their footsteps dogged by snow-white arctic foxes, inquisitive and entirely unafraid. They found no cairn or any other sign of the *Jeannette*'s crew, but in the frigid arctic twilight they could see the bluish bluffs of Wrangel Land some forty miles to the northwest.

The *Corwin* headed for Wrangel Land immediately, but not till August 12 could it draw near enough for a landing. The previous day the ship had followed a long open lane to within five miles of the beach, but the lane had ended with a seemingly impossible barrier of ice. Captain Hooper decided to send men over it the next day, but after they had slept, the barrier struck him as less forbidding. So he ordered a full head of steam, and the *Corwin* rammed through the ice and cast anchor near the mouth of a river fully seventy-five yards wide.

Muir was one of the landing party, and he wrote, "A land more severely solitary could hardly be found anywhere on the face of the globe." There were a few polar bear tracks on the beach, but not a sign of caribou or musk-oxen. Several marmot burrows pitted the hillock where the party planted the American flag and built a cairn for the record that Captain Hooper had claimed Wrangel Land for the United States. The claim was not destined to hold, however, and today Ostrov Vrangelya belongs to Russia.

Meanwhile, Muir found twenty species of plants there, and

Nelson listed over twenty kinds of birds, many duplicating those he had seen on Herald Island. But there was no cairn or other evidence of the *Jeannette*'s crew in the area of the party's restricted explorations. They could make no further search, however, lest the *Corwin* become locked in the ice. And when the cutter's whistle summoned them, they hastened back on board. The *Corwin* was soundly battered in her retreat, the lane by which she had steamed toward Wrangel Land having all but disappeared. "Had our retreat been cut off," Muir wrote, "we would not, perhaps, have suffered greatly for a year or thereabouts, inasmuch as we had nine months' provisions aboard," which could be stretched out indefinitely by hunting arctic game like seals, walruses, and polar bears.

Soon thereafter another attempt to reach Point Barrow succeeded, but no evidence of the *Jeannette* or the *Mount Wollaston* could be found there. Captain Hooper then made one more effort to attain the east coast of Wrangel Land in search of Commander De Long's projected cairns. But the ice proved impenetrable. In ramming it the *Corwin*'s icebreaker parted at a riveted seam and had to be discarded. Then on September 2, 1881, one of the rudder chains snapped, stopping all further progress, and two days later the *Corwin* was steaming back to San Francisco, months sooner than expected.

From his journal Muir had extracted twenty-one letters for the *Bulletin*. They were printed as received and not in the order of composition. But in 1917 W. F. Badè would publish them in correct sequence as *The Cruise of the Corwin,* after integrating with them unpublished parts of Muir's journal of the cruise. The book comprises straightforward reportage, constituting a factual travelogue. It teems with action and peril and, in line with Muir's scientific bent, abounds in botanical, zoological, geological, and ethnological details. A highlight of grisly interest is the chapter called "Village of the Dead," in which he detailed the tragedy of the Inuits of St. Lawrence Island. The book contains much other matter of historical significance, and if Muir had enjoyed a novelist's flair, it might have become an engrossing novel of adventure.

By early December he had learned the fate of the *Jeannette* and her crew. The ship had been frozen into the polar pack for nearly two years while the ice drifted to the north and west. Then on June 10, 1881, having moved with the currents nearly a third of the way to Sweden, the crushed hull had separated from the pack, only to sink in the icy water. Of the thirty-three men who had evacuated the *Jeannette,* only thirteen reached a Siberian settlement, and of the thirteen only eleven lived to tell their story, Commander De Long being among those who had perished. As for the *Mount Wollaston,* its fate remained a mystery.

CHAPTER 16

Fruit Grower

SOON after returning from the arctic in September 1881, Muir became absorbed in the autumn grape harvest, and when freed from that responsibility he turned to sorting out his collection of arctic plants, duplicate specimens of which he sent to Asa Gray at Harvard. One species proved to be new to science, a member of the compositae family whose blossom looked rather like a daisy. Gray named it *Erigeron muirii*. Muir also helped Captain Hooper compile his official report and prepared his own supplementary reports on the glaciation and the botany of the regions visited by the *Corwin*.

Then later that fall and winter he joined with several members of the California Academy of Sciences to draw up two bills for the consideration of Congress, the first to extend the boundaries of Yosemite State Park, the second to create a "public park" essentially duplicating in area the present-day Sequoia National Park and the Kings Canyon National Park combined. But 1882 saw the death of both bills in the Public Lands Committee of the Senate. Thus, Muir's career as a conservation activist was checked almost at the outset, and he was so disheartened that seven years were to pass before he would enter the lists again.

Meanwhile, he had made plans to convert the Muir-Strentzel ranch from a moderately profitable combination of experimental orchards and vineyards to a highly lucrative enterprise. His plans had the support of Dr. Strentzel, who in his declining years put complete faith in Muir's judgment, so that the whole ranch became in effect Muir's to run as he thought best. He converted hayfields into additional orchards and vineyards and pursued a course of purposeful grafting. Since Bartlett pears sold better than any other variety, he began to graft Bartletts on to all the other sixty-five kinds of pear trees that Dr. Strentzel had planted in his experimental orchards. He also specialized in cherries, of the sort the market demanded most, and as for grapes, Muir narrowed the choice down to tokay, zinfandel, and muscat, all excellent sellers. Under his management the ranch prospered, assuring his family an excellent income.

With Scots shrewdness and love of contention he became a legendary bargainer with the commission merchants who came from San Francisco to buy his produce at the Strentzel wharf in Martinez. There the enormous ranch wagons brought tons of Muir-Strentzel fruit to be shipped and sold throughout not only the West but also the East. Amid these operations a practice Muir consistently followed illustrated the tenor of his business methods. The crates in which the produce of several fruit growers of the area was shipped to San Francisco were regularly returned at midnight to the railroad station in Martinez. It was Muir's custom to rise before daybreak and go to the immense piles of lugs and crates and, although he never took more than his rightful number, he was able by being the early bird to select the best and strongest boxes for his grapes, pears, and cherries. This and other crafty practices caused some people to consider him a dubious oddity.

Muir became a familiar figure in Martinez, with his one-horse buggy, his frostbitten foot dangling over the side, and a laundry bag of greenbacks for deposit at the local bank. But the Martinez bank was not the only one in which he put his money. As his horticulture flourished, he laid away funds in several San Francisco banks, "until," he wrote, "I had more money than I thought I would ever need for my family or for all expenses of travel and study." After his death his estate would be evaluated at a quarter of a million dollars.

But the price of getting on was high. His bronchial cough racked him constantly at the ranch, and he lost so much weight that, in Louie's words, he looked "shadowy and ghostly." He grew irritable, too; for he was beset by an intolerable conflict. The more he improved his trees and vines by grafting, the more he contradicted his dearest principle—that the natural was superior to the cultivated. Then, too, there was the knowledge that the great spectacle of nature was unfolding in the wilderness while he remained chained to a thousand petty cares. For his conflict financial success was not a sufficient satisfaction, and once he railed, "I'm degenerating into a machine for making money." There seemed, however, no escape from the tether that bound him to the ranch.

But there were compensations—like young Wanda, his heart's delight, to whom he was ever the indulgent father. Sometimes Louie or Mrs. Strentzel would bring her to the orchard or the vineyard where Muir was hard at work, and he would lay his tools aside and carry her back to the house on his shoulders or take her to the nearby hills to see the "gowans," as he called the daisies there. He taught her the names of all the plants and flowers they met ("for how would you like it," he enquired of her, "if people didn't call you by your name?"), and such absorption in the child was a welcome relief from the grind and weariness of his ranch routine.

Further relief came in the evenings that he spent with books from the Strentzels' library or with books that he now acquired himself—the five-volume set of Humboldt's *Cosmos*, for example, or Carlyle's collected works in thirty volumes, the latter an apt index to the prevailingly British character of his literary taste. He still delighted in the poetry of Burns and in that of the English Romantics—Wordsworth, Coleridge, and Shelley. He preferred British novelists to American ones, except for Hawthorne, and still another exception to his Anglophile preferences was his enthusiasm for the historical works of Francis Parkman. All of his intensive reading during the 1880s would sharpen the focus and widen the scope of his opinions on what a friend would call "a surprisingly large number of topics," but he would generally express such bookish notions only in his torrential talk, and not in his future writing, which would continue to restrict itself to subjects he knew firsthand instead of from books.

Meanwhile, Louie worried about his health and urged him to go to the wilderness for its benefits. Sometimes he did, though probably not as often as he would suggest in old age. "Only in the early autumn," he would recall, possibly not entirely correctly, "when the table grapes were gathered, and in winter and in early spring, when vineyards and orchards were pruned and cultivated, was my personal supervision given to the work." Further, he declared that in the 1880s "explorations" had claimed him "every spring . . . until the approach of winter"—an assertion difficult to sustain. Muir left no journals or correspondence to confirm such frequent or prolonged excursions during this period, and most existing data seem irrelevant. Only a minimum of outings is certain, one of them occurring in July 1884, when to take him away from the cares of the ranch Louie insisted she needed a vacation with him in Yosemite.

Though the valley was Muir's special bailiwick, the trip was not a great success. Louie appreciated the grand features of Yosemite, true enough. But there was little of the mountaineer in her makeup, and so she found it difficult to follow where Muir was inclined to lead. All things considered, she much preferred the cultivated environs of the Alhambra Valley. Moreover, she continued to worry about the state of Muir's health. "I am anxious about John," she wrote to her mother. "The journey was hard for him, and he looks thin and pale." Then she added solicitously, "He must not leave the mountains until he is well and strong again." But that was not to be. Both were too concerned about Wanda, no matter how safe she was in the care of her grandparents. Therefore, they returned prematurely to the ranch, and Muir became more than ever snared in its management.

Meanwhile, at its lower end the Strentzels had built a Victorian mansion of sixteen rooms, with a fireplace in almost every one of them. At the same time Muir had improved the older house with dormer windows for more sunlight and with two spacious fireplaces for more warmth in the winter, the comfort of his family ever his concern, just as regard for their welfare kept him hard at work in the orchards and the vineyards. It took a premonition of his father's death to tear him from his ranch responsibilities for any extended period.

One day in August 1885, while writing in his study, he abruptly dropped his pen. He sought Louie out and told her of his presentiment, something like an inner command to go east at once if he wished to see his father alive. Though she was three months pregnant, she urged him to go, but for the sake of his health to go by way of Mount Shasta and Yellowstone National Park. Muir followed her advice and had such a delightful visit at Shasta that when the time came for his departure he claimed to feel like a drunkard swearing off the bottle. He had an equally happy time at Yellowstone, the fruit of his tour there a letter to the *Bulletin,* which he later revised for the *Atlantic Monthly* and finally included in *Our National Parks.*

Muir did not go directly to Kansas City, where his father now lived with Joanna, his favorite daughter. Instead, he first went to Portage, where his mother, two sisters, and brother David lived. He prevailed on David to leave his general merchandise business and go to Kansas City, along with Annie, but their mother and Sarah did not feel strong enough to make the trip. By wiring fare, Muir also induced his other two sisters and his younger brother Dan, now a medical doctor in Lincoln, Nebraska, to go and be with their father as well.

The family assembled at Joanna's house, where they found Daniel failing steadily and now in a confused stupor. Muir spoke to him in "braid Scots" to jog his memory, and Daniel would say, "Ye're a Scotchman, aren't you?" At last he recognized Muir and murmured, "Is this my dear John? . . . Oh, yes, my dear Wanderer." On the night of October 6 Muir waited alone at his father's bedside, the others having retired, worn out by their vigils; and at midnight he saw that the crisis had come. He called his brothers and sisters, and as the old man's spirit slipped away, seven of his eight children wept at his passing.

A decade before, Daniel had fallen on slippery ice and broken his hip. The bone had failed to knit properly, forcing him to walk on crutches. Thus incapacitated, he had returned to the United States, but instead of rejoining Anne, he had gone to Joanna's. His religious zealotry had continued until the birth of Joanna's daughter, and then a remarkable change had come over the old man, as if a child had led him to a new conversion. As Muir wrote to Louie, "His last years . . . were full of calm divine light, and he oftentimes spoke . . . of the cruel mistakes he had made in his relations towards his children, and spoke particularly of me, wondering how I had borne my burdens so well and patiently, and warned Joanna . . . to govern her children by love alone."

After the funeral Muir prepared to return to the West. He invited his mother to come and live with him, but she was so attached to her familiar sphere that she declined. However, Margaret and Sarah, both semi-invalids, and Annie, victim of tuberculosis, accepted invitations for an extended visit. Muir took them home by way of Yellowstone, where he widened his knowledge of the park. They arrived at the ranch in late October, and the sisters basked in the hospitality of Louie and her parents and fell in love with the Strentzel mansion.

Muir now found Louie in the midst of a difficult pregnancy. The baby, another girl, whom they named Helen Lillian, was born on January 24, 1886, a frail, sickly infant, subject to respiratory ailments like her father. Because of her uncertain health, Muir seldom left the ranch during the next year and a half, lest she fall ill and need him in an emergency. Her frailty would lead him to develop a partiality for her. Wanda realized this, but she was stable enough for it not to bother her, nor would it interfere with her acting as big-sister comforter and protector. In later years she would even sacrifice her college diploma to be with Helen in one of her bouts with pneumonia and its extended aftermath.

Meanwhile, Muir was more than ever engrossed in horticultural cares. He was also beset by outside pressures to return to public life. He received request after request to lead the crusade to save the forests across the land, and literary friends urged him to take up his pen again. The most persuasive was Robert Underwood Johnson, associate editor of the *Century Magazine,* successor to *Scribner's Monthly.* "Has the ink in your fountain-pen entirely dried up?" Johnson asked in one of his pleas for manuscripts. Muir neglected to answer, but there were signs that his urge to write was returning, signs like long letters to friends.

This gathering literary impulse led him in the spring of 1887 to accept the editorship of a two-volume coffee-table anthology

John Muir's two daughters, Wanda and Helen, as children, to whom he was completely devoted. He took special trouble in directing their nature study. Courtesy of Alfred A. Knopf.

modeled on William Cullen Bryant's *Picturesque America* and itself called *Picturesque California and the Region West of the Rocky Mountains, from Alaska to Mexico.* The production of this elaborate work would join a vast publicity campaign that had been launched in the middle eighties by railroads, steamship lines, land companies, commercial corporations, and chambers of commerce to spread the gospel of California's peerless climate and her bountiful natural resources. Even the state government had linked up with the advertising blitz by granting data through its commissioner of immigration on California's unequaled opportunities for prospective settlers as well as those already settled. Dewing & Co., the publisher, projected *Picturesque California* as a leading item in this flood of books, brochures, and pamphlets extolling the blessings of the Golden State, and it would do its part in helping to generate the immigration boom that was to double the state's population to 1,200,000 by 1890.

The literary content of the work would run heavily to descriptions of scenery, and it would be lavishly illustrated by leading artists, including Keith, Thomas Hill, and Thomas Moran. Muir would not only edit it; he would also write for it; and since he was unable to find an acceptable foreman for the ranch—for he was very choosy about whom to hire—he shouldered the double load of ranch management and literary endeavor. He found writing for *Picturesque California* pretty much a dead end, however; and acute literary critic that Louie was, she felt appalled at the uninspired pedestrianism of his initial contribution. She feared that years of grinding toil among the grapevines and pear trees had smothered Muir's inner fire. She had almost come to hate the ranch for what it seemed to do to him.

Fortunately, Muir did not have to do much new writing for *Picturesque California,* but made out with recycling former articles on the High Sierra, Yosemite Valley, Mount Shasta, and Alaska. Two entirely new pieces dealt with Washington State and Puget Sound and with the Columbia River basin. When the writing and editorial work grew onerous, Muir would retire to a hotel room in San Francisco and complete the chores in peace. Then back he would go to his labors in the orchards and the vineyards.

In June 1888 he wrote to Keith that he expected to go to the Northwest the following month in connection with *Picturesque California* and would like to have his company. The artist agreed, and they started off in July, spending two days at Mount Shasta. The commercialism playing havoc there induced Muir to weave into his Shasta revision its most significant passage—his emphatic recommendation that the Shasta area be made a national park. That would never happen, but in 1903, largely at Muir's insistence, the peak would be included in a national forest. Mean-

"Half Dome, Yosemite: View from Moran Point," as etched by Thomas Moran in 1887 and published in John Muir's *Picturesque California* the following year. Photograph by Caroline Lawson Hinkley.

while, the two friends went on to Oregon, where they reveled in magnificent forests filled with one of Muir's favorite trees, the majestic sugar pine, discovered in 1826 by David Douglas, a hardy Scots explorer of the Pacific Northwest. Keith and Muir stopped at Portland, with plans to climb Mount Hood, but Keith fell ill, and the ascent had to be canceled.

However, after Keith's recovery, they climbed Mount Rainier along with several other mountain climbers. "I gained the summit from the south side," Muir wrote, "in a day and a half from the timber-line, without encountering any desperate obstacles that could not in some way be passed in good weather. I was accompanied by Keith the artist, Professor [E. S.] Ingraham, and five ambitious young climbers from Seattle. We were led by the veteran mountaineer and guide [Philemon] Van Trump, of Yelm," who had made the first ascent in 1870 with General Hazard Stevens. Muir delighted in the glaciers they encountered, several that S. F. Emmons of Clarence King's corps had discovered in 1870 shortly after the Van Trump–Stevens ascent.

On going to Seattle John received a letter in which Louie announced a momentous decision she was contemplating. "A ranch that needs and takes the sacrifice of a noble life, or work," she wrote, "ought to be flung away beyond all reach and power for harm. . . . The Alaska book and the Yosemite book, dear John, must be written, and you need to be your own self, well and strong, to make them worthy of you. There is nothing that has a right to be considered beside this except the welfare of our children." When he reached home, Muir found her pondering what part of the ranch to keep, what part to lease, and what part to sell. It would take some time to accomplish this diverse arrangement, but he was assured of freedom at last—especially when in 1891 John Reid, Margaret's husband, tired of trying to make an arid Nebraska homestead pay, agreed to come and manage that part of the ranch that Muir and Louie would retain.

CHAPTER 17

Yosemite National Park

MUIR'S ideas on the education of his "bairns" were not strictly conventional. The girls—for even Helen was old enough by 1889 to learn her ABCs—were not sent to school, but were taught at home, Louie assuming most of the teaching chores, helped by occasional tutors. Muir took upon himself the responsibility for the girls' nature study, a subject he emphasized. "More wild knowledge," he said, "less arithmetic and grammar, keeps alive the heart, nourishes youth's enthusiasms, which in society die untimely." Relaxed, too, were his notions about religious instruction. He desired his children to love God as a benevolent spirit coexistent with the universe, not as a terrifying human-like *person* to be feared. With Louie's consent, he refrained from teaching the "bairns" to pray, except for a special instance when he asked that Wanda memorize the Lord's Prayer.

After Muir's ranch work and writing were finished for the day, he would join his daughters for relaxation. He would frolic with them and tell them amusing stories like the long, multi-installment saga of Paddy Grogan and his kangaroo steed. He also improvised doggerel verses for their entertainment. Wanda later wrote, "Father [was] the biggest, jolliest child of us all." How good he found it thus to secure relief from the drudgery not only of ranch duties but also of writing and editorial work, for though *Picturesque California* bore 1888 as its publication date, it was not actually finished for a year or more thereafter and still held Muir tightly in the editorial harness.

But now that it had reclaimed him from literary hibernation, Robert Underwood Johnson was determined to secure some articles from him for the *Century*. Therefore he got in touch with Muir on coming to San Francisco to line up "reminiscents" for a

Robert Underwood Johnson, associate editor of the *Century,* who suggested the creation of Yosemite National Park in 1889 and who became one of Muir's staunchest supporters in his crusade for preservation. Courtesy of the American Academy of Arts and Letters, New York City.

projected series called "The Gold Hunters of California." Muir responded by visiting Johnson at the Palace Hotel, where they conversed for three hours, with Muir managing to do most of the talking. In the process he invited the editor to visit the Muir-Strentzel ranch as soon as his work permitted.

When Johnson arrived at the Alhambra Valley, he saw at once why Muir had fallen silent during most of the 1880s. At the same time he discovered a likely ally in Louie, whom he called "a most intelligent woman" who "deplores the inactivity of Muir's pen." Muir himself, on learning of Johnson's love for the outdoors, invited him for an outing in Yosemite Valley and its backcountry. Johnson accepted the invitation and was so pleased with his host that he wrote home: "My great discovery here is John Muir." He was amused, no doubt, by Muir's description of himself as a "self-styled poetico-trampo-geologist-bot-& ornith-natural, etc.!!!"

They reached the valley on June 3, and Johnson was suitably impressed by Yosemite's grandeur. They spent a day or so there; then hiring burros and a camp cook, they climbed from the valley and made their way to Soda Springs in the Big Tuolumne Meadows. Muir planned to give Johnson a taste of the Great Tuolumne Canyon the following day. "But how much we will be able to accomplish," he had written to Louie, "will depend upon the snow, the legs, and the resolution of the Century." The *Century*'s legs and resolution held out until they found themselves confronted by a thousand-foot precipice, at which the editor declared, "Enough." Johnson's difficulties amused Muir at the time, but at their Soda Springs campfire that evening he was all solicitude, and the two talked long and earnestly about the problems of the mountains.

Johnson remarked that they had seen none of those luxuriant alpine gardens that Muir had described so lovingly in his early essays. "No," Muir replied, "we don't see those any more. Their extinction is due to the hoofed locusts." That was Johnson's first encounter with Muir's metaphor for sheep, and struck by its effect, he listened intently as Muir condemned the devastation wrought by sheep. Muir also deplored the destructiveness of sheepmen's fires, as well as the wastefulness of logging operations in the Sierra and their cost to the watershed.

Johnson was always ready for a crusade; he was also fertile with ideas, and according to his later memory of the event, he proposed one now that would make history. "Obviously," he said, "the thing to do is to make a Yosemite National Park around the valley on the plan of the Yellowstone." At first Muir was less than optimistic, or perhaps he merely pretended to be so. He explained how he had helped to draft a bill in 1881 to establish just such a park and how it had died from lack of public support. But from years of work on behalf of an international copyright law, Johnson had become an expert lobbyist, with influential friends on Capitol Hill; and with its more than two hundred thousand subscribers the *Century* was not only the finest magazine in America but also a potent molder of public opinion. These were aids that Muir and his friends had not enjoyed in 1881.

At their Soda Springs campfire Johnson offered Muir a proposition. If Muir would write two articles supporting the creation of Yosemite National Park and collect a portfolio of illustrative photographs, the *Century* would publish them, and as soon as the articles were in type, Johnson would take the proofs to Washington and see that a bill for the park was framed and pushed by the proper people. "Our meeting in 1889 not only struck fire in me," Johnson later wrote, "but in Muir himself." Muir consented wholeheartedly to Johnson's scheme, and thus writer, editor, and magazine came together, a superlatively effective coalition to sponsor the establishment of Yosemite National Park. Moreover, in his fifty-second year Muir entered the most productive period of his life, his years as a public figure.

His meeting with Johnson was of paramount importance for conservation in general and the national parks in particular. Their joining forces coincided with a flowering interest in conservation that contrasted sharply with the outmoded philosophy of public land use that then prevailed. The 1870s and 1880s had witnessed a high point for the myth of inexhaustible resources with its deification of "free enterprise" and its blind disregard for the future; caught up in that illusion, the westward-moving pioneers had assumed since the close of the Civil War that the public domain was theirs to deal with as they saw fit. It mattered little to most of them that their collective credo, marked often by cupidity, cynicism, and outrageous laxity, had made their involvement with the public domain, as a later historian would suggest, "a circus of inefficiency and corruption." On that keynote ended the American frontier, a reality that would soon be underscored by the U.S. Census of 1890; and with the frontier's termination, Muir and Johnson's cause could scarcely have germinated at a more propitious moment or rooted itself more fruitfully in the loam of amateur enthusiasm, long before a corps of professionals trained in conservation matters could develop.

As soon as Muir's last responsibility to *Picturesque California* was discharged, he began the articles he had promised Johnson. The two crusaders kept in touch with one another, Muir sending practical advice and information for Johnson's use in his maneuvers among the politicians in Washington. Moreover, on March 4, 1890, Muir forwarded his views on the extent of the proposed park, which he claimed should "comprehend all the basins of the streams pouring into the Valley." And on an enclosed map he indicated the Yosemite State Park and around it the area he considered a practical expectation for a national park and around that the area that might be added to make "an ideal reservation."

Two weeks later General William Vandever, a representative from southern California, introduced a Yosemite National Park bill in the House, but in Muir's opinion its prescribed area was much too limited—only 288 square miles. It omitted the Soda Springs campsite and the whole Tuolumne River watershed, as well as much of the Merced drainage system, including Lake Tenaya. Johnson quickly went to work to sell the notion to the Public Lands Committee of the House that the area specified by the Vandever bill was too restricted. At the same time he pressed Muir to write insistent letters recommending extension of the boundaries laid down by the bill.

Muir wrote on May 8 that "the Yosemite Reservation ought to include all the Yosemite fountains." He pointed out that these lay in a compact cluster of mountains that offered magnificent scenery and were of easy access from Yosemite Valley. These mountains were valuable only for the use of beauty, he argued of necessity, for only lands deemed economically "worthless" except for scenic purposes stood much chance of becoming a national park. The extension of the reservation's boundaries to include these peaks would cause no other interests to suffer. No mine of any value had been discovered in the summits along the axis of the range. Most of the granite basin would never be suitable for agriculture, but there were compelling reasons why the forests there should be preserved. He argued further that the park should include not only the Big Tuolumne Meadows "as the central camping-ground for the High Sierra adjacent to the Valley," but also the Great Tuolumne Canyon as well. Moreover, the lower boundary should be extended to include certain Big Tree groves south of the valley.

Muir's articles, in which he made it clear that the primary rationale for the park was the protection of wilderness, were ready by late spring, 1890, and he sent them east to Johnson, but not before influenza laid him low, making his bronchial cough more harrowing than ever. He was reduced to a shadow of himself, and since the cough did not improve in the area of Martinez, recuperation in the wilderness seemed imperative. Exploration of the Muir Glacier, he believed, would kill the culprit microbes. But when he told his doctor of his plan, the physician said, "If you go on this journey in your condition, you'll pay for it with your life."

"If I don't go," Muir replied, "I'll pay for it with my life."

He sailed from San Francisco on June 14. At Port Townsend he joined up with Henry Loomis, one of the young men from Seattle with whom he had climbed Mount Rainier in 1888, and together they voyaged in the tourist steamer *Queen* to Glacier Bay, arriving there on June 23. Their baggage was put ashore and they made camp on a rocky moraine a mile from the terminal wall of the Muir Glacier. During the next few days Muir made preliminary explorations of the glacier and climbed the adjacent mountains for views of its various tributaries in preparation for the exploring trip he planned to make along its surface.

At the next appearance of the S.S. *Queen* it brought the two of them lumber from Sitka, and they built a sturdy cabin. Then Muir prepared himself for his projected exploration of the glacier. From scraps of lumber and boughs of Sitka spruce he built a sled that measured eighteen inches in width and three feet in length, and he shod its runners with strips of iron. He found it conveniently maneuverable, weighing as it did only about a hundred pounds when fully loaded. Besides provisions and gear, he packed it with a sleeping bag made of a bearskin covered with a red blanket and a canvas sheath.

He began the trip on July 11, pushing the sled before him over the ice. His intention was "to obtain general views of the main upper part of the Muir Glacier and its seven principal tributaries" and also to rid himself of his oppressive cough. The first three days were uneventful, but on the fourth day in a camp he had made off the ice he heard the howling of wolves. They came nearer, and while out of sight themselves, he suspected that they had seen him. During his breakfast they began to howl again, so near that he developed a dread of their attacking him, and so he hastened to the protection of "a big square boulder," where he could fend them off with his alpenstock. But the wolves moved on, and so did Muir, after naming the locality Howling Valley.

That day he climbed a three-thousand-foot mountain, later known as the Snow Dome, to study the whole width of the glacier, in order to choose a course with the fewest difficulties. The hour grew late, and to shorten the way to his sled he decided to glissade down the mountainside. But on a bluish patch of ice he lost control and rolled and bounced like a ball till stopped by a bed of bare, loose gravel. Then, unhurt though somewhat dazed, he watched two ravens swoop from the sky with demoniacal cries, as if ready to pick his bones. He shook his fist and shouted, "Not yet, you black imps. Not yet!"

On the sixteenth he crossed the main glacier and spent the night on the ice, after making his smallest campfire yet, of shavings from the bottom of his sled, burned in a tin cup, over which he held another cup to brew his tea. His feet were wet and cold, the ice having worn his soles badly, and he considered resoling his shoes with wood. But his cough had vanished, exactly as he had hoped.

On the eighteenth, however, he began to see double from the glare on the ice, and the next day found him almost blind. He lay all day with poultices of snow on his eyes, and he made himself a pair of goggles, though of what he failed to record. Late in the afternoon he went ashore and gathered some "fossil wood" for a fire on the ice to make tea. The next day, the twentieth, he still saw double, but felt much better. He had been on his return trip for several days now, and he knew he was nearing Muir Inlet, where the S.S. *Queen* was expected at any time. And it was his intention that on reaching the inlet he would signal Henry Loomis to come and ferry him to their cabin.

He pushed forward that day, but late in the afternoon a cold wind rose, and he sought shelter in the lee of a nunatak island, rock that reared up insular-fashion through the ice. He had taken only a dozen steps when he suddenly plunged into a hidden crevasse filled with icy water. "Never before had I encountered a danger so completely concealed," he wrote. He struggled to pull himself onto the ice, and when he had done so, he shoved his sled to the leeside of the island, stripped off his clothes, and slipped into his sleeping bag "to shiver away the night."

He reached the Muir Inlet the following day, but decided to delay signaling to Loomis and spent the day examining the remains of a forest of Sitka spruce that had once grown near the southwest corner of the glacier. Then he had an early supper and was about to crawl into bed when he spied Loomis approaching with a companion across a nearby moraine. Loomis had seen Muir from their cabin and had come to row him back to their base. Thus ended a sled trip of eleven days into a region of ice where probably no white man had gone before.

When Muir returned home in early September 1890, aglow with health, he found the national park campaign in full swing. His first article—"The Treasures of the Yosemite"—had caused a sensation on appearing in the August number of the *Century*. After an enthusiastic account of Muir's first approach to Yosemite in 1868, the essay had described the magnificent sequoia groves that he had surveyed in 1875, before it settled down to its essential objective—an expansive, detailed portrayal of Yosemite Valley and its various features, set off by compressed recitals of several of Muir's adventures there. The scenes in question were illustrated in the finest *Century* manner with wood engravings and photographs in "process" reproductions. The article was reprinted far and wide, both whole and in part, and provoked a multitude of editorials.

Now in September the second article, somewhat shorter than the first, had just been published—"Features of the Proposed Yosemite National Park"—with Muir's map included among the illustrations. The essay devoted much attention to the Upper Tuolumne region, the Great Tuolumne Canyon, and Hetch Hetchy, while playing up the opportunities for hiking and camping that the Sierra afforded. At its climax Muir called for government intervention to save for posterity the wonderland he had described. "Unless preserved or protected," he declared, "the whole region will soon or late be devastated by lumbermen and sheepmen, and so of course made unfit for use as a pleasure ground." Altogether the articles constituted by far the most effective publicity the preservation cause had yet enjoyed, the response to the second essay proving even livelier than the reaction to the first. Suddenly the Southern Pacific lobby seems to have thrown its influence into the situation—covertly, so as to shield from SP tarnish the new bill (HR 12187) that now replaced the Vandever Bill and specified boundaries for Yosemite National Park which corresponded closely to the ideal limits proposed by Muir. Soon thereafter a flood of telegrams, letters, and petitions poured into the Capitol in favor of its passage.

There was opposition, which libeled Muir *ad hominem,* the chief maligner being a San Francisco Bay area politico and newspaper editor named Colonel John P. Irish, who happened also to serve as the secretary-treasurer of the Yosemite State Park Commission. He spearheaded a campaign of innuendo that accused Muir of sins ranging from marital infidelity and unlawfully felling trees in Yosemite Valley to sentimental emptyheadedness and being "a pseudo-naturalist." The virus would linger on long

after Muir's death and would even be used to help block the
Kings Canyon National Park from being named in his honor
when it was finally established in 1940. But Irish's calumny failed
of its immediate end, especially in the face of Southern Pacific
clout. On September 30, 1890, the substitute bill to create Yosemite National Park (bearing the misleading title "Yosemite Forest
Reservation") was passed by both houses of Congress, and President Harrison signed it into law the following day.

The act provided for a park more than five times as large as
that specified by the original Vandever Bill—a huge pleasure
ground of 1,512 square miles, an area even larger than the park today and nearly the size of Rhode Island. "Even the soulless Southern Pacific R. R. Co.," Muir acknowledged years afterward,
"never counted on for anything good, helped nobly in pushing
the bill for this park through Congress." To his satisfaction a
cavalry patrol was soon sent to guard the park against undesirable
trespassers.

CHAPTER 18

The Sierra Club

YOSEMITE National Park was not the only national park that Congress established in the fall of 1890. Two other bills introduced by General Vandever were enacted and signed into law—the first making the General Grant Grove a national park of 3.9 square miles; the second creating the Sequoia National Park, a reservation of 604 square miles in the Kaweah and Kern rivers area. Both Muir and Johnson, however, considered the area allotted to the latter much too small, and they resolved to launch a campaign to enlarge Sequoia National Park by including the Kings Canyon region and certain Kaweah and Tule River Big Tree groves. They would strike in favor of the extension while their Yosemite National Park victory was still fresh. Muir's main contribution to the effort would be an article for the *Century* on the Kings Canyon; and in preparation for it he projected a trip to the region to refresh his memory and to gather new impressions. But before he could get under way, Dr. Strentzel took seriously ill, and the trip had to be postponed.

Muir's father-in-law died on the last day of October 1890. He was buried on the ranch; and in order for Louie to look after her mother, the Muirs moved from the house where they had lived for the past ten years to the Strentzels' big Victorian mansion on the knoll at the lower end of the ranch. The delay caused by the combination of Dr. Strentzel's death and the move to the big house made it necessary for Muir to cancel the Kings Canyon trip entirely for the year.

Johnson, however, did not wait for Muir's article before going into action. In the spring of 1891 he took the matter up with John W. Noble, Secretary of the Interior, who declared himself in favor of enlarging Sequoia National Park. Moreover, he was prepared "to withdraw the [relevant] region from entry"—by homesteaders and by those who filed under the provisions of other land laws— "if Muir would delimit upon land office maps the territory that should go into a park." This Muir did about the middle of May, sending the map to Johnson. Then without further delay he made the deferred trip to the Kings Canyon country in the company of the artist Charles D. Robinson, with whom he spent most of his time in the South Fork. The result was an article that combined both his old and new impressions in describing the South Fork of the Kings Canyon under the title "A Rival of the Yosemite." It turned out to be the most elaborately illustrated of all Muir's articles, mostly from Robinson's sketches, but in some cases from sketches by Muir himself.

As soon as the essay was in type, Johnson rushed galley proofs to Secretary Noble, who made Muir's statement a part of his own report to Congress, with an emphatic recommendation for action. But the opposition was fully mobilized, and the plan died in committee. Muir's writing had neverthess convinced Noble of the need to waste no time in preserving wilderness, and resourceful administrator that he was, he had a substitute plan up his sleeve in case the Kings Canyon measure failed. In accordance with his wishes, a subordinate named Edward A. Bowers had drafted a sixty-word clause by which the president might reserve by proclamation any forest land in the public domain. With historic roots that reached back for decades,* the clause

---

*These roots were varied. Before the Civil War, the protoconservationists like former President John Quincy Adams, George B. Emerson of Massachusetts, and Dr. Increase Lapham of Wisconsin had preached against the evils of tree destruction. But George P. Marsh's *Man and Nature,* published in 1864, generally receives the major credit for launching the movement to protect American forests. In 1873, in the wake of Marsh's classic, Franklin B. Hough of New York discussed the forests of the United States before the American Association for the Advancement of Science and moved that organization to appoint a committee "to memorialize Congress and State Legislatures regarding the cultivation of timber and the preservation of forests." Hough chaired the committee, and its work initiated his influential series, *Reports on Forestry.* In 1877, on becoming Secretary of the Interior, Carl Schurz made a vigorous attempt to secure the protection of forests in the public domain, and in 1878 Major John Wesley Powell released his heretical report on the arid lands of the

would be known as Section 24 or the Forest Reserve Act, and master political stroke that it was, it would ensure a fundmental change in the future of American forests when the bill to which it was attached—a bill to revise the general land laws of the United States—had passed through Congress on March 2, 1891. Owing to the cultural lag in the West that perceived wilderness and the public domain in much the same light as they had been regarded in the East a century before (with a deep-seated animus toward wild lands and a cavalier carelessness about their "improvement"), Section 24 might well have died instead of becoming one of the most far-ranging conservation measures ever implemented.

But its backers, including Secretary Noble himself, who was present at the meeting of the joint conference committee of both congressional houses that aimed to adjust differences on the land laws bill, were willing to bend the rules under which they operated. At Noble's suggestion they attached the Bowers clause to the bill under consideration even though such a move at such a late date flouted congressional rules. In making this concession, the lawmakers acted in line with several factors that pointed to the advisability of accommodating the rider.

Not the least of these was the decade-long campaign of the American Forestry Association and the American Association for the Advancement of Science to modify federal policies that allowed timberlands in the public domain to fall into the hands of western lumber interests by fraudulent means, instead of their being conserved in permanent reserves to ensure favorable hydrological conditions in associated rivers. No doubt, a principal impetus that spurred the legislators on was the outcry of western

---

West, in which he specified timberlands as one of the five major categories in his land classification scheme. Powell was in the vanguard of those who pointed out the dangers of forest fires and advocated the need for protecting forests from fire. In 1882 Charles S. Sargent of Harvard urged state legislatures to pass laws for the protection of forests in the East and the federal government to withdraw forests from the public domain in the West and preserve them in permanent reserves. Four years later a Division of Forestry was established in the Department of Agriculture, headed by Bernhard E. Fernow, a professional forester. Fernow's agency was small and primarily research oriented, but it helped to pave the way for the Forest Reserve Act of 1891.

farmers, who, dependent as they were on irrigation, had learned from bitter experience a precept that Muir had preached for years—that mountain forests served as "nature's reservoirs," holding water for gradual release to use on farmlands below. Indeed, the chairman of the congressional conference committee confirmed that the rationale for the creation of forest reserves was the need to protect the watersheds of the Far West from profligate lumbering, overgrazing, and frequent forest fires in order "that the water supply in the country may be preserved."

The bill to revise the public land laws, with Section 24 incorporated (shaky grammar and all), was rushed through the Senate without being printed; it provoked mild objection in the House, but with the session drawing to a close the time for debate was limited and in the resulting haste Section 24 slipped through the legislative process as a "sleeper." Had its true intent as a forest reserve measure been more generally recognized, it might well have been killed. But in the end-of-session rush Congress passed the omnibus bill for land laws revision, and President Harrison signed it into law with Section 24 intact.

Nudged by Noble, the President lost no time in taking advantage of the legislation to set aside the Yellowstone Forest Reserve of 1,239,040 acres in Wyoming. Later, in the fall, he set aside the White River Forest Reserve of 1,198,000 acres in Colorado. Then, on February 14, 1893, shortly before retiring from office, he set aside a sweeping total of thirteen million acres, including four million that made up the Sierra Forest Reserve, stretching from the southern edge of Yosemite National Park to the latitude of Bakersfield.

The Sierra Forest Reserve had resulted from a suggestion sown by Johnson in June 1891 when he saw Noble in New Haven, where both had received honorary degrees from Yale. "When I spoke to the Secretary in advocacy of Muir's idea of reserving the whole of the upper regions of the Sierra," Johnson would write in his memoirs, "he was most sympathetic, . . . but I had no idea to what length he would go in his recommendations to President Harrison. It was through Noble's effort that all the reservations in California of that administration were made." Johnson wrote further that "Muir and Noble were the two salient leaders and pioneers of forest preservation, and Noble's torch, like those of most of us, was kindled at the flame of Muir's enthusiasm,"—in recognition of which (although there were other leaders in the movement) it was to become fashionable to single Muir out as a symbol of forest preservation in America and sometime even to stretch the point a little and call him "the father of our national forests." With the *Century* Johnson had the means of turning Muir into a culture hero, and over the years he did not hesitate to do so.

Meanwhile, the fifteen forest reserves that President Harrison had created before leaving the White House notwithstanding, victory was far from complete. Congress had failed to specify the purpose of the reserves, and provision had not been made for their management other than their assignment to the jurisdiction of the Secretary of the Interior. Neither had steps been taken to protect them from fire, timber theft, or misuse by sheep and cattle grazers. Therefore, five hundred thousand sheep still invaded the Sierra Forest Reserve, causing inestimable damage and indelibly pointing up the unprotected state of the forests there.

At the same time the national parks were not beyond danger. Cavalry patrols under tough-minded officers might keep flocks and herds beyond their boundaries; but not content with access to the forest reserves, sheepmen and cattle grazers, with an assortment of interested allies, had mobilized to subvert the inviolability of the parks. As early as August 28, 1891, Secretary Noble had alerted Johnson to imminent trouble for "the Yosemite Reservation . . . and there will be an attack, I think, next winter."

It was clear that the preservationists needed to found a protective organization to counter such opposition—a course that Johnson had recommended as early as the fall of 1889, when he urged Muir "to start an association for preserving California's monuments and natural wonders—or at least Yosemite." Muir was sympathetic to the idea, seeing advantage in association, but he was unsure of his qualities of leadership. "I would gladly do anything in my power to preserve Nature's sayings and doings here or elsewhere," he responded, "but have no genius for man-

aging societies." Therefore, he declined to take the initiative, but
when in the spring of 1892 J. Henry Senger, professor of German
at the University of California, consulted him about forming "an
alpine club for mountain lovers," Muir encouraged him to contact a Berkeley colleague, William D. Armes of the English department. This meeting led to a fruitful alliance. By March the
projected society had a name—the Sierra Club.

But before it could actually be organized, Muir was called to
Wisconsin in connection with the bankruptcy of Parry & Muir,
the general merchandise firm of which his brother David was the
active partner. Parry & Muir had failed through the recklessness
of David's partner, a Wisconsin legislator involved in Lake Superior land schemes. To shore up his real estate investments he had
borrowed heavily from the firm's reserve funds, and when lean
times came, the company was unable to meet its obligations and
slid into bankruptcy.

Muir went to Portage under the impression that by investing
in the firm he could save David's share, but on surveying the
wreckage he found the company beyond salvage. David, though
ill with so-called "brain fever," agreed to pay off half the firm's
indebtedness; and this Muir made possible by inviting him to
work "on shares" a portion of the Muir ranch. Meanwhile, John
took him to Lincoln, Nebraska, to receive the care of their brother
Dan, the medical doctor. Muir went on to California, where
David followed as soon as he regained his health.

While Muir was away, plans for the mountain club had matured, and on May 25 Professors Senger and Armes sent out
invitations to a meeting three days later in the office of Warren
Olney, a San Francisco attorney, "for the purpose of forming a
'Sierra Club.'" The letter added, "Mr. John Muir will preside."
At the meeting the new club was organized along the lines of the
Appalachian Mountain Club, and on June 4, 1892, twenty-seven
prominent citizens signed the articles of incorporation that Olney
and Senger had drawn up. The articles made it clear that the
Sierra Club's purpose was threefold—recreational, educational,
and conservationist—namely, "to explore, enjoy and render accessible the mountain regions of the Pacific Coast; to publish

authentic information concerning them; [and] to enlist the support and cooperation of the people and the government in preserving the forests and other natural features of the Sierra Nevada." Muir was elected president, an office he would hold for
the rest of his life. He went home exultant, sure that the or-
ganizers of the club had done "something for wildness and [to]
make the mountains glad." His high spirits were prophetic; over
the years the club would become one of the most effective organizations in the preservation movement, its membership reaching 622,000 by November 1990.

Soon after its founding the club listed 182 charter members,
whose enthusiasm ran high when John Wesley Powell attended
an early meeting and spoke on his explorations of the Green and
Colorado rivers. No doubt most of the charter members had
joined the club out of earnest feeling for wilderness, without
great interest in the politics of land use; but a hard core of
activists considered the club as a "Defense Association" (in the
sense of Johnson's original proposal) for Yosemite in particular
and the Sierra Nevada in general. As a consequence, the club
soon found itself actively cast as the defender of Yosemite National Park.

The opposition to the park, an alliance of stock, timber, and
mining interests, had found a cat's-paw in Representative An-
thony Caminetti, who in the late spring of 1892 had introduced a
bill in the House to shear away nearly half the area of Yosemite
National Park. As soon as alerted, Muir and two other charter
members of the club began to oppose the bill by letters, telegrams, and published interviews. They pushed the fight until
November 5, when the club voted a resolution instructing "the
Board of Directors . . . to prepare a memorial to Congress against
the bill and to use every effort to defeat it." The Sierra Club's
campaign was successful; the Caminetti Bill never emerged from
committee, though a modified version of it would be introduced
in the next Congress, only to die also as a result of further Sierra
Club opposition.

Perhaps the success of the anti-Caminetti campaign in 1893
caused Muir to feel that he could now take a well-earned vaca-

tion. For ten years Keith and he had planned to visit Europe together, and now one morning in May Muir received a telegram from Keith to the effect that he could wait no longer. Muir could meet him at the World's Fair in Chicago. Within a day or so Muir was able to leave in pursuit of the artist, feeling that with John Reid and his brother David he was leaving the ranch in capable hands. On reaching Chicago, after a visit with his mother on the way, he found a scrawled note from Keith: "Couldn't stand the crowd. Will wait in New York."

Muir took time to sample the fair, finding it, as he wrote to Louie, "a cosmopolitan rat's nest." He soon arrived in New York, where he found Keith caught up in a dazzle of parties thrown by dealers and art patrons. Muir quickly discovered himself in a similar situation, for Johnson was determined to give him "exposure" to the elite, in order to make him a more effective crusader for preservation. First he met Richard Watson Gilder, editor in chief of the *Century*. Then came his fellow naturalist John Burroughs, who was queasy from bad food that had been served at a dinner of the Walt Whitman Club the night before and so "gave no sign of his fine qualities." But in spite of this inauspicious beginning they became fast, though ever sparring friends.

Among the other writers Muir met were George Washington Cable, Rudyard Kipling, Thomas Bailey Aldrich, Mark Twain and his collaborator on *The Gilded Age*, Charles Dudley Warner. Johnson also introduced him to the electronics wizard, Nikola Tesla. "With all his Scotch wit and his democratic feeling," Johnson wrote, "Muir bore himself with dignity in every company, readily adjusting himself to any environment." On a sultry June day the editor took him up the Hudson River to the home of Henry Fairfield Osborn, then serving as dean of pure science at Columbia University. Muir discovered a natural affinity between himself and Osborn, and so began a friendship that would last for the rest of Muir's life.

After Muir had examined glacial scorings in Central Park, Johnson whisked him up to the Cambridge area. At Concord they visited Emerson's house, Hawthorne's Old Manse, and the Concord bridge, where "the shot heard round the world" was

fired. They also visited the Sleepy Hollow Cemetery, where Hawthorne, Thoreau, and the Sage of Concord were all buried; and
Muir admired the uncut mass of white quartz that marked Emerson's grave. He then strolled with Johnson out to Walden Pond,
which inspired him to hyperbole. "No wonder Thoreau lived
here two years. I could have enjoyed living here two hundred or
two thousand."

But the highlight of the trip was their visit to the Brookline
estate of Charles S. Sargent, author of the many-volumed *Silva
of North America* and director of Harvard's Arnold Arboretum.
Muir had met Sargent through Asa Gray in 1878 and had recognized in him a kindred spirit by virtue of their mutual love of
trees. Their friendship now flowered, to endure like that with
Osborn to the end of Muir's life. At Sargent's dinner table he
told Stickeen's story with such effect that the liveried servants
listened rapt behind half-closed doors. Not even Muir's digres-
sions (a friend once said that when he tells "his famous dog story,
you get the whole theory of glaciation thrown in") could mar the
impression.

Then it was back to New York City and a continued round of
socializing until June 26, when Muir followed Keith, who had
already sailed for Europe. John arrived in Liverpool early in July
and went on to Edinburgh the same day. There he visited the
elderly publisher David Douglas, to whom Johnson had given
him a letter of introduction. Douglas proved to be "a fountain of
fun, humor, and stories of the old Scotch writers." He showed
Muir around Edinburgh, including many places that had figured
in Scott's novels. Then Muir took the train for Dunbar, reaching
the town of his birth in just an hour and going to the Lorne
Temperance Hotel, which had been his boyhood home, "if for
nothing else [than] to take a look at that dormer window I
climbed in my nightgown, to see what kind of adventure it really
was." While in town, he sauntered about the streets, looked up
cousins and old friends, visited Dunbar Castle and the Davel Brae
School, and even dined with the contemporary schoolmaster.

After visits to other localities in Scotland, his itinerary took
him successively to the glacier-carved fiords of Norway, the En-

glish Lake District with its reminders of Wordsworth, London
for a visit to Parliament, Switzerland (where he considered climbing the Matterhorn), then back to London, where he stopped at
Kew Gardens to call on Sir Joseph Hooker, only to be whisked off
for an overnight stay at the botanist's country house, Sunning-
dale. Back in Scotland, Muir basked in the heather in full bloom
around Thurso. Then he crossed the Irish Sea for an inspection of
the bogs of Ireland and a short rest at the lakes of Killarney. He
never caught up with Keith and returned to America without him,
but not before paying Edinburgh and Dunbar each a second visit.

On his arrival in the United States, he spent a week with
Johnson in Washington, conferring with strategic officials on the
national parks and forest reservations, his interviews contribut-
ing much to the success that conservation would have with the
Cleveland administration. And then on leaving the capital he
went home by way of Portage in order to see his mother and
sisters again.

Before sailing for Europe, he had promised his first book to
Johnson and the Century Company, and now in late September
1893 he made haste to put it in shape. He worked in his "scribble
den" at a large desk beside a window that overlooked the orchards
and the vista down the valley to Carquinez Strait. He would
begin his work day shortly after sunrise, after cooking the eggs
and heating the coffee left for him by the Chinese servant. He
customarily worked until ten o'clock, when the family had their
breakfast, after which he would read the morning's work for
Louie's criticism. Then he would go to his desk again.

In this fashion, toiling as much like an editor as a creative
writer, he had the manuscript ready for submission by April 1894.
It consisted mostly of revised and edited articles that had seen
previous publication ("A Windstorm in the Forests of the Yuba,"
for instance, and the essays on the water ouzel and the Douglas
squirrel). But he informed Johnson, "I have worked hard on every
one of them, leaning them against each other, adding lots of new
stuff, and killing adjectives and adverbs of redundant growth. . . . I
feel sure the little alpine thing will not disappoint you."

The Mountains of California was published in the fall of 1894,

when Muir was fifty-six years old. The reviews were excellent,
and the first printing was soon sold out. "I have never read
descriptions of trees that so picture them to the mind as yours
do," Charles S. Sargent wrote. "Your book is one of the great
productions of its kind." In England Sir Joseph Hooker was
equally enthusiastic, as if he recognized that the book contained
much of Muir's best writing. It emphatically belied Muir's statement that "No amount of word-making will ever [cause] a single
soul to *know* these mountains"; and as more of his books were
published, many admirers would decide that *The Mountains of
California* remained his finest work. Its influence was far reaching; it helped to mobilize public sentiment in favor of conservation
and to stiffen the public will to preserve the vanishing wilderness.

CHAPTER 19

The National Forestry Commission

JOHN Muir was not always easy to live with, but Louie adjusted understandingly to his eccentricities and to his periods of irascibility, even where it concerned her beloved Steinway. The piano jangled on Muir's nerves, especially when he was writing. Ever self-effacing, Louie solved the problem by playing only when he was out of the house; but when the girls began to take music lessons, she had a music room soundproofed across the house from Muir's study.

Yet even with the house made quiet, his writing went as slowly as ever. That was particularly true of an article he composed late in 1894 and early in 1895. On February 6 he wrote in his journal, "This day I finished 'The Discovery of Glacier Bay.' . . . It seems strange that a paper that reads smoothly and may be finished in ten minutes should require months to write."

With the article on Glacier Bay completed, Muir turned to the long-delayed book on Yosemite. He set about arranging his notes, but to refresh his memory and to secure new impressions he decided to visit the park again in late July. August 7 found him camped at the head of the Grand Cascade in the Great Tuolumne Canyon, after which he followed bear trails through Muir Gorge to Hetch Hetchy. He remained until September in Yosemite National Park, closely observing conditions there, especially the effect of the army's patrolling the area, and he approved of what he saw.

The contrast was sad, however, between the frowziness of the floor of Yosemite Valley under the management of the state commission and the healthy condition of the surrounding national park. Equally sad was the destruction of trees in the adjacent Sierra Forest Reserve, where sawmills operated brazenly, and the "hoofed locusts" had grown more devastating than ever, and sheepmen continued to set ruinous fires for their own designs. It was imperative that the government adopt correctives for such evils, and in the East, Charles S. Sargent, Robert Underwood Johnson, and a young professional forester named Gifford Pinchot (whom Muir had met in New York in 1893) decided in their consultations together that Sargent's proposal for a national forestry commission should be implemented to survey the problems of the western forests and recommend solutions—a decision that won the approval of Muir and the Sierra Club. "The Sargent plan of salvation of trees," Muir wrote to Johnson, "will prove, I think, a glorious reformation and make the pine needles tingle with joy." Unfortunately, when key members of Congress were approached on the question of authorizing such a commission, they showed no interest.

The next best thing to do, the reformers decided, was to persuade the Secretary of the Interior to request the National Academy of Sciences to appoint such a commission in its capacity as scientific advisor to the government. Sargent had great faith in Johnson's persuasive powers and so asked him to approach the secretary. This Johnson did, conferring with Hoke Smith from eleven one evening until one in the morning, and at the end of their session Secretary Smith assured him that he would lodge the official request with the National Academy, especially since the American Forestry Association favored the step.

At Smith's request Wolcott Gibbs, president of the academy, appointed the National Forestry Commission of 1896, whose unpaid service, as the memoirs of Gifford Pinchot later suggested, would "put government forestry on the map." Sargent was named chairman, a position for which his devotion to trees well suited him. Gibbs served ex officio, and there were five other members— William H. Brewer of Yale; General Henry L. Abbott, engineer and hydrologist; Alexander Agassiz of Harvard; Arnold Hague of the U.S. Geological Survey; and Gifford Pinchot, who would act as the secretary of the commission. Because of ill health, Muir had asked to be passed over for appointment, but he was willing to serve as an unofficial advisor, and Sargent urged him to do so, declaring that his understanding of trees was indispensable. Muir had mutual feelings and would later write that Sargent was "the only one of the Commission that knew & loved trees as I loved them."

At this time Harvard invited Muir to attend its June 1896 commencement to receive an honorary master's degree in recognition of his conservation work. At first he decided that his ailing health forbade the trip to Cambridge, but one of his mysterious flashes of psychic perception changed his mind. During work in his "scribble den," a sudden premonition, like that about his father, bade him hurry to Portage if he wished to see his mother before her death. He had had no previous warning that her health was failing, but he felt so strongly that he caught the next train to Wisconsin. En route he wired his brother Dan at Lincoln, Nebraska, and his sister Mary at Kearney. Mary and her daughter met him at the station, and he pulled them aboard the train, but Dan took no stock in hunches and declined to go.

As Muir entered the yard at Portage, along with Mary and her daughter, Sarah rushed from the door, crying, "Oh, John, surely God has sent you. Mother is terribly ill!" Anne Muir had suffered a heart seizure shortly before and was now becoming comatose. When Sarah made her understand, however, that John and Mary had come, she somehow roused herself and whispered, "My ain bairns, my ain bairns!"

Anne Muir rallied; but as Muir was inclined to run no risks, he wired railroad fare to Dan and bade him come at once. Dan caught the first train, only to find when he reached Portage that their mother seemed out of danger. So Dan and the Portage doctor considered it safe for Muir to go on to the Harvard commencement. Before departing, however, he left addresses where he could be telegraphed in New York and Cambridge in case of trouble; and on June 23, while still in New York, he received word that his mother had died peacefully in her sleep. He wired back that he would return for the funeral, then hurried up to Harvard to receive his degree the following day.

After the funeral he went to Chicago, where on July 5 he joined the National Forestry Commission for its western tour,

Congress having appropriated $25,000 for its expenses. The commission was concerned not only with the forest reserves previously set aside but also with such timberlands that still remained in the public domain, after millions of acres had been given away (notably as grants to the western railroads), sold for a song to special interests, or even stolen outright by every sleazy means of manipulating the various land laws. It would be impossible to obliterate such a record of heedlessness and shameless exploitation, but to preserve and to make judicious use of those forests that remained and to demonstrate that the nation could learn from its past mistakes was a feasible goal, and to help in its achievement was the commission's commendable aim.

Two commissioners were absent—Alexander Agassiz, Louis Agassiz's son, who would never join the tour, and Gifford Pinchot, who would join it only after the commission had reached Montana. At that time Muir and Pinchot, the latter a tall, sharp-featured man with a drooping mustache and piercing blue eyes, would find themselves strongly drawn to one another, in marked contrast to their frigid relations later on.

In the meantime, Muir traveled with four of the commissioners to the scene of their first inquiry, the ponderosa forests of the Black Hills. There they found trees ravaged by fire, mining operations, and illegal logging; and the story would continue much the same wherever they went—the Bighorn Mountains in Wyoming, the Bitterroot Range in Idaho and Montana, and the Cascade Mountains in Washington. In Spokane, Muir temporarily left the commission, for a brief trip to Alaska with Henry Fairfield Osborn, whom he joined in Tacoma. It had been their intention "to learn something of the inlets of St. Elias & Prince William Sound," but something unforeseen upset their plans, "so I returned like a tourist," Muir wrote to Johnson. "However, I gained a good review of the ground I visited so long ago & got back in time to join the forestry commission in Oregon. . . . I hope to . . . remain with them for the balance of the season."

He toured with the commission through the Cascades of Oregon, where, according to Pinchot, "Muir and Professor Brewer made the journey short with talk that was worth crossing the

Gifford Pinchot, who served on the National Forestry Commission in 1896 and who became the first chief forester of the U.S. Forest Service in 1905. He was leader of the utilitarian wing of the early conservationist movement. Courtesy of the Yale University Archives, Manuscripts and Archives, Yale University Library.

continent to hear." Next the commission visited the coast red-
wood belt in northern California, several Big Tree groves in the
Sierra Nevada, and the San Bernardino Reserve in southern California. They also visited the nearby San Jacinto Mountains, whose
forest, they decided, should be set aside. Then they went to the
Grand Canyon, where on the rim Muir discouraged Pinchot from
killing a large tarantula, because "it had as much right there as
we did." That night Muir and Pinchot camped in a stand of
cedars, away from the rest of the commission, "and there [Muir]
talked until midnight," Pinchot would write in his memoirs. "It
was such an evening as I have never had before or since." For
Muir the tour ended at the Grand Canyon, but on their way
home the commission made brief acquaintances with five reserves in Colorado.

In the East, Sargent and the commission began at once to
systematize their findings. They met at places like the Brevoort
House and the Century Club in New York City, and at times
their proceedings resembled genteel civil war. Muir kept in touch
with them, and as an advisor his chief service was that of media-
tor between the narrowly dendrological position of Sargent and
the utilitarian orientation of Pinchot, the two emergent poles of
contention in the ongoing deliberations. Part of the difficulty
traced back to the Forest Reserve Act, which merely authorized
the creation of reserves, without spelling out the manner of their
management.

Even during the tour, with the question of administration un-
resolved, a fundamental division of opinion had developed on one
point. Sargent and Abbott—seconded by Muir—favored army supervision of the reserves as the most effective means of protection
and the least subject to political pressure. Muir could—and probably did—extoll the efficiency of the U.S. Cavalry in patrolling the
Yosemite National Park and keeping out timber thieves, stock
operators, and other undesirable trespassers.

But Pinchot opposed military oversight, having been converted to the civilian-guard system of Germany, where he had
studied forestry. Brewer and Hague, especially Hague, sided with
Pinchot. Hence, for the sake of harmony and to head off a mi-

nority report by Pinchot, Sargent worked out a compromise that made neither faction happy. The final report of the commission would recommend military supervision, but only until an authorized, trained, and organized Forest Corps could be formed to administer the reserves under civil service. Meanwhile, Sargent sent drafts to Muir for "ideas and inspiration." Muir in turn consulted with members of the Sierra Club, and from their huddles came a recommendation—originally the idea of President David Starr Jordan of Stanford University—to establish the Stanislaus Forest Reserve north of Yosemite. Muir favored the proposal and sent it on to Sargent. At the same time he approved further decisions of the commission, notably that reached on October 24, 1896, at the house of Arnold Hague in Newport, to recommend the creation of thirteen new forest reserves and two national parks—Mount Rainier and the Grand Canyon.

Although the final report of the commission would not be ready for submission until May 1, 1897, a preliminary draft was sent on January 29 to Wolcott Gibbs, who forwarded it to President Cleveland during his last days in office. With diverting irony the president decided to celebrate the 165th birthday of Washington, the fabled chopper of cherry trees, by issuing executive orders to withdraw from the public domain, with no mention of their purpose, the thirteen forest reserves recommended by the commission. They totaled more than twenty-two million acres and included two reservations in California, the Stanislaus and the San Jacinto forest reserves.

Cleveland's act burst like a bombshell on the public consciousness, and without preparation (not even the politicians had been consulted) many in the West developed a sudden alarm that the reserves were going to be locked up tight, a fear in large measure justified in the absence of an effective policy on what the reserves were intended for. Conservation thus became a burning issue, and opposition to Cleveland's edicts exploded throughout the West. There were sustained barrages of protest against the "useless protection of dead timber"; newspapers frothed, claiming that "wiseacres" and "impractical dreamers" out of touch with western realities had advised the president. Many of the western protesters upheld the old-time custom of helping oneself to timber in the public domain on the grounds that it built up the nation and put a premium on enterprise. Many, moreover, were adherents of William Jennings Bryan and the Free Silver crusade and were therefore hostile already toward Cleveland and the "Gold Democrats" of the East.

Thus erupted what Pinchot would call "the most considerable storm in the whole history of Forestry in America"—a deafening hullabaloo that resounded throughout the West. It might have been averted had the president heeded Pinchot's advice that a management plan be devised before the forests were actually set aside, or even that lumber and sheep interests, miners, and others be prepared by the timely publication of an effective proviso such as that which would appear in the final report. "These great bodies of reserved lands cannot be withdrawn from all occupation or use," this proviso read. "They must be made to perform their part in the economy of the nation. Unless the reserved lands of the public domain are made to contribute to the welfare and prosperity of the country they should be thrown open to settlement and the whole system of reserved forests be abandoned."

But, kept in the dark as to the purpose of the reservations, stock, mining, and timber barons registered their wrath in streams of telegrams to their allies on Capitol Hill, and their allies reacted vehemently. Sargent advised Muir: "The Western politicians are out for blood"; and understandably so in view of several deeply rooted factors. The depression of 1893 had hit the West particularly hard and caused a number of state governments to teeter on the brink of insolvency. Capital had grown so tight that hosts of western constituents feared that the boom of the eighties might never return. They claimed that the monetary policies of the federal government had hamstrung the silver mining industry, and now that the western forests had been locked from public access, they feared that the grazing, timber, and railroad interests would be sabotaged as well. At the same time the public perceived that Cleveland's proclamations had caused the badly

strapped governments of the states in which the reserves were located to lose a substantial part of their tax base, a fact that supposedly made their financial plight worse than ever.

Hard-pressed by their angry constituents, congressmen struggled for two whole days to impeach the outgoing president.
When that effort failed, the Senate attached to the Sundry Civil
Bill a rider that annulled all the reserves that Cleveland had created. "Ye Gods!" Muir fulminated to Johnson. "What's to be
done with the crazy Senate? Voting unanimously in the face of
the admirable report of the Academy Commission. The Western
Senators are a bad lot, but we will win at last. But how long, O
Lord, how long must destruction go on?" To his delight Cleveland scotched by means of a pocket veto the Senate's move to
annul the reserves. That was how the matter stood—entirely un-
resolved—when the president left office and Congress adjourned
on March 4, 1897.

The new president, William McKinley, called a special session
of Congress not long after his inauguration, and a main object of
its attention was Cleveland's thirteen forest reserves. No action
was taken, however, before Sargent submitted the Forestry Commission's final report, too late for the best effect, true enough,
but hardly amounting, in Pinchot's words, to "nothing more
than so much waste paper." It may not have formulated what one
pioneer writer on conservation called "a comprehensive plan for
the extension and development of the forest reservations." But it
did recommend among other things the amendment or repeal of
timber and mining legislation that fostered fraud, the banning of
sheep from the reserves, and the systematic management of forests to insure a permanent and sustained yield of timber.

Yet much to Pinchot's disgust, it left other important matters
unaddressed, especially the details of forest use. Still, he had
signed it in the end, "bad as it is," and remained to be mollified
when the report was largely superceded by the Forest Management Act, passed by a bickering Congress on June 4, 1897. To
Muir's dismay, this measure, pending further study, suspended
Cleveland's forest reserves until March 1, 1898, with the exception
of the two in California, which were allowed to stand at the re-

quest of both senators from that state. It was, thus, a matter of intense gratification to Muir that his forest gospel had made significant progress at least in his home state.

The plight of the suspended reserves was another matter, and it distressed him deeply to witness the stampede of speculators and timber, mining, and grazing interests to file entries, grabbing land in the suspended areas while the grabbing was opportune, and in addition perpetrating without check various underhanded manipulations that had been winked at for generations as expedient means of taming the frontier.

But the Forest Management Act presented other more heartening tangibles. It solidly established the principle that, while timber in the existing reserves might be sold, the land itself could not; and two clauses of the act clarified the purpose of the reserves on the one hand and granted authority on the other to the Secretary of the Interior to devise measures to protect the forests. At the same time it cleared the political atmosphere, so that western hostility receded, while the McKinley administration, along with Congress, accepted the suspension period as propitious for a survey of the forest lands by the U.S. Geological Survey.

Still, 1897 clearly marked a setback and a time of gloom for Muir's crusade, and the best course for him and his preservationist colleagues to follow seemed to be a strenuous effort to minimize the toll on the forests in the reserves. To this end, and to foster national parks, Muir now produced some of his finest writing. By the time March 1, 1898, rolled around (the date on which the suspension of Cleveland's reserves was lifted), he had published three more conservation articles—two in the *Atlantic Monthly*—and they bore so much influence on public opinion that Congress would reject moves to abolish Cleveland's eleven remaining reserves outright. Thus, the outlook for conservation was again encouraging.

The first of Muir's three articles, his most explicitly political writing to date, had appeared in *Harper's Weekly* under the title "The National Parks and Forest Reservations." In it he described a horse he had once seen "snorting, groaning [and] plunging back and forth in blind fury"—a horse with a yellow jacket in his ear. He compared the animal's mad commotion with the storm of protest that had rocked the West against the forest reserves that President Cleveland had proclaimed. "I thought of that poor horse," he added, "and said, 'These men must have yellow jackets in their ears.' Gold stings worse than the wasps of the woods, and gives rise to far more unreasonable and unexplainable behavior." The plunderers might protest, but Muir announced his confidence that a majority of Americans approved of forest protection by the federal government. He then proceeded to describe the aims of the Forestry Commission and concluded that "not only should all the reserves established be maintained, but that every remaining acre of unentered forest-bearing land . . . should be reserved, protected, and administered by the Federal Government for the public good forever."

But even more effective were the articles published in the *Atlantic Monthly,* the opening pair in a series solicited from Muir by the *Atlantic*'s editor, Walter Hines Page, future U.S. ambassador to Great Britain. The series would use much of Muir's Yosemite material, and in 1901 he would gather it in a book called *Our National Parks.* The first essay, published in August 1897 under the title "The American Forests," described the primeval wilderness of the continent as it must have existed before the coming of Europeans—forests that contained some five hundred species of trees and that could be adversely affected by native peoples with their stone implements no more than by the "gnawing beaver" or the "browsing moose." "But when the steel axe of the white man rang out on the startled air their doom was sealed." Most of the essay dealt with the fate of American forests at the hands of white settlers, and in the course of it Muir made one of his most telling statements on behalf of the preservation of trees.

"Any fool can destroy trees," he declared. "They cannot run away; and if they could, they would still be destroyed,—chased and hunted down as long as fun or a dollar could be got out of their bark hides, branching horns, or magnificent bole backbones." He pointed out that it had taken three thousand years to grow certain giants in the forests of the West. God had protected those trees through the millennia from all sorts of natural disasters; "but he cannot save them from fools,—only Uncle Sam can do that." So effective were Muir's appeals on behalf of trees that Johnson would abandon all restraint in his memoirs and name Muir as "the real father of the forest reservations of America."

Muir mailed "The American Forests" to Page in time to go to Madison to receive an honorary LL.D. from his alma mater. Then in August 1897 he joined Sargent and another botanist, William Canby, on a trip to examine the trees of western Canada and southeastern Alaska, where he would have ample opportunity to hear Sargent's voluminous catalogue of grievances against Pinchot, his former protégé. At Victoria they were caught in the rush of gold hunters stampeding toward the Klondike, and among them Muir saw his old friend Hall Young, who aimed to do Christian work among them. Muir viewed the gold seekers and their outfits with amused contempt. "A horde of fools," Young would report his saying.

Then while homeward bound he stopped in Seattle, where he read in a local newspaper a statement that sheep grazing in forest reserves did no harm. He was startled to note that the opinion was attributed to Gifford Pinchot, who had been appointed as a "confidential forest agent" by the Secretary of the Interior the day after the signing of the Forest Management Act and who had come west to make an economic survey of Cleveland's suspended reserves. Muir and Pinchot had stopped at the same hotel, and when Muir saw him in the lobby, surrounded by a pack of reporters, he stepped up to him with the newspaper in hand and asked, "Are you correctly quoted here?"

"Yes," Pinchot admitted.

"Then," Muir replied, ". . . I don't want anything more to do with you."

On that day more than a friendship suffered; the nascent, as-yet-unnamed conservation movement began to divide. The rift grew even wider in January 1898 when Muir's second article for the *Atlantic* was published—"Wild Parks and Forest Reservations of the West." It was an impassioned plea for the preservation of wildness and its blessings, making clear from the preservationist point of view why national parks and forest reserves had been and should be created. "The tendency nowadays to wander in wilderness," the essay began, "is delightful to see. Thousands of tired, nerve-shaken, over-civilized people are beginning to find out that going to the mountains is going home; that wildness is a necessity; and that mountain parks and reservations are useful not only as fountains of timber and irrigating rivers, but as fountains of life."

Muir then proceeded to describe unusual features in certain reservations and, like the Forestry Commission's report, recommended that Mount Rainier and the Grand Canyon be made national parks. The article was entirely silent in respect to Pinchot's objectives. Nevertheless, it was widely perceived as a frontal attack on his "wise use" policies. Therefore, while the two would occasionally meet (largely through the mediation of Johnson) and even go to the woods together, cooperation between them waned, and their break foreshadowed a fundamental schism in the conservation movement.

Strain had already developed in conservationist ranks by the time Congress had passed the Forest Management Act, and the measure in fixing the purpose of forest reserves—"to furnish a continuous supply of timber for the use and necessities of citizens of the United States"—hewed exactly to Pinchot's aims, which he would later explain at a meeting of the Society of American Foresters: "The object of our forest policy," he said, "is not to preserve the forests because they are beautiful or wild or the habitat of wild animals; it is to ensure a steady supply of timber for human prosperity. Every other consideration comes as secondary." Thus, Pinchot's policies drew a sharp line against the aestheticism of Muir's preservationist stance and specifically ruled out Muir's goal of recreation and the enjoyment of scenic beauty as a paramount use of the forest reserves.

At first, however, Muir tried to straddle the issue and keep one foot in the utilitarian bailiwick. But after a period of indecisive wavering he accepted the fact that keeping wilderness intact and the utilitarian management of forests were simply incompatible, making it impossible for him to continue supporting the aims of professional forestry and at the same time remain true to his own ideals. Therefore, he rejected the Pinchot version of conservation and opted for uncompromising preservationist principles. The result was that, as time went on, the less promise for wilderness preservation that he saw in the foresters' programs, the more he would concentrate on promoting and defending the national parks.

Such efforts coincided with developments in the Department of Agriculture that strengthened Pinchot's hand, first by making him chief of the Division of Forestry in 1898, then by expanding his division into the Bureau of Forestry in 1901. Four years later Congress would replace the bureau with the U.S. Forest Service and transfer to its administration all the forest reserves (renamed national forests) from the Department of the Interior, thus enshrining Pinchot's "wise use" program as the official policy of the federal government. Soon the chief forester would magnify the breach between the two factions of the conservation movement by appropriating the term "conservation" for his wing of the movement and would even make the unsustainable claim that he had coined the expression. Thus, by this time the originally synonymous terms "conservation" and "preservation" had diverged in meaning and represented two increasingly dissonant points of view.

Meanwhile, late in the summer of 1898, Sargent invited Muir on another tour with him and Canby—this time to the forests of the Southeast; and Muir accepted enthusiastically. The trio started out in September, and on occasion their itinerary crossed Muir's route of 1867, while somewhere along the way Muir read with immense enthusiasm the copy that Sargent gave him of the *Travels* of William Bartram, a work that described the country (with its flora) through which they now moved, but as it had looked a century before. Now in October, 1898, the Southern forests blazed in brilliant autumn colors. Muir reveled in fine views of them from many Appalachian vantage points and was especially moved by the vista from Grandfather Mountain in North Carolina. He later remarked that he could not hold himself in and jumped about in his enthusiasm. That is, until he glanced at Sargent, who stood completely silent, but with a bemused expression.

"Why don't you let yourself out at a sight like that?" Muir asked.

"I don't wear my heart on my sleeve," Sargent answered.

"Who cares where you wear your little heart, mon? There you stand in the face of all Heaven come down to earth, like a critic of the universe, as if to say, 'Come, Nature, bring on the best you have. I'm from BOSTON!'"

The tour was interrupted when Sargent fell ill, but on his recovery the three set out again, spending a day in Baltimore and another in Washington, where they examined parks along with the surrounding woods. At last they proceeded to Florida, and at Cedar Key Muir enquired of the Hodgsons, who had nursed him back to life in 1867. Mr. Hodgson was dead, he learned, but his wife was still alive. Muir looked her up at Archer, Florida, a meeting that he described to Louie: "I asked if she knew me. She answered no, and asked my name. I said Muir. '*John* Muir?' she almost screamed. '*My* California John Muir? My California John?' 'Why, yes, I promised to come back and visit you in about twenty-five years, and though a little late I've come.'"

The tour ended at Archer, where Muir and his companions parted company. Muir had wanted to go on to Mexico to see "the grand Taxodiums" there, but the others declared that they had traveled enough. Muir went on alone as far as Live Oak, Florida; then he also turned back and, feeling suddenly home-sick, headed west by way of New Orleans.

CHAPTER 20

The Harriman-Alaska Expedition

BY spring 1899 Muir had another article ready for Walter Hines Page, one about Yosemite National Park. Moreover, he had still others under way for the *Atlantic* series, and he informed Page, "I wanted to complete these and get the book *[Our National Parks]* put together and off my hands this summer, and now that I have all the material well in hand and on the move, I hate to leave it."

What he was leaving the series for was a project of Edward H. Harriman, president of the Union Pacific Railroad, and soon to be the president of the Southern Pacific as well. "I first heard of him . . . ," Muir later explained, "when my friend Dr. [C. Hart] Merriam wrote that I was invited to join a scientific expedition to Alaska which Mr. Harriman was organizing." Harriman had asked Merriam, chief of the U.S. Biological Survey, to select scientists for the expedition, and Merriam had chosen Muir in his role as "student of glaciers."

When Muir asked for details, Merriam said that Harriman's doctors had ordered him on a leave from overwork, and so he had planned a cruise to Alaska. This would involve "a good sea-going steamer," Merriam pointed out, and so Harriman had decided to put the ship to double duty and public service, with an expedition "devoted to the interests of science. . . . Accordingly, as many scientific explorers as could be accommodated had been invited, about twenty-five biologists, naturalists, ornithologists, geologists, artists, etc . . . assembled for work in a magnificent wilderness and under most favorable auspices."

At first Muir considered turning the invitation down, but on learning that Yakutat Bay, Prince William Sound, and Cook Inlet would be among the places visited, he reconsidered, for these regions comprised stretches of Alaska coast he had never seen. He left San Francisco on May 26 with Charles Keeler, ornithologist and director of the Museum of the California Academy of Sciences. On their way to Portland, Muir found Keeler "a charming companion," a fortunate discovery, for they were to be roommates throughout the cruise. They stopped at the Portland Hotel and on May 30 went to the railroad station to meet the Harriman Special on its arrival from the East. The next day the Special took the Harriman party on to Seattle, where they boarded the *George W. Elder*, a tourist steamer refurbished for the expedition. Harriman had ordered it fitted out with a library, laboratories, and instruments for the scientists. There were 125 people aboard, counting the crew, when it sailed.

At first Muir felt "rather repelled" by Harriman, or so he later confessed to John Burroughs, but "at last learned to love him." He soon found the tycoon "was uncommon. He was taking a trip for rest, and at the same time managing his exploring guests as if we were a grateful, soothing, essential part of his rest-cure. . . . He kept us all in smooth working order."

The stateroom Muir shared with Keeler was somewhat cramped, and so Keeler wrote home "how great a privilege [it was] to be cooped up for two months in a little room with John Muir." William H. Brewer, the botanist Muir had come to know on the tour of the National Forestry Commission, and for whom he had developed a great admiration, was housed next door; and John Burroughs, historian of the expedition, was located three rooms away. Others among the scientists included not only Merriam but also William H. Dall, paleontologist of the U.S. Geological Survey; Robert Ridgway, curator of birds at the U.S. National Museum; Henry Gannett, chief geographer of the U.S. Geological Survey; George Bird Grinnell, ethnologist and editor of *Forest and Stream;* and G. K. Gilbert, geologist of the U.S. Geological Survey. The artists were R. Swain Gifford, Fred S. Dellenbaugh, and Louis Agassiz Fuertes, famous for his portraits of birds. The principal photographer was Edward S. Curtis, who would later be known as one of the foremost photo-ethnographers of the American Indian. "In John Muir," wrote Burroughs, "we had an authority on glaciers, and a thorough one—so thorough that he would not allow the rest of the party to have an opinion on the subject."

The presence of Harriman's family helped make the voyage a pleasant experience—Mrs. Harriman and her three high-spirited daughters and two young sons. There were several close relatives, and rounding off the party were various cronies of the tycoon, who had come to shoot big game.

In steaming north, the *Elder* took the inland passage, and almost at once began a routine that Muir would describe in his later tribute to Harriman. He would "put us ashore wherever we liked, in all sorts of places—bays, coves, the mouths of streams, etc.,—to suit the convenience of the different parties into which we naturally separated, dropping each with suitable provisions, taking us aboard again at given times, looking after everything to the minutest detail; work enough to bring nervous prostration to ordinary mortals instead of rest."

The expedition spent five days at Glacier Bay, where the *Elder* cast anchor near the cabin Muir and Loomis had built nine years before. Most of the passengers hastened to disembark to admire the Muir Glacier's wondrous calving of bergs, while at the same time a party of hunters, spurred by Muir's tale of wolves in Howling Valley, set out on an ultimately fruitless search for wolves and bears. On the second day Muir led a small group that included G. K. Gilbert and Charles Palache, a Harvard minerologist, on a three-day boat trip to the head of the bay. They visited such glaciers as the Hugh Miller and the Grand Pacific, which Muir had named on previous visits. The latter, they found, had retreated several miles since 1890 and had divided into three separate glaciers. The largest of these Muir named after Harriman, the news of which elicited enthusiastic cheers when he announced it in a talk aboard the *Elder*.

The ship next stopped at Yakutat Bay and then steamed on to Prince William Sound, where Muir's geological expertise led to an interesting discovery. The sound was an intricate expanse of water with shores indented deeply by glacial fiords. As the *Elder* neared the mouth of one of these, the inlet appeared to be en-

tirely blocked by the combination of a giant glacier and a jutting
headland. A map of the U.S. Coast and Geodetic Survey indicated that navigable waters ended at the glacier, and the local
pilot, who had come aboard at Sitka, turned to Captain Peter
Doran and said, "Here, take your ship." He declined further
responsibility for the *Elder* if she were going to be run into
"every uncharted frog marsh."

Captain Doran ordered the *Elder* to proceed more slowly,
and Harriman asked Muir for his opinion of the situation. "Judging from the trends of this fiord and glacier," Muir replied,
"there must be a corresponding fiord or glacier to the southward." He then suggested that a boat be lowered, so that he
might "take a look around that headland into the hidden half of
the landscape." Instead, Harriman proposed that maybe they
could run the ship there and ordered the captain to try. The
narrows proved forbidding, but they soon opened into a fiord
some twelve miles long and unmarked on any map, a magnificent
inlet that by right of discovery Muir named for Harriman. Since
the sounding line indicated safe water, the millionaire ordered the
captain to steam forward through the inlet, a maneuver in the
evening sunshine that Muir would call "the most exciting experience of the whole trip."

But in line with the pilot's misgivings, the *Elder* broke one of
its propellers on a submerged rock and had to find a smooth
beach in order that repairs might be made. Muir therefore asked
to go ashore with a small party to study the environs of the
Harriman Fiord during the overhauling of the propeller. Several
glaciers were discharging bergs into the fiord, and Muir gave
Harriman's name to the largest glacier. By this time a warm
friendship had developed between him and the tycoon, and the
latter was enormously pleased that the fiord and two glaciers
would now bear his name.

After the propeller was repaired, the *Elder* visited Cook Inlet,
then steamed to Kodiak Island, where the hunters hoped to shoot
Kodiak bears. They had moderate luck, and Muir noted on July 4,
"Mr. Harriman returned last evening after killing two bears,
mother and child." Muir's disgust at hunting was as strong as

ever, and in another note he expressed his scorn for the hunters' "pleasure [in] making a hole in the animal [and] satisfying the savage instincts that should be kept down . . . after civilization has gone far enough for trousers and prayers."

It was while anchored off Kodiak Island that certain of the scientists began to praise "the blessed ministry of wealth, especially in Mr. Harriman's case." As the praise crescendoed, Muir interrupted whimsically, "I don't think Mr. Harriman is very rich. He has not as much money as I have. I have all I want and Mr. Harriman has not." Someone relayed Muir's remark to the magnate, and he came to Muir that evening. "I never cared for money except as power for work," he said. ". . . What I most enjoy is the power of creation, getting into partnership with Nature in doing good, helping to feed man and beast, and making everybody and everything a little better." Muir accepted Harriman at his word, whatever his reservations at the mode of the millionaire's "partnership with Nature."

The ship crossed Bering Sea to Plover Bay in foul weather, since Mrs. Harriman had decided she must see the Siberian coast after Muir's spirited description of it. Then they recrossed the Bering Sea to Port Clarence, Alaska, the northernmost reach of the cruise. After that the *Elder* sailed south, stopping at St. Lawrence Island to allow the passengers to visit the villages of the dead. Muir felt rather glum over the meager scientific accomplishment of the expedition in contrast with its spectacular outlay. "We had a long talk on book-making," he confided in his journal on July 19, "with much twaddle about a grand scientific monument of this trip. . . . Much ado about little. . . . Game hunting, the chief aim, has been unsuccessful. The rest of the story will be mere reconnaissance." The "monument," edited by C. Hart Merriam, would comprise thirteen volumes when publication was completed years after the first of them appeared in 1901—volumes that led off with Burroughs' "Narrative" and Muir's paper "Notes on the Pacific Coast Glaciers," less than a spectacular contribution to science.

No doubt, Muir was largely right in predicting that the "monument" would be "much ado about little," as illustrated by his own contribution. Still, the Harriman Expedition volumes laid a foundation for future scientific work in Alaska. It would not become clear, however, till after the Glacier Bay earthquake of September 10, 1899, that the most immediately significant contributions of the expedition were probably Henry Gannett's maps of glaciers and the photographs of Edward Curtis and G. K. Gilbert. The earthquake changed the Muir Glacier beyond recognition, but Gannett, Curtis and Gilbert had left a permanent record of how it had looked before the quake.

Meanwhile, the passengers went ashore several times as the *Elder* steamed southward. They revisited Cook Inlet and Yakutat Bay. Then they sailed into Cross Sound, and Muir wrote on July 24: "I got a view of the island-blocked entrance to Taylor Bay, and thought of my wild storm day there on the glacier with Stickeen." The ship reached Seattle on the twenty-ninth, and Muir arrived in the Alhambra Valley in early August. Within the month he played host to friends from the expedition—Captain Doran, who brought his wife; G. K. Gilbert, Henry Gannett, and C. Hart Merriam, with the last of whom he talked about everything from glacial sculpture to wild heather.

CHAPTER 21

Roosevelt, Round the World, and Recession

NOT long after Muir's return from the Harriman-Alaska Expedition he again busied himself with the *Atlantic* series and completed it by the end of 1900. It contained his revised essay on Yellowstone National Park, as well as several others on Yosemite, its animals, birds, forests, streams, and wild gardens. The concluding article, called "Hunting Big Redwoods," concerned for the most part the region of the General Grant and Sequoia national parks and was published in September 1901. *Our National Parks,* which collected the entire series, appeared the same year under the imprint of Houghton Mifflin. It presented the most sustained argument yet made for creating national parks and forest reserves for spiritual, aesthetic, and recreational purposes and would be reprinted a dozen times in half as many years, confirming Muir as the leading spokesman for the preservation of wilderness.

The book's emphasis on Yosemite ensured a push for the recession of the valley and the Mariposa Grove to the jurisdiction of the federal government and their amalgamation with Yosemite National Park. As a whole, however, the book left fewer readers as satisfied as did *The Mountains of California,* even though passage after passage was as brilliant as any writing Muir had ever done. He himself remarked about the book: "I have done the best I could to show forth the beauty, grandeur and all-embracing usefulness of our wild mountain forest reservations and parks, with a view to inviting the people to come and enjoy them, and get them into their hearts, [so that] at length their preservation and right use might be made sure."

In the meantime, a sore point had developed between Muir and Wanda. One of his Victorian convictions was that college was not suitable for women, and when Wanda decided that she wanted a higher education, he opposed her wishes, a surprising attitude in view of his having encouraged Mary to attend the University of Wisconsin and of his having defrayed her expenses there. When Wanda persisted, he characterized her as "a faithful, steady scholar, not in the least odd or brilliant, but earnest and unstoppable as an avalanche." Interestingly enough, a friend of Wanda's subsequently wrote that "of her defiance of his stern Scotch dictum, and of her persistence, he was later very proud."

In order to qualify as a freshman at the University of California, Wanda was required to take preparatory work at the prestigious Anna Head School in Berkeley; and when she left home for that purpose, a coolness developed between Muir and her, their correspondence trailing off for several years. She entered the university in January 1902 and did well there in her studies, at the same time reveling in the musical life of Berkeley. But she was not to receive her bachelor's degree, since she would leave school prematurely to help care for Helen in one of her attacks of pneumonia and its extended aftermath.

Meanwhile, the Sierra Club, in concentrating on propaganda and political action, had begun to languish, much to Muir's distress. In 1900, however, William E. Colby, a young mining attorney and son of Gilbert W. Colby of Benicia, was elected secretary. In that capacity he became close to Muir, who encouraged his plan to organize a program of summer outings to resuscitate the club. The first outing, planned on the lines of those sponsored by the Appalachian Mountain Club, was announced for July 1901, and for the occasion Muir reached a truce with Wanda. He and both his daughters were present when ninety-six club members camped for a month in the Big Tuolumne Meadows, rambling through the park by daylight and returning in the evening to a campfire and food prepared by a fabulous Chinese cook named Charley Tuck. The summer outing was such a success that it became an annual affair, giving the club new vigor and doubling its membership within three years.

Muir and Louie with their two grown daughters, Wanda and Helen, on the porch of their ranch house near Martinez, California. The photograph was taken in 1901 by Muir's scientist friend, C. Hart Merriam. Courtesy of the Bancroft Library, University of California, Berkeley.

Meanwhile, on September 14, 1901, not long after the first Sierra Club outing, Theodore Roosevelt became president of the United States. He was a complex personality of flabbergasting breadth, who felt enormous concern about the stranglehold that a small minority held on the country's sources of wealth, and as part of the progressive policies that he would put in place during his administration, he embraced Pinchot's gospel of the wise use of natural resources. It was a cause toward which he had long leaned, having put the preservation of wild game on the agenda of the Boone and Crockett Club, which he had founded along with George Bird Grinnell in 1888.

Shortly after taking the oath of office, Roosevelt announced himself determined to come to grips with the nation's deeply entrenched philosophy of *laissez-faire,* at least so far as it encouraged entrepreneurs to waste the nation's natural resources. He was moved to do something about the alarming extent to which special interests monopolized the country's water power and about the fact that grazing lands and mineral wealth and oil deposits in the public domain brought profits to only a few, instead of to their rightful owners, the people at large. But he was especially moved to action against the wholesale rifling of the nation's timberlands through the circumvention of the letter of federal land laws—manipulations Muir had underscored in *Our National Parks.*

Almost immediately after entering the White House Roosevelt began to seek advice about such matters from men of knowledge and expertise, and as early as October, C. Hart Merriam wrote to Muir from Washington: "The President is heartily with us in the matter of preserving the forests and keeping out the sheep. He wants to know the facts and is particularly anxious to learn them from men like yourself." Muir lost no time in responding. He informed the president of the situation in the reserves and urged that the management of the forests be assigned to the Bureau of Forestry in the Department of Agriculture. On December 3 Roosevelt's first annual message to Congress made conservation a principal theme and described the preservation of forests as an economic necessity. "The forest and water problems," Roosevelt declared, "are perhaps the most vital internal questions of the United States at the present time." On that keynote TR's message to Congress marked the outset of one of the brightest periods in conservation history, making conservation a paramount issue in American politics.

Early in 1903 reports circulated that the president aimed to visit California on a western tour during the coming spring. Then, having met with TR, Robert Underwood Johnson informed Muir that Roosevelt wished him as a guide through Yosemite. Muir replied, "Should the President invite me, I'll go and preach recession like . . . a Century editor." Soon Roosevelt himself wrote to Muir, "I do not want anyone but you, and I want to drop politics absolutely for four days, and just be out in the open with you."

That settled the matter, except that Muir had promised to go on a world tour with Sargent and his son. He therefore wrote to Sargent that "an influential man from Washington wants to make a trip to the Sierra with me, and I might be able to *do some forest good* in talking freely about the campfire." In his reply Sargent postponed the trip, but could not resist a jab at the president, saying that Roosevelt took only a "sloppy, unintelligent interest in forests" and was "altogether too much under the influence of that creature Pinchot."

Roosevelt reached San Francisco by May 14, and Muir, in a new suit bought specially for the occasion, met him the following morning. The official party rode by train to Raymond. Then the president, with Muir at his side to point out the sights, took the stage to the Mariposa Grove of Big Trees, where they planned to camp for the night. At the grove, Roosevelt learned that his suitcase had been sent to Wawona, where the commissioners to manage Yosemite Valley planned to wine and dine him. *"Get it!"* Roosevelt snapped, and Muir later remarked, "Never did I hear two words spoken so much like bullets." Roosevelt had meant it when he said he wanted to be alone with Muir.

Muir built a campfire under the giant sequoias and constructed beds of fern and Big Tree plumes. "It was clear weather," Roosevelt later wrote for the *Outlook,* "and we lay in the open,

President Theodore Roosevelt and Muir at Glacier Point in Yosemite, which they toured together in May, 1903. At the president's request Muir gave him much valuable advice. Courtesy of the Bancroft Library, University of California, Berkeley.

the enormous cinnamon-colored trunks rising about us like the columns of a vaster and more beautiful cathedral than was ever conceived by any human architect." Like Muir, Roosevelt was a nonstop monologist, but Muir managed to do his share of the talking, his forest gospel giving Roosevelt the basis for his judgment that "John Muir talked even better that he wrote." On Muir's agenda was the recession of Yosemite Valley to federal control, a subject on which he spoke so convincingly that Roosevelt became a staunch recessionist and promised to sign any bill to that effect that reached his desk.

On the second day they rode horseback through shallow mantles of snow to Glacier Point on the south rim of the valley. They camped that night in a nearby clump of firs, cooking by campfire large beefsteaks that had been stowed there during the day. As the president sniffed the steaks and the brewing coffee, he exclaimed, "Now this is bully!" After dinner Muir set fire to a dead pine standing alone in an open flat, and the tree became a pillar of flame. "Hurrah!" Roosevelt shouted. "That's a candle it took five hundred years to make." Later they slept through a storm that covered their blankets with four inches of snow, and as they rose, the president cried, "This is bullier yet! I wouldn't miss this for anything."

The politicians were still intent on entertaining Roosevelt with a reception and a banquet and even fireworks afterward. But again TR ignored them, camping the third night with Muir at Bridalveil Meadow, near the foot of El Capitan. The president's perception of the slovenly condition into which the valley floor had fallen under the management of the State Board of Commissioners reinforced his commitment to recession. He seconded Muir's abhorence of the commissioners' complete insensitivity to the beauty of the valley and their consequent encouragement of such mercenary activities as grazing, plowing, planting orchards, building fences, and felling timber—practices that Muir inveighed against to Roosevelt with his sharpest rhetoric. TR felt in such complete rapport with him that when shaking hands in farewell he said, "Goodbye, John. Come and see me in Washington. I've had the time of my life."

Muir had made his points so tellingly that when the presidential train paused in Sacramento, Roosevelt gave a short speech on forest preservation that sounded curiously like a quotation from John Muir. In citing the need to protect American forests, he claimed as his goal not to build "this country of ours for a day" but "to last through the ages." As a step in that direction he instructed Ethan Allen Hitchcock, his Secretary of the Interior, to prepare an executive order that would extend the Sierra Forest Reserve as far north as Mount Shasta. This measure, which Muir had long advocated, was but the beginning of Roosevelt's remarkable record of creating forest reserves. Before his presidency would end, he would expand the area of the national forests from forty-three million to more than 150 million acres.*

But after 1905 the utilitarian emphasis of Gifford Pinchot's "wise use" management, with its slogan "wilderness is waste," would antagonize Muir more than ever, and while he would never discourage the creation of further national forests, he would see more clearly than ever that Pinchot's administration of them would afford little insurance there for the preservation of wilderness intact. It was rather in the national parks that optimism for unspoiled wilderness lay. In that direction Muir's hopes continued to gravitate, encouraged by the fact that, in a large part due to his own efforts as publicist for the national parks idea, the movement for their establishment had enjoyed two heartening successes around the century's end. In 1899 Congress had created Mount Rainier National Park in Washington State, as Muir had advocated, and three years later Crater Lake in Oregon had achieved national park status. In Muir's lifetime, moreover, Congress would also establish Glacier National Park in Montana.

Meanwhile, Muir was free for his world tour. He reached

*The extent of TR's additions to the forest reservations so agitated Congress that in 1907 it outlawed the executive creation of further national forests in a half-dozen western states without its express authorization. That did not deter Roosevelt, however; for before the law took effect, he doubled the area of the national forests by either creating or enlarging thirty-two reserves for a total of 75,000,000 acres. Notwithstanding all of Roosevelt's additions to the national forests, however, fully eighty percent of the nation's commercial timber remained under private control.

Sargent's Brookline mansion on May 24, and wearing a tuxedo for the first time in his life, he was entertained at a formal dinner. Then with Sargent and his son Robeson, he went to New York, where he visited E. H. Harriman, since 1901 president of the Southern Pacific Railroad as well as the Union Pacific. The magnate was the soul of hospitality, explaining that he was also the president of two steamship lines in the Orient and that he would see "that they do everything possible for you when you reach that part of the world."

Muir and the Sargents sailed for Europe without delay. In a letter to Johnson from Moscow, Muir wrote: "I'm still alive after [a] most monstrous dose of civilization, London, Paris, Moscow, Berlin etc. etc. with their miles of art galleries, museums full of old armor and murder implements, endless architecture, parks, gardens, palaces." He spoke of visiting St. Petersburg, then of a trip to the Crimea and the Caucasus and back to Moscow before a projected rail trip across Siberia to Manchuria, Japan, and finally Shanghai.

He might have added that he had felt keen pleasure on visiting the forest of Lindula in Finland, but that on starting for the Crimea he had been so ill he had to be carried aboard the train on a stretcher. Moreover, he arrived at Vladivostok with a case of ptomaine poisoning that had reduced his weight to ninety pounds. Possibly it was his illness that prevented his enthusiasm from kindling at some of the other forests they visited, a fact that would prompt Sargent to say in the memorial he would write after Muir's death: "Together we saw the forests of southern Russia and the Caucasus and those of eastern Siberia, but in all these wanderings Muir's heart never strayed very far from the California Sierra. He loved the Sierra trees the best."

At Shanghai he left the Sargents, not wishing to go with them to central China, and then, as he would write Johnson, "My main trip began," with his transportation arranged largely by Harriman's agents. He traveled alone from Shanghai to Singapore, then on to India, where he visited several large cities and their ancient temples. At Darjeeling he rejoiced in magnificent views "of the highest Himalaya Mountains," and about Simla he

delighted in enormous deodar trees. He left India by way of
Bombay, heading for the cedars of Lebanon, only to be deflected
by a cholera epidemic. Therefore he made for Egypt and as-
cended the Nile as far south as Aswan. He then doubled back to
Port Said and traveled down the Suez Canal, making his way to
Ceylon before sailing "to the south end of the world," including
New Zealand, which he sandwiched between two visits to Australia. There he claimed to have had a "glorious time" and began
his "botanical studies over again with all the wildness and enthusiasm of youth."

The purpose of his second trip to Australia was to observe
two species of araucaria in the mountains of Queensland. He
found both species prodigious, but to his satisfaction neither
could eclipse the giant sequoia. From Australia he moved on to
Port Darwin and Timor, then through the Malay Archipelago to
Manila. His stay was brief in the Philippines, and from there he
sailed to Hong Kong and Canton. At the latter city he received
a cable from Harriman, inviting him to voyage home on the
S.S. *Siberia* of the Pacific Steamship Line. This Muir did, and was
treated like a prince aboard ship. Slightly more than a year after
his departure, he arrived in San Francisco, where Wanda and
Helen met him on the dock. His appearance delighted them, for
he had regained his health so fully that he now weighed 148
pounds, more than he had ever weighed before.

But he would need every ounce of his good health, for during
his absence the contest over the recession of Yosemite Valley had
come to a boil. For the rest of 1904 he was engaged with William
E. Colby and other members of the Sierra Club in preparing for
the next year's session of the state legislature, at which they
schemed to introduce a bill to cede Yosemite Valley and the Mariposa Grove back to the federal government. Governor George C.
Pardee, like President Roosevelt, assured Muir that he favored
recession and would gladly sign such a bill.

The opposition, backed by William Randolph Hearst's *Ex-
aminer*, was strong and active. But the example of President
Roosevelt and Governor Pardee spurred other Republican leaders
to support recession, and since 1901 *Our National Parks* had done

its part in swinging public sentiment behind the cause. For years the Sierra Club, in spite of internal dissension, had worked for recession, with such effective allies as the Sons of the Golden West and the State Board of Trade, with covert support from the Southern Pacific. Still, those with a vested interest in retaining the slipshod administration of the Park Commission were so powerfully vocal and whipped up so much provincialism in California that the recessionists knew they needed more effective assistance.

So late in 1904 Colby urged Muir to call on his friend Harriman to increase the support of the Southern Pacific. As president of that railroad, Harriman had control of the most puissant lobby in the state. Muir may not have approved of the Southern Pacific's political record, the epitome of corruption, especially under the Big Four before Harriman had taken control. But he knew that the SP supported conservation for reasons of its own and had long been interested in Yosemite. Besides, his idealism was tempered with realism, and he was willing to accept help from anyone who held the proper view of his heart's desire, the preservation of wilderness. Therefore he wrote for Harriman's help. The financier reacted favorably, and thereafter the Southern Pacific became more than ever a force, however clandestine, in the campaign for recession.

William H. Mills, chief land agent of the railroad, helped Colby draft the recession bill that Muir had requested, and it was introduced in the legislature in January 1905. The chief lobbyist of the railroad instructed SP pawns in the Senate and Assembly to speak against the bill during debates but to vote for it in the end. Muir and Colby made nine trips to Sacramento to lobby for the measure, and during the contest Colby was Muir's staunchest aide, "the only one of all the club," Muir wrote, "who stood by me in the downright effective fighting."

The Assembly passed the bill by a comfortable margin, but on February 23, 1905, it squeaked through the Senate by a single vote, proving Muir's contention that the "love of Nature among Californians is desperately modest, consuming enthusiasm almost wholly unknown." Still, in the end the preservationists had won, and to Johnson, Muir could write, "I am now an experienced lobbyist; my political education is complete . . . and now that the fight is finished . . . I am almost finished myself."

But the fight was not finished—at least not yet. Hostile maneuvers in Congress delayed federal occupation of Yosemite Valley and the Mariposa Grove for over a year, and again Muir found it necessary to ask for Harriman's help to push a resolution of acceptance through Congress. On June 11, 1906, however, Yosemite Valley and the grove formally became parts of the enclosing national park. "Yes, my dear Johnson," Muir wrote, "sound the loud timbrel and let every Yosemite tree and stream rejoice! . . . The fight you planned by that famous Tuolumne camp-fire seventeen years ago is at last fairly, gloriously won."

CHAPTER 22

The Contest for Hetch Hetchy

CONDITIONS in the Muir household contrasted forlornly with the success of the recession campaign. During the legislative contest Helen had again been put to bed with pneumonia, and her doctor had decreed a year in the desert for her to strengthen her lungs. So in May 1905 Muir and Wanda took her to the Sierra Bonita Ranch near Wilcox, Arizona, where they camped in the open air.

But on June 24 a telegram informed them that Louie was desperately ill. They hurried home to find that she had cancer of the lung and that her doctor considered her condition hopeless. Then within days Helen's serious state made it necessary for her to return to the desert with a hired companion. "The leave taking from my mother was a terrible thing for both of us," she later wrote. "She knew as well as I that we would never see each other again."

By August 6 Louie was dead, and Muir buried her on the ranch in a shaded plot beside her parents, her mother having died eight years before. Louie's death shook Muir severely, for while his love for her had apparently been no more than lukewarm when they were married, his devotion had grown profoundly over the years. But in his grief he said little about her passing, and in death she remained as obscure as when alive. She had been so shy, reticent, and retiring that she had left no vivid impression on friend or acquaintance to fuel her memory. Muir himself had said little about her in letters to others, nor would he leave any written memorial of her. Thus, while her death marked a major turn in his life, the record about Louie was to remain sparse to the point of skimpiness.*

Her health had not been robust, so that she had almost never traveled with Muir, remaining at the ranch, a confirmed "homebody," as a friend had described her. But in that role she had also been described as "the mainstay of the Muir household." Muir had come to rely on her increasingly, not only as a loving and sympathetic wife, but also as a confidante, advisor, and literary critic. She had been so unobtrusive, however, that few acquaintances realized the force she had exerted in his life.

As soon as feasible after the funeral Muir and Wanda joined Helen at Adamana in the northeast part of Arizona, putting up at the Forest Hotel six miles from the Petrified Forest. Helen's tent was pitched beside the hotel, and she slept in the open air. Her lungs improved rapidly in the dry climate, and the two sisters often rode horseback across the sands, an extension of the Painted Desert.

Sometimes Muir rode with them, and on one occasion he and Helen discovered a plateau strewn with the huge trunks of petrified trees. The blue cast of the silicified wood led him to name their find the Blue Forest—to be known later as the Blue Mesa. He returned to the stone trunks again and again, for they gave him an interest in which to forget his bereavement; and on further exploring the surrounding countryside, he came upon other deposits of petrified wood that would, in time, be called the Rainbow, Black, Jasper, and Crystal forests. And when he returned to the Alhambra Valley, his anodyne for loneliness and mourning was to bury himself in the Triassic Period of over 200 million years ago when the stone trees had lived and flourished. He corresponded with authorities on petrified forests, bought books on the subject, and spent several days a week reading about it in the library of the University of California.

Muir was disturbed by the Santa Fe Railroad's practice of carting petrified logs away to be hacked and polished into bau-

---

*After sifting the primary record for his detailed biography of John Muir, Frederick Turner wrote, "The dearth of evidence on [Louie]—even of photographs— amazes me."

bles for the tourist trade, but there was a solution for that problem. In 1906 Representative John F. Lacey, probably the most
active conservationist in the House, sponsored in Congress the
Antiquities Act, which empowered the president to set aside areas
of special scenic, scientific, and historic significance. At Muir's
suggestion Roosevelt decreed the Petrified Forest a national monument, with the Blue Forest and the other areas that Muir had
explored soon added to the original reserve, all destined ultimately to become a national park. Meanwhile, in 1908 Roosevelt
would again act at Muir's nudging and make a portion of the
Grand Canyon a national monument, a prelude to its becoming a
national park in 1919.*

Meanwhile, in June 1906, Muir saw Wanda married to Thomas
R. Hanna, a civil engineer whom she had met at the university in
Berkeley. The newlyweds began housekeeping in the old adobe
that had been the home of the original owner of the ranch, while
Muir continued to live in the big house, alone except for Ah
Fong, his Chinese servant. He refused to let any furniture be
moved, wanting everything to remain as Louie had left it; he did
no writing in his lonely, unproductive frame of mind. His loneliness came to an end in August, however, when Helen returned
from the desert, apparently cured. She immediately began to
help him put some order into his "scribble den."

---

*This development, like the making of the Petrified Forest a national park in 1962,
would have delighted Muir, while the establishment of the National Park Service in
1916 as a counterpart to the U.S. Forest Service would have delighted him even more,
fulfilling as it did one of his most cherished dreams. No doubt, he would have
approved the appointment to the directorship of Stephen Mather, a valued friend and
a dedicated member of the Sierra Club, who would develop and administer the Park
Service in the Muir tradition. "[To the national parks movement] many persons and
organizations have contributed," Johnson would observe, only to add, without undue
exaggeration, that "Muir's writing and enthusiasm were the chief forces that inspired
the movement. All other torches were lighted from his." Granted that national parks
would have been created had Muir never lived, still his influence was crucial and
long-lasting. In a perceptive study of the American conservation movement, Stephen
Fox would find seven decades after Muir's death that "of the early pioneers in
conservation, only one—John Muir of the Sierra Club—still seemed an actual force
in the movement today, with his books in print and his name familiar to contemporary activists."

Muir also resumed his outdoor fellowship with Helen, with whom he had often walked in the open air for the sake of her fragile health. They strolled through the hills, seeking out wild flowers and imitating the songs of birds, both being expert whistlers. Muir encouraged all of her enthusiasms, especially that for railroad operation, heir that she was to his mechanical bent. He sometimes rode with her in the cab of the Santa Fe locomotive that stopped at Muir Station near the ranch. Having made friends with the engineer, Helen took the throttle and learned to operate the locomotive and on one occasion made the run from Stockton to Muir Station. Muir even bought her technical books on railroad matters.

But by the fall of 1907 her health was failing again, her cough having returned as oppressive as ever. A week's trip that Muir took with Keith to Hetch Hetchy in October was nearly ruined by his concern for her welfare; and on his return to the ranch, he found her state alarming. The specialist again decreed the desert for her—this time for a two-year stay. So Muir took her to the Mojave, where he had a cabin built for her near the town of Daggett; and to look after her he hired a nurse-companion. He also had Helen's pony and their shepherd dog, Stickeen II, brought from the ranch for additional company.

Perhaps Muir had chosen Hetch Hetchy for his outing with Keith in order to familiarize himself again with its character, to defend it all the better from the designs of San Francisco. To escape from the monopolistic gouges of the Spring Valley Water Company, the city had long sought an independent source of water. Eventually Hetch Hetchy had come to the attention of the city fathers, who had learned from personnel of the U.S. Geological Survey that the valley, with its high walls and narrow exit, was an ideal site for a dam and—what was especially attractive—a prospective source of hydroelectric power. Also desirable was Lake Eleanor on a tributary a short distance down the Tuolumne.

On October 16, 1901, Mayor James D. Phelan had filed with the Stockton Land Office an application for reservoir rights in both Hetch Hetchy and Lake Eleanor. Muir did not learn of the city's designs upon these sites until early 1905 when Colby heard of them from Gifford Pinchot, who, as chief forester of the newly-formed U.S. Forest Service, threw his weight squarely behind San Francisco's aims. Muir and Colby's alarm over the city's move was temporarily allayed, however, when they learned that Secretary Ethan Allen Hitchcock of the Interior Department had rejected the city's application three times on the grounds that it violated the law of 1890 that guaranteed the integrity of Yosemite National Park.

At first Muir did not realize how fragile this technicality was. Hitchcock's course had been undercut by the Right-of-Way Act of 1901 that Marion De Vries of Stockton had quietly seen through Congress (probably with Phelan's connivance) to authorize the secretary to grant the right to locate dams and reservoirs in national parks, as well as water conduits of any sort. "The act," according to a later commentator, "was . . . perfectly tailored for looters of the parks," and Muir and Colby soon realized they had a battle for Hetch Hetchy on their hands much more formidable than the fight for the recession of Yosemite Valley. They immediately began a campaign of letters, telegrams, speeches, interviews, and published pamphlets.

Simply put, the issue at stake was the welfare of the city or "civilization" versus the preservation of wilderness, and before the final resolution of the controversy Hetch Hetchy would become a cause célèbre, by far the most conspicuous conservation battle up to that time and for years to come. A favorite argument of the dam's proponents was that Hetch Hetchy was not unique and so could be spared, that indeed the mosquito-ridden meadows there would be transformed into a beautiful lake. Aware that Roosevelt would be receptive to their case, Muir countered their contentions much as he was to argue in the final chapter of *The Yosemite:* "Hetch Hetchy Valley, far from being a plain, common rock-bound meadow, as many who have not seen it seem to suppose, is a grand landscape garden, one of Nature's rarest and most precious mountain temples." It would be a despicable desecration, he contended, to turn it into a reservoir.

Meanwhile, to aggravate the situation, the fires from the earthquake of 1906 had made the people of San Francisco more water-conscious than ever, and taking advantage of the hysteria that had developed, Phelan had speciously charged that had his application been promptly approved, water from the Tuolumne would have been available to fight the flames. It made no difference that those who understood the facts realized that no water could have arrived from the Tuolumne for years to come. Besides, there had been no lack of water; rather, there had been an abundance of it. The problem had been that the quake had ruptured all the mains, and the water had run off, to make mud instead of fighting fires. But in the prevailing atmosphere Phelan was widely believed, and citizens rallied behind the municipality's bid for Hetch Hetchy. Moreover, by 1906 Pinchot had gone a long way toward convincing the president that San Francisco had a legitimate need for the Tuolumne sites.

In the wake of the fires of 1906 an opinion of Roosevelt's assistant attorney general came to light that the secretary of the interior had authority to confer on the city the rights to Lake Eleanor and Hetch Hetchy without need for congressional approval. As long as Hitchcock had remained in office, there had had been no danger of that occurring, but in 1906 he left the cabinet; and when he was replaced by James R. Garfield, son of the former president, the situation changed.

Pinchot, Garfield's friend, advised the city engineer of San Francisco to renew the application for the desired sites and "to assume that [the Secretary's] attitude will be favorable." Accordingly, the Board of Supervisors submitted the petition again, and Pinchot's tip became a reality, though not before Roosevelt tried to backtrack at an appeal from Muir on April 21, 1908, which pointed out that "all the water required can be obtained from sources outside the park." As a compromise, TR suggested that Garfield limit his permit to Lake Eleanor. But the secretary felt too deeply committed to renege, and on May 11, 1908, he issued "a revocable permit" to San Francisco for reservoir rights at both Hetch Hetchy and Lake Eleanor. Garfield hedged his permit, however, with the condition that the Lake Eleanor site be developed first, and only then might Hetch Hetchy be dammed.

In many respects the Hetch Hetchy controversy was a strug-

John Muir at age seventy in a photograph by J. Edward B. Greene, circa 1908. Courtesy of the State Historical Society of Wisconsin, neg. no. WHi(X3)24295.

gle between the two wings of the conservation movement—Muir's preservationists on the one hand, seeking to save a "temple" of exceptional magnificence, and Pinchot's utilitarians on the other, their position epitomized by the chief forester's claim that the contested valley's scenic beauty was "altogether unim-

portant compared with the benefits to be derived from its use as
a reservoir." Both aspects of this antithesis were pressed with
such determination that the contest was guaranteed a long and
acrimonious life. Each faction argued that it thus represented the
"public interest," true in each case, for the controversy raged
between the proponents of two public uses of Hetch Hetchy.

In the *Outlook* Muir pressed the preservation of the valley on
the aesthetic grounds that "everybody needs beauty as well as
bread, places to play in and pray in where Nature may heal and
cheer and give strength to body and soul alike." The national
press played numerous variations on this theme, for except in the
San Francisco area, newspapers were almost without exception
behind the preservationist cause, inspiring its advocates with the
conviction that they were fighting a battle between fundamental
right and wrong and sometimes leading them to outbursts of
vituperation. Just as often the proponents of the dam responded
in kind, as likely as not to provoke Muir into self-righteous retal-
iation of such partisan inflexibility that it sometimes turned even
potential allies into adversaries.

Nothing revealed so well how bitter the struggle had grown
as the pointed exclusions Pinchot decreed at the great showpiece
of Roosevelt's last year in office, the Governors' Conference on
Conservation, held at the White House two days after Garfield
had signed the permit in favor of San Francisco and said to be the
most illustrious body of dignitaries yet assembled for any single
event of American history. To accent its significance TR himself
spelled out its theme—"That the conservation of natural resources . . . is yet a part of another and greater problem . . . the
problem of national efficiency, the patriotic duty of insuring the
safety and continuance of the nation." Johnson later claimed that
he had suggested the conference, a claim that the administra-
tions's statements failed to substantiate. At any rate, Roosevelt
had let it become Pinchot's elaborately orchestrated show, largely
financed from his private fortune in the absence of an appropria-
tion from a predominantly hostile Congress. Pinchot, with the
help of his assistant W J McGee, whom he called "the scientific
brains" of their movement, drew up not only the agenda but the

guest list as well. Forty-four state and territorial governors and other officials plus hundreds of experts attended, often making speeches written by Pinchot and McGee. But preservationists were conspicuous by their absence. Johnson attended only in his capacity as a representative of the press.

Not only were Muir and Sargent excluded but also, as Johnson observed, "nearly all the [other] men who had been prominently associated with forestry before [Pinchot's] entrance into public life." When Johnson protested such omissions, Pinchot gave the cavalier reply that there was "no more room." As a consequence, the overwhelming number of addresses reflected only the essential Pinchot-Roosevelt emphasis on "rational planning to promote efficient development and use of all natural resources." Only a handful of conferees, including J. Horace McFarland of the American Civic Association and Charles Evans Hughes, governor of New York and later chief justice of the U.S. Supreme Court, spoke in favor of "preservation."

The Governors' Conference was a resounding success. It underscored Roosevelt's claim that the conservation of natural resources was "the most weighty question now before the people of the United States" and made that question the leading subject of discussion throughout the land. Soon afterward the National Conservation Conference was convened to draw up an inventory of all the nation's natural resources, the first of its kind in the United States. Still other conservation conclaves followed, in which Pinchot played a key role, but Muir was ignored and took no part at all.

Paradoxically, in contrast with the enthusiastic favor that Roosevelt's conservation initiatives enjoyed in many quarters, no other program of his administration received more bitter opposition, especially during his second term. Sailing for it had grown increasingly rough in the West, where it principally applied. By the time of the Governors' Conference, the president's relations with Congress had reached a virtual stalemate where conservation was concerned, and to break it TR launched a campaign for popular support of his resources policies. This effort brought into the movement increasing numbers of enthusiasts who looked on conservation as a kind of religious crusade to rescue America from rampant materialism. Nothing could have heartened Muir and his colleagues more in their languishing battle for Hetch Hetchy.

Thus, the preservationist outlook became less bleak in the latter months of 1908, and the fight was far from over. One encouraging factor was that Garfield's permit was revocable, and in the second place its terms required it to be approved by Congress. A most favorable development occurred in January 1909 when, after lively hearings, a bill was pigeonholed on Capitol Hill to authorize the city to exchange certain marginal lands for the floor of Hetch Hetchy, which Muir and Colby claimed was "worth a thousand times more than the land to be given up [for it]." According to a report of the House Committee on Public Lands, the action of scuttling the bill had come as a result of widespread protest "by scientists, naturalists, mountain climbers, travelers, and others," made in person and by letters and telegrams, and in newspapers and magazine editorials. The status quo remained unchanged for the rest of Roosevelt's term of office.

The Hetch Hetchy controversy took a new turn on March 4, 1909, when William Howard Taft, TR's secretary of war, became president. Roosevelt had handpicked Taft as his successor and had vigorously supported his candidacy on the understanding that Taft would carry on Rooseveltian policies and retain the Roosevelt cabinet. But once elected, Taft assumed an unexpected independence and turned all but two of his inherited cabinet out of office. In place of Garfield, he chose Richard A. Ballinger of Seattle as his secretary of the interior.

This development gave Muir new hopes for Hetch Hetchy, especially when in September 1909 Taft invited Muir to go with him to Yosemite Valley. Muir accepted the invitation wholeheartedly. On reaching San Francisco the president endured an elaborate entertainment in his honor. Then on October 6 he was off to Yosemite, with not only Muir in his retinue but also Congressman James C. Needham, an opponent of the Hetch Hetchy dam. The presence of Muir and Needham in the president's party filled the proponents of the dam with consternation, and Taft himself remarked, "I suppose you know, Mr. Muir, that several people in San Francisco are very much worried because I asked you to come here with me today."

Taft's party visited Glacier Point, and on the trail back into the valley the president, though bathed in profuse sweat, could not refrain from teasing Muir. He suggested that the floor of the valley would make an excellent farm. "Why!" Muir exploded, "this is Nature's cathedral, a place to worship in." That was the sort of rise the president had anticipated from Muir, and it delighted him. He continued, pointing to the great rock gateway through which the Merced left the valley. "Now that," he said, "would be a fine place for a dam!"

Muir was furious, or pretended to be. "A dam!" he cried, ". . . the man who would dam that would be damning himself!"

The one-day tour with Taft was not as intimate as the outing with Roosevelt had been. Taft remained surrounded by people until he managed to free an hour to be alone with Muir. The president grew serious as Muir outlined a plan for the future of Yosemite National Park, showing by means of maps a system of projected roads and trails that would connect all areas of the park. The plan impressed Taft; he was also convinced by Muir's arguments on behalf of Hetch Hetchy and confessed himself opposed to the dam. He requested that Muir go to Hetch Hetchy the next day with Secretary Ballinger, along with two government engineers and George Otis Smith, director of the U.S. Geological Survey. This trip resulted in Ballinger's finding himself impressed with the beauty of Hetch Hetchy and predisposed in its favor. The trip also resulted in a report that led to the president's appointing a board of engineers to study the Lake Eleanor site to determine if it could supply San Francisco with water enough to make Hetch Hetchy unnecessary. The board reported that Lake Eleanor was sufficient to the city's needs, and after studying the report Ballinger scheduled a hearing and required San Francisco to show cause why the Hetch Hetchy site should not be withdrawn from Garfield's permit. This development gave Muir and his associates great encouragement.

Meanwhile, the Sierra Club was not free from dissension in its role as defender of Hetch Hetchy. A rather large contingent of members considered themselves San Franciscans first and club members only afterward and objected to the board of directors' stand. Earlier in 1909 Muir had become so frustrated by the internal opposition and felt so sure that his zeal made matters worse by provoking reaction that he considered resigning, both as president and as a regular member. Colby pointed out that such action would only precipitate the collapse of their campaign, and his solution to the problem was the formation of a separate rump society from the positive members of the club— the Society for the Preservation of National Parks, with Muir as president. Such an organization would be united and could more easily take the initiative in the fight, as well as taking the brunt. Muir agreed, and so they organized the society in the spring of 1909. Colby was the prime mover in the organization, the real workhorse, but he had to be so covertly, since the law firm that employed him was an active promoter of the Hetch Hetchy dam.

As for the Sierra Club, Muir and Colby decided that the directors' stand on Hetch Hetchy should be put to a vote of the membership. This was done on December 18, 1909, with the result that, in a membership of about thirteen hundred, 589 votes were cast in favor of retaining Hetch Hetchy in its natural state, to 161 in favor of damming it. Fifty members resigned, and thereafter dissension ceased to be a problem. The preservationist campaign continued in high gear, not even slackening when San Francisco dragged its feet in showing cause why Hetch Hetchy should not be eliminated from Garfield's permit. The Board of Supervisors asked for more time to gather facts. In all five extensions would be granted, and the Hetch Hetchy contest reached a stalemate for the rest of the Taft administration. It was the city's object to prolong the controversy until the advent of a new and possibly more sympathetic administration.

During this lull, an interim of anxiety though it was for the preservationists, Muir felt it safe to take time out to realize finally the Humboldtian dream of his early manhood, and in April 1911 he announced his intention of going to South America—all alone. Friends, family, and his doctor tried to discourage him, all assuming that at seventy-three he was too old for such a venture. He merely said, "God will take care of me and bring me home safely."

He went first to New York and weathered an extravagant round of dinners, interviews, and speeches both there and at Washington, where he conferred again with President Taft and other officials, before hurrying up to New Haven to receive an honorary doctorate from Yale. Then on August 11 he sailed for South America, without telling anyone of his intention of also going on to Africa to see the exotic baobab tree.

On reaching the Amazon on August 31, he took a steamboat a thousand miles up the river, the vessel often hugging the bank so closely that he could reach out and touch the luxuriant foliage. In due course he branched off into the Rio Negro in an unsuccessful search for *Victoria regia,* a rare water lily with a large white flower. There in the interior he was at no time disappointed in the splendor of the dense rain forest, delighting in its prodigal variety of greens and tropical lushness. But at last he steamed back to the mouth of the Amazon and sailed down the coast to Santos. He was surprised at how friendly everybody seemed, not realizing that President Taft had opened doors for him by alerting the U.S. Consular Service in South America to look after a "national treasure." When a party of lumbermen invited him to accompany them up the Iguaçu River, he accepted their invitation in order to see a tree of geometrical shape called *Araucaria braziliana.* Then after a brief stay in Buenos Aires, he rode the train across the pampas and over the Andes and was greeted by the American minister in Santiago. Muir's purpose in visiting Chile, interested as he was in all varieties of trees, was to seek the curious monkey puzzle tree, a relative of *Araucaria braziliana.* No one seemed to know where it grew, but by piecing together various bits of information and following his hunches, he found a forest of the trees high in the Andes and spent a night beneath their imbricated branches.

From Chile he went to Montevideo, where he soon caught a steamer for Africa. He reached Cape Town in January 1912 and rode by rail to Victoria Falls. At a local hotel he enquired of the baobab tree, and the manager could only wonder what it was. But in the street a small black boy said he knew where it grew and led Muir to a grove close by Victoria Falls. Muir wrote to Helen that the baobab was "easily recognized by its skin-like bark, and its massive trunk and branches. The bark . . . looks like leather, or the skin of a hippopotamus."

At Beira Muir embarked on a Dutch steamer and sailed along the eastern coast of Africa to Mombasa, from where he made his way inland to the sources of the Nile. Thereupon he returned to America by way of the Mediterranean, reaching New York on March 26, 1912, the end of a seven-month pilgrimage. He hurried home and was soon embroiled deeper than ever in "the political quagg" of the Hetch Hetchy controversy.

He continued to refute San Francisco's case as he had done in the final pages of *The Yosemite*. "The proponents of the dam scheme," he had written there, "bring forward a lot of bad arguments to prove that the only righteous thing to do with the people's parks is to destroy them bit by bit." His analysis found only a minimum of their arguments even partially true, and all, he contended, were misleading. He branded the advocates of the dam as "temple destroyers, devotees of ravaging commercialism," having "a perfect contempt for Nature." His condemnation contended further that "instead of lifting their eyes to the God of the mountains, [they] lift them to the Almighty Dollar. Dam Hetch Hetchy! As well dam for water-tanks the people's cathedrals and churches, for no holier temple has ever been consecrated by the heart of man."

Somewhere along the way Muir and Colby had come to suspect that the profitable distribution of the hydroelectric power that the Hetch Hetchy dam would generate was perhaps more the issue at stake than the much debated supply of pure water for San Francisco. Congress became suspicious, too, of the city's motives in this respect, and when considering the final formulation of the Raker Bill to fix by law the rights that the Garfield permit had granted to San Francisco, the House addressed the water-power issue by adding an amendment (Section 6) that would require the city to distribute the Tuolumne-generated power directly to its ultimate consumers and not through the agency of such private utilities as the Pacific Gas and Electric Company. It was ironic, in view of future developments, that the PG&E's intention to develop a power monopoly on the West Coast inspired its own designs on Hetch Hetchy and made it the implacable opponent of San Francisco, so that Muir and his preservationist colleagues were often cited as its pawns.*

The handful of politicians and financiers who billed themselves as "the City of San Francisco" continued to emphasize the city's need for a source of pure water, but at the same time they remained peculiarly indifferent about taking into account other sites less adapted to the production of power. Colby suspected that it was the prospect of a power bonanza from Hetch Hetchy that kept them motivated to remain active in the fray, and were it not for that bountiful prospect, which promised to pay the construction costs for the entire project and more, San Francisco might have withdrawn its claim, since water alone from the Tuolumne (especially with other sources available elsewhere) might not

---

*It was one of the greater paradoxical twists of the so-called "Hetch Hetchy steal" that perhaps its greatest corporate adversary should become its hugest profiteer through the circumvention of Section 6 of the Raker Act. In the New Deal era Secretary of the Interior Harold Ickes took San Francisco before the U.S. Supreme Court for the flagrant violation of the Raker Act in selling to the Pacific Gas and Electric Company all the power generated at the Hetch Hetchy dam, instead of making it available on inexpensive terms to the people of the city. Under the arrangement worked out, PG&E resold the power to San Franciscans for treble the price it paid. In his autobiography Senator George Norris of Nebraska wrote that when he helped push the Raker Bill through the Senate, he "underestimated the resources of the Pacific Gas and Electric Company." He went on to explain: "After the dam was built the honest promoters of it in Congress discovered that the power transmission lines instead of terminating in San Francisco, where there was a market, actually delivered the [Hetch Hetchy] electricity . . . to Newark, where the Pacific Gas and Electric Company had transmission facilities and where there was no market except through [that] Company. Although San Francisco furnished water to the citizens without any profit to a private company, it did not develop the electric capacities and from the beginning violated [the law] by selling electric power to private companies. In 1925 the City supervisors turned over the Hetch Hetchy power to the Pacific Gas and Electric Company, which began to re-sell power and light to the consumer at a handsome profit. The citizens became aroused and a fight began which has lasted for years and up to the present [1945], the Pacific Company finding ways to circumvent even the decisions of the Supreme Court."

have made the dam worth the fight. Thus, while water remained
the overt objective, the question of hydroelectric power hovered
on the sidelines, an ongoing root of suspicion for the preservationists.

Meanwhile, what San Francisco had been waiting for occurred in November 1912 when Woodrow Wilson was elected
president. Three days before he took the oath of office, the final
step of the Taft administration was taken in the Hetch Hetchy
affair when outgoing Secretary Fisher informed the mayor of San
Francisco that he had determined that Ballinger's order for the
city to "show cause" should remain in force pending the city's
application for congressional action to the contrary. That was
the shape of the Hetch Hetchy matter when Wilson entered the
White House on March 4, 1913. But he had chosen as his secretary
of the interior Franklin K. Lane, who had served as the city
attorney of San Francisco during the Phelan administration, and
who, as an enthusiastic supporter of the Hetch Hetchy project,
lost no time making known his position on the dam. All at once
the situation was in rapid flux, and as Johnson would write, "The
summer of 1913 was the turning point in the contest."

Muir summoned all his resources for the battle, and the more
the situation deteriorated the harder he fought, seeming to lose
perspective in his intensity. Nothing illustrated so well the inflex-
ible rigidity with which he pursued his aims as his tendency to
think of himself as always right and his opponents as always
wrong, his side as entirely good, the opposing side as entirely
evil. In the last stages of the controversy even Congressman William Kent, who had donated to the republic as a national monument a grove of coast redwoods on the flank of Mount Tamalpais
and named it Muir Woods, characterized Muir as a cranky, self-
righteous old fanatic. "With him," Kent wrote, "it is me and
God and the rock where God put it, and that's the end of the
story."

Cartoons in Bay area newspapers pictured Muir as a surly old
churl, and there were frequent remarks as uncomplimentary as
that which Phelan had made in the House hearings of January
1909—that Muir "would sacrifice his own family for the preser-

John Muir in a late photograph by W. Dassonville, taken probably in 1912 near the close of the Hetch Hetchy controversy. Courtesy of the Bancroft Library, University of California, Berkeley.

vation of beauty." Undaunted he fought on, while discouraged friends dropped away, even Colby to a degree, his livelihood threatened by the pro-dam stand of his employers. Toward the end the strain took its toll, and Muir wrote to Helen, "I'll be relieved when it's settled, for it's killing me."

The anguish did not last long. The Raker Bill was brought to a vote earlier than scheduled, catching offguard many opposing congressmen, so that they were not present for the vote in September. The House passed the bill 183 to 43, with 205 congressmen absent. Muir wrote to a friend, "The Raker Bill has been meanly skulked and railroaded and logrolled through the House, but we are hoping it will be checked in the Senate."

Muir and his associates mustered all their resources for the final battle. It was their strategy "to flood the Senate with letters from influential people"; and to that end, the Society for the Preservation of National Parks, along with the newly organized National Committee for the Preservation of Yosemite National Park, published and distributed leaflets and circulars in lots of five thousand up to twenty thousand, calling on the recipients (including everyone mentioned in *Who's Who in America*) to write the president and their senators in opposition to the Raker Bill. The response was so brisk that, by the time the bill was scheduled for debate in the Senate, Hetch Hetchy had become a national issue of major proportions, inasmuch as a large segment of the American public was all ready to be aroused on the side of wild nature.

Hundreds of newspapers throughout the land, as well as several leading magazines like the *Century* and the *Atlantic Monthly,* joined the issue with editorials and articles, mostly on behalf of preservation. The Senate, as planned, was flooded with letters and telegrams, one senator indicating that he had received more than five thousand letters opposing the bill. Protests also came from organizations of varied descriptions, especially women's clubs. As a consequence, Muir had high hopes that the vote in the Senate would go in preservation's favor. But he had not counted on how effectively the San Francisco lobbyists had done their quiet work. At midnight on December 6 the Senate voted 43 to

Hetch Hetchy Valley, a yosemite second only to Yosemite Valley, as it looked when flooded by the dam built by the city of San Francisco. Muir spent most of his final years in its defense. Courtesy of the Bancroft Library, University of California, Berkeley.

25 in favor of the bill, with 29 senators either absent or abstaining from voting. A rumored presidential veto was Muir's last hope, but thirteen days later President Wilson signed the bill into law, and it was widely believed that the Raker Bill had become an "administration measure," with Hetch Hetchy going to San Francisco as a reward for California having cast its votes for Wilson in November 1912.

Thus, Muir's preservationist philosophy had lost to Pinchot's catchphrase "the greatest good for the greatest number for the longest time." This was the worst defeat of Muir's life, with something he supremely valued condemned to what he considered rape. He would, of course, not live to see the consequences of the Raker Act's granting to San Francisco perpetual water and power rights on 420,000 acres of Hetch Hetchy's floor. It would take eighteen years for Tuolumne River water to reach the city. The reservoir itself would never become, as the dam defenders had promised, "a beautiful mountain lake, blue, deep, and clear, in which fishes swim and on the surface of which rowboats and sailboats glide." Rather it would become a perpetual eyesore, a synonym for error along the lines of Muir's prediction of how "it would be gradually drained [in summer], exposing the slimey sides of the basin and the shallower parts of the bottom with the gathered drift of waste, death and decay." Disenchanted campers would go elsewhere to unroll their sleeping bags or pitch their tents, while Yosemite Valley, visited to excess, would desperately need the overflow space of the once resplendent yosemite of the Tuolumne.

Meanwhile, Muir took his defeat with noteworthy resilience of spirit and turned to his writing again—his long-deferred book on Alaska. But in a physical sense the story was different, and friends perceived how much the heartbreak cost him. "Our defeat has weighed heavily on Mr. Muir . . . ," Colby informed a mutual friend sometime in 1914. "At least he has been seriously ill two or three times since the action against us and is now so feeble that he seldom comes to the city."

CHAPTER 23

Home-Going

THE outcome of the Hetch Hetchy controversy set an ominous precedent for preservationists—that the national parks were not inviolable when citizens and bureaucrats found other uses for their land; if allowed to operate freely, such a precedent might well destroy the parks. (As Muir once said of Yosemite, there would be little left if everyone got what he coveted.) But other forces were also at work, and in an optimistic moment Muir wrote to Johnson that "the long drawn out battle-work for Nature's gardens has not been thrown away. The conscience of the whole country has been aroused from sleep, and from outrageous evil compensating good in some form must surely come."

The public conscience had been aroused so thoroughly, in fact, that when the defenders of the parks increased their emphasis on tourism as the principal rationale for national parks, no violation of a park on such a scale as the damming of Hetch Hetchy would occur again. At the same time the popular enthusiasm for wilderness preservation had long since grown to the proportions of a national cult, with Muir enshrined at its heart. It might therefore be said that, while he had lost a most important battle, he had won the war.

Much as the Hetch Hetchy question had dominated Muir's later years, it did not completely fill that period of his life. There had been other concerns, and one involved the outings of the Sierra Club. Muir attended many of them, making frequent campfire talks, though speeches scheduled in advance still gave him nervous chills. Program planners, deferring to this difficulty, ceased to schedule talks by him and would merely ask him questions to get him started. Then all went beautifully. "Never was there a naturalist who could hold his hearers so well," noted Bailey Millard, a journalist friend, "and none had so much to tell."

Soon after a club outing in Yosemite in July 1907,* Muir received an invitation from the Harrimans to spend the rest of the summer at their country lodge at Pelican Bay on Klamath Lake, Oregon. When he chanced to meet Harriman in San Francisco, the tycoon asked him if he planned to go to Pelican Bay. "Yes," Muir said. "I shall be very glad to pay my respects to Mrs. Harriman and the family and stay a few days, but I cannot afford to spend the summer there." When Harriman asked why not, Muir replied that he was writing a book.

"Well," the millionaire declared, "you come up to the Lodge and I will show you how to write books."

So Muir went to Pelican Lodge with the intention of staying a week, but when he prepared to leave, Harriman told him to wait and get to work. Having recognized the literary potential in Muir's fluent talk, the magnate ordered his private secretary to follow him about and record in shorthand everything he said. "Dictating to a stenographer," Muir confessed, ". . . proved rather awkward at first, but in a couple of months a sort of foundation for more than one volume was laid."

Soon the secretary sent Muir a typescript of over a thousand pages, whose many asides failed to wreck its fundamental coherence. It was autobiographical, the basis for Muir's life story. At first, however, he was too pressured by the Hetch Hetchy imbroglio to undertake the editing and revising necessary to make the narrative publishable. And then another book claimed his attention, *My First Summer in the Sierra*, which Houghton Mifflin brought out in 1911, after serializing it in the *Atlantic Monthly*.

Then while working on *The Yosemite*, one of Muir's least interesting and least accomplished volumes (a kind of guidebook compiled largely from formerly published materials), he carved from the Pelican Bay transcript *The Story of My Boyhood and*

---

*Following the lead of Linnie Marsh Wolfe, some biographies of Muir give this date as 1908, but in the 1978 edition of *Edward Henry Harriman* both Averell Harriman and Muir cite the year as 1907.

Youth, a chronicle of the first quarter-century of his life, told in an easy, conversational manner. It was striking for its integration of Darwinian concepts within a pantheistic, biocentric context. From the Osborns' Hudson River estate he wrote to John Burroughs on July 14, 1911: "I have got a volume of my autobiography finished. Houghton Mifflin are to bring it out. They want to [do so] immediately, but I would like to have at least part of it run through some suitable magazine, and thus gain ten or twenty times more readers than would be likely to see it in a book." As *My First Summer in the Sierra* had pleased the editors of the *Atlantic,* it followed that Muir would arrange for them to also serialize *My Boyhood and Youth,* in four excerpts.

The Century Company published *The Yosemite* in 1912, but because of its magazine run, *My Boyhood and Youth* did not appear in book form until a year later, just twenty-one months before Muir's death. As he had dictated the raw material of the book when he was seventy years old, the story had necessarily been filtered though a mindset developed over a lifetime, and this had inevitable effects on the finished product. Notwithstanding Muir's prodigious memory, some readers felt that many of the details had been invented (like Muir's claim that he had studied for four years at the University of Wisconsin instead of only five semesters) and were the stuff of legend rather than factual truth. At the same time readers were sometimes shocked by the accounts of his father's harshness, but if they queried Muir on that score, he would always assure them that he had told the strictest truth. This was borne out by his sister Joanna, who wrote to him, "The portion relating to yourself and the family was read in tears, and I wish with all my heart it had not been so true. In other words, that the hard things had never occurred so that they would not be there to record."

Muir considered the volume a narrative for young readers about the lessons he had learned while growing up, and as such it told of his transit from the idyll of boyhood through the dismal concerns of farm life (relieved by happy contacts with wild nature and the excitement of contriving bizarre inventions) to the climax of his studies at the university. Its method of development

involved the juxtaposition of themes, basically an alternation between the motif of culture and that of nature (one of his favorite
approaches), as well as a relentless opposition of two iron wills—
that of his father on the one hand and his own on the other; but
probably owing to its peculiar method of composition, the story
failed to become one of Muir's best books. It lacks the degree of
sober self-analysis expected of the best autobiography, and it suf-
fers other defects like the exaggerations in the account of his
triumphal trip to Madison, which sound basically unconvincing.
Perhaps the book's most appealing and characteristic features are
the incidents in which Muir captures the human-like characteristics of animals, both wild and domesticated.

Meanwhile, in late February 1909, he made another trip to
the Petrified Forest, to await the arrival of John Burroughs and
his physician, Dr. Clara Barrus, and her woman companion. After a day together, spent among the stone trunks, the party went
to the Grand Canyon, arriving early in the morning, tired and
hungry. Muir twitted the others for wanting breakfast before
they beheld the wonders of the canyon. He had described these
for the *Century* in 1902—"the toughest job I ever tackled," he
had assured Sargent at the time. Now, the petrified trees and the
Grand Canyon were just the spectacles to set Muir off on nonstop monologues, and Dr. Barrus found him "one of the most
engaging talkers imaginable, discursive, grave, and gay." Then,
on their departure from the canyon, he traveled with the party as
far as Pasadena, where he promised to be their host at Yosemite
Valley that coming spring.

In the interim he accompanied E. H. Harriman back to Arizona in the magnate's private railroad car. The tycoon wanted
Muir's advice as a geologist on a flood-control project that followed upon the disastrous breach in the bank of the Colorado
River that created the Salton Sea—a breach that Harriman had
dammed by running trainloads of boulders into it after the federal government had failed to solve the problem. But Harriman
was now at the end of his tether, as Muir could sense on seeing
how exhausted the slightest effort left his friend; and he wrote,
"There fell a foreboding shadow that I could never shake off."

He would never see Harriman again, but would publish a tribute to him in 1911.

Meanwhile, Muir rejoined the Burroughs party in May. "It was particularly gratifying to Mr. Muir," wrote Dr. Barrus, "to show Mr. Burroughs the glories of the Yosemite and make him admit that he had nothing like it in Esopus Valley, or in the Catskills." But the party had to be content with enjoying views from the valley floor, for the trails to the rim were clogged with snow, and Muir could not take them to favorite places of vantage like Glacier Point. They did camp out in the upper reaches of the valley, however, and then "sauntered" to Vernal and Nevada falls on what Dr. Barrus described as "the most idyllic of our Yosemite days." J. B. found even such limited walks too strenuous, however, though Dr. Barrus could report that on at least one occasion "the two Johnnies" behaved like ten-year-olds.

They argued fiercely on many subjects, including animal instinct. Burroughs took the rigidly mechanistic view then so popular, while Muir regarded instinct as unconsciously transmitted wisdom or racial memory, the residue of ancestral experience. Their arguments also included geology, on which Muir put Burroughs down unsparingly. "Aw, Johnnie," Muir said, "ye may tak' all your geology and tie it in a bundle and cast it into the sea, and it wouldna mak' a ripple."

This remark illustrated how impolitic Muir could be on occasion, in contrast with his usual kindness. Burroughs later wrote in his journal that conversation with Muir was "a sparring match with gads." He claimed that Muir loved to give "the first cut" and then follow it up "to see you wince." Tender though he was with animals, he yet "likes to walk over the flesh of his fellow men with spurs in his soles." As for J. B.'s geological disagreement with Muir, especially his doubts about Muir's theory of the glacial origin of Yosemite, he grumbled, "Muir rides his ice hobby till the tongue of the poor beast hangs out and he is ready to lie down and give up the ghost. Ice is by no means the only agency at work here." But whatever their differences, Muir and Burroughs agreed on the wonder of the valley.

Muir's visit to Yosemite with "John o' Birds" was not a routine matter, for during these later years it was no longer Muir's custom to make frequent visits there. He went more often to see Helen, still living near Daggett and married to Buel A. Funk, a cattleman's son. Muir's health improved whenever he left the environs of Martinez, and perhaps that was why he now spent so much time with Helen, as well as with certain friends in Pasadena and Los Angeles. A wealthy crony in the latter city, John D. Hooker, fitted up a study for him in the Hooker house—"my Palace Garret," as Muir described it; and there he worked on his various manuscripts, and it was from there that he was called to be with his sister Margaret during her final illness in the summer of 1910.

Meanwhile, several honors came to Muir during these later years. In 1909 he was elected to the American Academy of Arts and Letters, after having been a member of its associate organization, the American Institute of Arts and Letters, since 1898. He also enjoyed membership in the Washington Academy of Sciences and was a fellow of the American Association for the Advancement of Science. He served as president of the American Alpine Club. Then on May 14, 1913, to add to his honorary degrees from Harvard, Yale, and the University of Wisconsin, he received the Doctor of Laws degree from the University of California, with John Swett enjoying the same honor on the same day. Muir was touched by such recognition from the major school of his home state. Yet the honor that moved him most deeply seems to have been the creation of the Muir Woods National Monument in 1908.

Of even greater satisfaction, however, was the "boy undergrowth," as he fondly called the sons of Wanda and Helen. In May 1913 he wrote to a friend, "Both of my girls are happily married and have homes of their own. Wanda has three lively boys, Helen has two and is living at Daggett, California. Wanda is living on the ranch in the old adobe." There he saw much of her and her children and enjoyed playing with the youngsters. His grandsons were the greatest pleasure of his old age, and to his satisfaction, Wanda and Helen would each have another boy during his lifetime.

But as if to counterbalance the flourishing "boy undergrowth" came the deaths of intimate friends, climaxing with that of John Swett in August 1913. During the Hetch Hetchy contest the grave had claimed some of his dearest associates—Jeanne Carr and Catharine Merrill, Colonel A. H. Sellers of Pasadena, E. H. Harriman, Willie Keith, John D. Hooker, and Sir Joseph Hooker, to name a few. At Keith's death he had wondered in a letter to Helen "if leaves feel lonely when they see their neighbors falling." His mood often grew pensive in such a manner during the last rounds of the Hetch Hetchy controversy and also after its conclusion with his return to his "ice-crystal book," *Travels in Alaska*.

Worn and exhausted from the Hetch Hetchy battle, with his right lung badly infected and his cough more harrowing than ever, he made only negligible progress on the manuscript. The book seemed beyond completion, and friends who noted his frustration were deeply troubled on his behalf. William Colby then had an idea, one that grew out of his concern not only for Muir but also for Marion Randall Parsons, now at loose ends since the death of her husband, Edward T. Parsons, a stalwart of the Sierra Club. Why not have them work together, Mrs. Parsons as a kind of secretary to Muir? The idea was broached to both, and both accepted it. Thereafter Mrs. Parsons came to the big house on the ranch several times a week. "The arrangement proved unexpectedly happy and congenial to us both," she later wrote, "and lasted until a week of his death."

The state of Muir's health did not keep him from beginning work as early as seven each morning, after breakfast at Wanda's, and he stayed with the task till ten at night, with only short breaks to romp with his grandsons. Mrs. Parsons, an excellent typist, was of immense help; and the work went well, with Muir stowing every finished chapter in an orange crate. "Each sentence, each phrase, each word underwent his critical scrutiny," Mrs. Parsons wrote. "His rare critical faculty was unimpaired to the end. So too was the freshness and vigor of his whole outlook on life." His newfound equanimity was affected only by the outbreak of World War I in the summer of 1914. To read of the

German ravages of Belgium made him smolder with anger. But only bouts of illness associated with his infected lung interrupted progress on the manuscript.

Travels in Alaska, which Houghton Mifflin would not publish until 1915, dealt in chronological order with three of Muir's seven trips to Alaska, those of 1879, 1880, and 1890, with almost two-thirds of the book devoted to the initial journey. The study of glaciers preoccupied, in one degree or another, all of those tours, for after years of tracing the effects of ancient glaciers in the Sierra Nevada, Alaska had afforded Muir the exciting opportunity to observe the activity of advancing ice even as it occurred. His studies of Alaskan glaciers confirmed the conclusions he had reached about glaciation in California, but he made little further scientific advance in this direction. Therefore *Travels in Alaska* must stand more as travel and nature literature than as scientific writing. So judged, it compares favorably with Muir's better writing, but fails to achieve the stature of his best, one reason being that he was never able to familiarize himself as thoroughly with the immense landscape of Alaska as he had with that of California. High points of the book include Muir's account of his rescuing Hall Young on Glenora Peak, a compressed version of Stickeen's story, and a breathtaking description of the aurora borealis at the end of the volume.

At one point Muir interrupted his progress on the manuscript when he was seized by an idea strange and unexpected in view of how zealously he had insisted on keeping everything in the house as Louie had left it. He now went on an orgy of renovation, with Ah Fong's help. He replaced old furniture, built new cupboards and bookcases, and banished candles and kerosene lamps in favor of electrification. Then he went to San Francisco and bought new carpets and velvet drapes. Muir never revealed his motive for this rehabilitation, but no doubt he had put the house in order in hope that one of his daughters would live there after his death, as indeed Wanda was to do.

Helen's third son was born in June 1914. Muir longed to see him, but waited until *Travels in Alaska* was all but finished. Then in mid-December he told Wanda that he wished to go and see his

John Muir's house, formerly the Strentzel mansion, which is now the principal building at the John Muir National Historic Site, located on nine acres of the former Muir-Strentzel ranch near Martinez, California. Courtesy of Jack Harris/National Park Service.

new grandson. She packed his suitcase, in which he stowed his typed manuscript, with the intent of working on it at Helen's house. He rode the train south, arriving at Daggett at 2:30 in the morning. A cold, blustery wind blew, and before he reached the Funk ranch he had taken cold. The next day, however, he seemed better and went for a long walk with Helen, talking in his old familiar manner to the "plant friends" they met along the way. But the improvement proved illusory. That evening, after working on his manuscript beside the fireplace, he staggered as he rose.

Helen put him to bed and called the local physician, who found that Muir had contracted pneumonia. Dr. George L. Cole, a friend in Los Angeles, was then summoned, and he made an even graver diagnosis—double pneumonia. He recommended that Muir be taken by train to the California Hospital in Los Angeles, where he—Dr. Cole—could supervise the treatment. The move was made (Wanda having been sent for in the meantime), and Muir entered the hospital on the evening of December 23.

Again he rallied. The next morning he chatted affably with Dr. Cole and the attending nurse, while sheets of manuscript lay spread across his bed. But again the rally was a false assurance, and later that day, Christmas Eve, with neither Helen nor Wanda present, nor doctor nor nurse, he went quietly "home." He had once written that the Norse "spoke of death as *Heimgang*—home-going. So the snow flowers go home when they melt and flow to the sea, and the rock ferns, after unrolling their fronds to the light and beautifying the rocks, roll them up close again in the autumn and blend with the soil."

Friends suggested that only Yosemite was the proper place for Muir's grave. But he had once told Wanda that he wished to rest beside Louie, and so they buried him there in the family plot, in the shade of a lofty eucalyptus tree.

CHAPTER 24

Lore of a Literary Naturalist

THE deference paid to Muir at his death as the acknowledged leader of the preservation movement was not forgotten as time went on, and in 1965 *Time* Magazine named him, with understandable hyperbole, as "the real father of conservation." The same year this verdict was essentially sustained when Muir was made the second member, after Theodore Roosevelt, of the Conservation Hall of Fame, sponsored by the National Wildlife Federation. Pinchot, on the other hand, would eventually win position number eight. The perception of Muir's ascendancy as star of the conservation movement, making him a potent icon in the American consciousness, persists until the present day, with him sometimes serving as a folk hero for popular television.

Much of Muir's present prestige stems from the impact of his sizable body of writing, and this raises the question of his identity as an author, which preoccupied Edwin Way Teale when studying Muir's works. After pondering a contemporary debate on whether Muir was an effective scientist, he suggested that Muir's perception of environmental interrelationships was precise enough for him to be legitimately called a pioneer ecologist. Indeed, Muir's first book, *The Mountains of California*, was later described as "a general ecology of the Sierra Nevada," and Muir probably would have found considerable satisfaction in that description, since he liked to think of himself as a scientist.

But as a writer, he has been most frequently termed a literary naturalist (in the tradition of Gilbert White of Selborne), owing largely to the popular cast of his contributions to natural history. His reputation, thus, is generally that of a naturalist less in the sense of "scientist" than in the sense of "literary nature lover" who frequently poetized his closely observed facts; or put in another fashion, his identity as a scientist tended to submerge itself in his identity as a belletrist. Even in the field of his first love, botany, Muir's observations, in the opinion of Hugh Iltis, curator of the botanical collection of the University of Wisconsin, were neither specific enough nor systematic enough to have "more than minimal value" as a contribution to science.

Not even his single strictly scientific treatise *Studies in the Sierra* could escape the smack of a literary naturalist at work, for all of Muir's scientific caution could not prevent the Sierra Nevada from standing forth therein as a divinely archetypal range that symbolized poetically the truth of mountains everywhere. Moreover, Muir was to lift from the "Studies" motif after motif for incorporation into other works less scientific and more popular in character. For instance, the "Studies" provided numerous details on glaciation for *The Mountains of California, The Yosemite,* and to a lesser extent *Our National Parks.* But all such scientific information could hardly transform the character of the latter works into science or keep them from being essentially popular natural history, and the same may be said of still another book that emphasized ice and its action, *Travels in Alaska.*

In the chapter of *The Mountains of California* on the prodigious snows of the Sierra, a pointed example of how a potentially scientific statement may emerge as a passage of popular belles lettres is Muir's description of the wondrous snow banners he had observed in the winter of 1873, as well as his explanation of how they were formed. He found that the principal causes of their beauty and perfection "were the favorable direction of the wind, the abundance of snow-dust, and the peculiar conformation of the slopes of the peaks." The wind had not only to blow with enough velocity and steadiness to whip up a sufficiently abundant and constant flow of snow-dust, but also had to blow from the north. A gale that blew from the south, Muir pointed out, would produce "only a dull, confused, fog-like drift . . . ; for the snow, instead of being spouted up over the tops of the peaks, in concentrated currents, would have been shed off around the sides, and piled into the glacier wombs." It was the special contours of the northern faces of the peaks, where the cirques of residual glaciers lay, that determined the crucial "concentrated action of the north wind."

In the same way that Muir's remarks on snow banners exemplified his use of details from geology and related disciplines for purposes of belletristic natural history, a large part of his writing drew upon the details of biology, especially botany. In so doing, his approach often gave importance to the "habits" of plants and their relations with their neighbors and the environment, thus producing an ecological effect. This followed from the condition that his botanical data, like his geological facts, derived largely from a firsthand study of nature. Consequently, it made little difference that he remained a dedicated reader for all his mature life; his reading never caused his natural history to become bookish in the way that John Burroughs' often was. Like Emerson, Muir regarded books as fare for the scholar's idle hours, and on one occasion he wrote, "One day's exposure to the mountains is better than a cartload of books." The direct accounts he wrote of his immersions in mountains, meadows, and forests naturally introduced an autobiographical flavor into his works, though from the first he kept his physical presence within modest bounds. Even later, when his editor encouraged him to lace his narratives more frequently with first-person remarks, his writing remained a suitably objective record of his observations of the things and doings of nature, however deeply emotional their expression.

Strong feeling patently infused his references to plants and flowers in such works as *My Boyhood and Youth, A Thousand-Mile Walk,* and *My First Summer,* as well as many pages on bee pastures in *The Mountains of California* and the entire chapter that *The Yosemite* (like *Our National Parks*) devotes to the flora of that park. "Yosemite," he wrote, "was all one glorious flower garden before plows and scythes and trampling, biting horses came to make its wide open spaces look like farmers' pasture fields." Nevertheless, he contended that a profusion of flowers still blossomed every spring on the talus slopes and wall benches as well as in the cool side canyons up to the Valley's rim, and even to the summits beyond.

Muir's paragraph on the snow plant is a piquant example of

his individual profiles of such flora. This plant *(Sarcodes san-guinea)*, he wrote, "is more admired by tourists than any other in California. It is red, fleshy and watery and looks like a gigantic asparagus shoot. Soon after the snow is off the ground it rises through the dead needles and humus in the pine and fir woods like a bright glowing pillar of fire." It reaches eight or twelve inches in height within a week or so, Muir went on to say, and its diameter measures an inch and a half or two. At that time its bracts, long and fringed, twist aside, letting the multilobed and bell-shaped flowers open directly from the axis. Muir denied the common claim that the snow plant ordinarily grows up through lingering snow. Instead, he pointed out, it invariably waits until the ground is bare, though spring storms sometimes bury it for a day or two, like other early flowers. Notwithstanding all the flaming red of its stem and blossoms, bracts and root, Muir considered it "a singularly cold and unsympathetic plant," and he could readily understand why almost everyone could admire it as a special curiosity without feeling any love for it in the way that roses and daisies, lilies and violets were taken to heart.

Muir's description of the snow plant conveys considerable information in a brief compass, while presenting a vivid picture in characteristic adjective-laden prose. At the same time the passage represents the common sequential graduation of Muir's writing, from notebook entry to periodical publication before inclusion in a book. The description of the snow plant was first published in an essay called "The Wild Gardens of Yosemite" in the *Atlantic Monthly*, after which it appeared in *Our National Parks*, only to be revised for further publication in *The Yosemite*. In several ways, then, it may be considered representative of the botanical details of Muir's nature writing.

Trees more than flowers and shrubs, however, were Muir's enduring enthusiasm; and as his friend C. Hart Merriam declared with pardonable exaggeration, "These he knew as no other man has ever known them." His deep devotion went to the giant sequoia and the sugar pine perhaps in equal degree, but no doubt Muir's most significant writing on trees stemmed from his tour in 1875 of the groves of giant redwoods south of Yosemite. This tour resulted in the most detailed report yet made of the giant sequoia and its distribution, and it makes little difference to Muir's standing as a naturalist that later scientists would find errors in his pioneer analysis of the Big Tree's ecology. He achieved his primary purpose in writing about the giant sequoia—to lead the public to a greater appreciation of its stands and groves, enough to generate efforts to save them.

But Muir wrote about other Sierra conifers as well. They "are the grandest and most beautiful in the world," he claimed, "and grow in a delightful climate on the most interesting and accessible of mountain ranges, yet strange to say they are not well known." In "The Forests," by far the longest chapter in *The Mountains of California,* he included an extensive catalogue of the Sierra's various cone-bearing trees, after first specifying the general order of their distribution. Muir's catalogue included sixteen different species in addition to the giant sequoia, notably the sugar pine, the yellow pine, the Douglas fir (which he called the Douglas spruce), and the incense cedar. The pattern of his dealing with each species involved the specification of its zone of occurrence, a picturesque description of its characteristic appearance, and an expansive retailing of any special information that it might be noted for. For all the conifers he listed the scientific names, some of which would change with time, and he closed the chapter with a running discussion of California trees other than cone-bearers. Charles S. Sargent was so impressed with the quality of this chapter that he suggested that Muir should have written the *Silva of North America,* rather than himself.

Muir also discussed trees in *The Yosemite,* duplicating information in both *The Mountains of California* and *Our National Parks,* the latter also containing a revised account of Muir's 1875 survey of the Big Tree groves south of Yosemite. Moreover, in essays gathered in *Picturesque California* and *Steep Trails,* he described the forests he had examined in Washington, Oregon, Utah, and Nevada. All in all, then, Muir's writing on trees constituted, with little doubt, his single most significant legacy to natural history. In *Impressions of Great Naturalists* Henry Fairfield Osborn claims that Muir "wrote about trees as no one else in the whole history of trees, chiefly because he loved them as he loved men and women." Muir himself pointed up the veritable religious significance that trees held for him when he said, "The clearest way into the universe is through a forest wilderness."

But at the same time he charmed his readers with the loving attention his writing paid to birds and animals, recognizing not only their essential importance for the wilderness but also what they had to offer humanity. "Any glimpse into the life of an animal," he observed, "quickens our own and makes it so much the larger and better in every way." Yet it must be said that of the zoological and ornithological aspects of Muir's natural history, C. Hart Merriam of the U.S. Biological Survey had definite reservations. Merriam wrote, "One often hears Muir spoken of as an authority on the animal life of the mountains. This is an error. For while he liked to see birds and animals in the wilderness and about his camps, he rarely troubled himself to learn their proper names and relationships." President Roosevelt, an ornithology buff, bore out Merriam's judgment when writing in his auto-biography that, at the time he camped with Muir in the Mariposa Grove, Muir seemed oblivious to all the birds around them.

Muir himself creates a different impression with his words of sympathy for birds and animals in the story of his boyhood years. The passage on the skylarks of his native Dunbar reveals an un-folding love of birds that further remarks in *My Boyhood and Youth* tend to confirm, especially the interesting anecdote about the shrike and the gophers and the chapter called "A Paradise of Birds," with such lively descriptions as those of the loon and the passenger pigeons. Of the pigeons Muir wrote, "I have seen flocks streaming south in the fall so large that they were flowing over from horizon to horizon in an almost continuous river in the sky, widening, contracting, descending like falls and cata-racts, and rising suddenly here and there in huge ragged masses like high-plashing spray"—a sentence freighted with irony, since the last surviving passenger pigeon would die between 1912, the copyright date of the passage, and Muir's own death two years later.

As if to belie President Roosevelt's allegation that he ignored

the birds in the Mariposa Grove, Muir punctuates his conversations with plants and flowers in *A Thousand-Mile Walk* by frequent though fleeting mentions of birds—cranes, bald and golden
eagles, bluebirds, and mourning doves. He also notes wild geese,
sparrow hawks, meadowlarks, owls, pelicans, bobwhites, and robins. He makes fewer remarks about birds in the journal for his
first summer in the Sierra, but his favorite feathered creature, the
water ouzel or American dipper, makes its debut there, to reappear glorified in one of Muir's most celebrated essays, "The
Humming-Bird of the California Water-Falls." First published in
Scribner's Monthly in 1878, the essay was later collected as a climaxing feature in *The Mountains of California.*

Retitled simply "The Water Ouzel," it begins with the observation that only one bird frequented the waterfalls of the Sierra—
"the Ouzel or Water Thrush (*Cinclus mexicanus,* Sw.). He is a
singularly joyous and lovable little fellow, about the size of a
robin, clad in a plain waterproof suit of bluish gray, with a tinge
of chocolate on the head and shoulders. In form he is about as
smoothly plump and compact as a pebble that has been whirled
in a pot-hole, the flowing contour of of his body being interrupted only by his strong feet and bill, the crisp wing-tips, and
the up-slanted wren-like tail." Muir went on to claim that during
his ten-year ranging of the Sierra he had never found a waterfall
without its attendant ouzel. "No cañon is too cold for this little
bird, none too lonely, provided it be rich in falling water. Find a
fall, or cascade, or rushing rapid, anywhere upon a clear stream,
and there you will surely find its complementary Ouzel, flitting
about in the spray, diving in foaming eddies, whirling like a leaf
among beaten foam-bells; ever vigorous and enthusiastic, yet self-
contained and neither seeking nor shunning your company." In
this chapter Muir achieved perhaps the highest point of his nature writing, and on finishing it, the reader feels intimately acquainted with the sprightly little bird.

The ouzel reappears in both *Our National Parks* and *The
Yosemite,* along with references to Clarke crows, robins, wild
geese, Steller's jays, kingfishers, and wild pigeons. There are also
glancing mentions of snowbirds, wild ducks, eagles, hawks,

plovers, woodpeckers, and mountain and valley quail. Muir described no other bird as lovingly as the ouzel, however, though he devoted two whole chapters to the birds of Yosemite in the abovementioned books.

He also interspersed his remarks about trees, plants, and birds with comments on mammals, mostly wild ones. Of the few animals that he mentioned in his journal of the walk to the Gulf, he had most to say about alligators, repulsive creatures that filled him with dread, but which, he believed, were beloved of God and enjoyed a respectable niche in creation "as part of God's family." He included in the same journal an interesting brief passage on the dolphins that preyed on flying fish during his voyage from Cuba to New York.

He discovered more to say about wild mammals after his arrival in California, beginning with the coyote, "a beautiful animal, graceful in motion," which he sometimes called "a wolf." On becoming a shepherd for Smoky Jack he found it necessary to guard the sheep from coyotes, but his sympathy lay with this audacious predator. "This morning," he wrote in his journal for January 23, 1869, "while observing the movements of my flock . . . I saw a coyote stealing from a thicket of dead weeds and earnestly watching the opportunity for a lamb. I did not make any allowance for his morning hunger, but almost wished I had not seen him, that he might have a lamb in peace." Muir's sympathy for the coyote was so great that he later planned to publish an essay about the beast, but this he never did, perhaps because he felt that prejudice would prevent it from being well received. Such caution on Muir's part led to a certain one-sidedness in his portrayal of wildlife and to a considered emphasis on inoffensive creatures like deer and squirrels, bighorns, and nonraptorial birds.

In line with this selective tendency in Muir's writing, the chapter in *Our National Parks* called "Among the Animals of the Yosemite," first published in the *Atlantic Monthly,* gives extended prominence to genteel species like the Sierra blacktail deer, two varieties of California squirrels, striped chipmunks, and woodrats, amid fleeting mentions of such innocuous animals as foxes,

badgers, porcupines, beavers, and pikas. But at the same time
Muir made a deliberate exception to his usual choice of inoffensive animals for portrayal and featured in this chapter the bears of
the Sierra, both cinnamon and grizzly, calling them "the sequoia
of the animals." The chapter devotes seventeen pages in all to
these often dangerous creatures, including attention to bear hunts
and bear hunters. What Muir had to say in this context about his
personal encounters with bears makes for riveting reading, as do
his brushes with them in *My First Summer*, but he supplements
such exciting passages with more mundane contributions to natural history like his remarks about bruin's unprejudiced feeding
habits. "In this happy land," Muir wrote, "no famine comes nigh
him. All the year round his bread is sure, for some of the thousand
kinds that he likes are always in season and accessible, ranged on
the shelves of the mountains like stores in a pantry. From one to
another, from climate to climate, up and down, he climbs, feast-
ing on each in turn,—enjoying as great variety as if he traveled to
far-off countries north and south." Muir then wryly summed the
matter up by suggesting that bears found almost everything fit
to eat "except granite."

The snow-white polar bears he met during the cruise of the
Corwin in 1881 received brief attention from his pen, along with
rapid mentions of reindeer (his name for caribou), walruses, and
arctic foxes. But among all the fauna Muir described, he had the
most to say about the bighorn sheep of the Sierra, principally in
two essays first run in the *Overland Monthly*—"Wild Sheep of
California," republished in *The Mountains of California*, and
"Wild Wool," posthumously gathered in *Steep Trails*. The first
essay opens with the claim that "The wild sheep ranks highest
among the animal mountaineers of the Sierra." In support of this
contention Muir stressed the bighorn's strong legs and keen sight
and sense of smell, by means of which "he dwells secure amid the
loftiest summits, leaping unscathed from crag to crag, up and
down the fronts of giddy precipices, crossing foaming torrents
and slopes of frozen snow, exposed to the wildest storms, yet
maintaining a brave, warm life, and developing from generation
to generation in perfect strength and beauty."

"Wild Sheep of California" stands as one of Muir's most satisfying contributions to natural history, but "Wild Wool" rates even higher, with its trenchant comparison between the wild bighorn and its bedraggled domestic cousin. Therein Muir made the bighorn, so perfectly adapted to its austere environment, the robust symbol for the wildness that he consistently juxtaposed against the brazen culture and civilization of Lord Man, the juxtaposition that constituted the central conflict in his writing.

No doubt, however, an even more appealing statement on mammals was Muir's essay on the Douglas squirrel, a rival in popular appreciation to his treatment of the water ouzel. He found the Douglas squirrel "by far the most interesting and influential of the California sciuridae, surpassing every other species in force of character, numbers, and extent of range, and in the amount of influence he brings to bear upon the health and distribution of the vast forests he inhabits." Muir brought a rich harvest of closely observed details to his portrait of this "principal forester" of the mountains, but about a prominent highlight of the essay some readers have registered reservations.

This was Muir's anecdote about the squirrel's reaction to whistled tunes, "more than a dozen airs, and as the music changed his eyes sparkled, and he turned his head quickly from side to side, but made no other response" until Muir whistled the doleful Protestant hymn "Old Hundredth" (the Doxology), and then "he screamed his Indian name Pillillooeet, turned tail, and darted with ludicrous haste up the tree out of sight, his voice and actions . . . leaving a somewhat profane impression, as if he had said, 'I'll be hanged if you get me to hear anything so solemn and unpiny.'" Muir claimed that he conducted the experiment on a later occasion with a similar result, another instance of the case he often made for the intelligence and individuality of animals. But Hart Merriam, who had the reputation of knowing what he was talking about when it came to birds and animals, bolstered his detraction of Muir as an authority on wildlife by asserting that in his portrait of the Douglas squirrel he had confused the Douglas squirrel of the Coast Range with the red squirrel of the Sierra.

Muir intended to write more about wild animals than he

actually did. In 1910, during the Hetch Hetchy controversy, he began a manuscript about them, but did not live to complete it. The brief passages on the porcupine, the coyote, and a jackrabbit hunt that Lisa Mighetto extracted from the existing fragment and published in her 1986 anthology *John Muir Among the Animals* have only a limited interest and do not materially increase Muir's stature as a naturalist.

The same may also be said about his entomological remarks, beginning with the letter to Jeanne Carr that revealed his early interest in insects by recording the curious pattern of a grasshopper's tracks. He also included in *My First Summer,* along with passing remarks about butterflies, bluebottle flies, gallflies, mosquitoes, and borers, a whimsical passage on the grasshopper he encountered at the top of North Dome. But aside from his many references to wild honeybees, the great pollinators of flowers in the lush bee pastures of California, his nature writing said little more about insects.

One notable exception, however, dealt with the jet black ants he met in the Sierra during the summer of 1869. Try as he might, he found it impossible to fit these creatures into his scheme of divine benevolence that infused nature. "These fearless, restless, wandering imps," he wrote, "though only about a quarter of an inch long, are fonder of fighting and biting than any [other] beast I know. They attack every living thing around their homes, often without cause as far as I can see. Their bodies are mostly jaws curved like ice-hooks, and to get work for these weapons seems to be their chief aim and pleasure." Their ferocity seemed to Muir to lack all common sense. "As soon as a vulnerable spot is discovered on man or beast, they stand on their heads and sink their jaws, and though torn limb from limb, they will yet hold on and die biting deeper."

Muir's acerbic portrait of these black ants was an atypical, even isolated indictment of a living creature of the wilds. It was not his habit to be thus hypercritical about the actors he observed in the great theater of nature. Indeed, vastly more often than not his comments on such things and beings amounted to long-drawn paeans of praise.

The enthusiastic reception of Muir's observations on nature was assured by the spirit of the times, as embodied in the sedulous nature cult of the day. The reception was facilitated by the religious aura Muir diffused over his communions with nature, couched in reverential generalities that obscured the exact character of his religious views and simultaneously guarded against disturbing those of his orthodox Christian readers, with the result that he was frequently accepted as an ordinary Christian. At the same time, though Muir remained a confirmed evolutionist to the end of his days, his brand of natural history rejected the mechanistic interpretation of Darwinism fostered by freethinkers like Ernst Haeckel and Thomas Henry Huxley, which tended to associate the doctrine with agnosticism and a universe devoid of a knowable God. The Godful universe that Muir himself espoused did not encourage in him a passive veneration, but rather a dedicated immersion in nature's bounty, leading in turn to a compulsion to conserve and preserve that bounty for distant posterity. And that, according to Alan Devoe, a devotee of Thoreau and Muir, was what made Muir stand out and loom large— the point and profound feeling of his nature evangelism. "Of all the prophets of the nature-faith," Devoe declared in 1945, "Muir was the most religiously exalted and sustained."

Epilogue

UNDERPINNING Muir's role in the conservation movement was his philosophy of nature (sometimes called his wilderness ethic). Its seeds were sown in his boyhood and youth, but crystallization of his thinking got seriously under way during his walk to the Gulf in 1867. Not that his thoughts on man and the natural wilds were systematized, either then or later; but thereafter his philosophy became an intermittent though persistent ingredient of his journals, then of his essays and books, and from them emerge several specific principles.

A central tenet raised the profound ethical question as to the proper or ideal relationship between humanity and nature or, framed in another manner, between civilization and wilderness. Muir's philosophy exalted wild nature over human culture and civilization and maintained that all life was sacred, even if not equal, and that the earth was never made primarily for human use; from which it followed that to survive, people must develop more humility and a greater respect for the rest of life and realize a juster perception of their own status in creation.

In contradicting the traditional doctrine of human dominion over all the world, as specified in Genesis 1:26 and 28, Muir wrote, "No dogma taught by the present civilization seems to form so insuperable an obstacle in the way of right understanding of the relations which culture sustains to wildness, as that which declares that the world was made for the uses of man. Every animal, plant, and crystal controverts it in the plainest terms. Yet it is taught from century to century as something ever new and precious, and in the resulting darkness the enormous conceit is allowed to go unchallenged."

A primary aim of Muir's nature philosophy was nothing less

than to challenge that "enormous conceit," and in so doing, he moved beyond the Transcendentalism of Emerson to a biocentric perspective on the world, an affirmation expressed in a quasi-theological vocabulary, making wild nature "a conductor of divinity." Thus, while still speaking as a theist, his youthful religious position, he referred to the manifestations of nature as the words, thoughts, or vestments of God; but when speaking as a pantheist, his more mature position, he made nature synonymous with God (God in everlasting process). Muir's philosophy of nature, then, was essentially religious, the expression of a liberal point of view that had replaced the fundamentalism of his father and that freed Muir forever from churches, traditional theology, and theological disputes. It remained thoroughly Romantic, however, especially in view of Muir's increasing inclination to substitute for God the word "nature" with a capital N or "beauty" with a capital B.

Muir discussed certain essential aspects of his nature philosophy in an expansive journal entry dated March 15, 1873; and these ideas would undergo little change during the rest of his life, in part because so much of his later writing mined his earlier journals. The statement in question welded influences from religion and science, including biology and geology, and climaxed on a quasi-Darwinian notion of human evolution. "What is 'higher,' what is 'lower' in Nature?" Muir asked. "We speak of higher forms, higher types, etc., in the fields of scientific inquiry. Now all of the individual 'things' or 'beings' into which the world is wrought are sparks of the Divine Soul variously clothed upon [sic] with flesh, leaves, or that harder tissue called rock." He thus expressed his pantheistic point of view, which in an animistic fashion allowed mind and soul not only to plants, trees, and animals, but even to rocks because of what he termed "instonation."

"Now," he continued in amplification, "we observe that, in cold mountain altitudes, Spirit is but thinly and plainly clothed. As we descend down their many sides to the valleys, the clothing of all plants and beasts and of the forms of rock becomes more abundant and complicated. When a portion of spirit clothes itself with a sheet of lichen tissue, colored simply red or yellow, or gray or black, we say that it is a low form of life." That observation prompted him to raise the question, was that more rudimentary form of life "more or less radically Divine than another portion of Spirit that has gathered garments of leaf and fairy flower and adorned them with all the colors of light, though we say that the latter creature is of a higher degree of life?" In answer to this question he generalized that every one of these varied forms, either high or low, is a portion of God radiated with modifications from "the God essence itself."

But he concluded that "the more extensively terrestrial a being becomes, the higher it ranks among its fellows, and the most terrestrial being is the one that contains all the others, that has, indeed, flowed through all the others and borne away parts of them, building them into itself." Muir found the human to be just such a being, a microcosm that had flowed through myriad other molds of being, assimilating elements of them, thereby becoming "most richly Divine because most richly terrestrial." By way of illustration, he likened humanity to a river that "becomes rich by flowing on and on through varied climes and rocks, through many mountains and vales, constantly appropriating portions to itself, rising higher in the scale of rivers as it grows rich in the absorption of the soils and smaller streams."

Not that our advanced evolution, as Muir had perceived on his walk to the Gulf, licensed us to arrogate to ourselves the role of the Lord of Creation and to domineer over all other species and recklessly squander the resources of the earth for greedy, materialistic ends. Muir's demotion of Lord Man in 1867 to a less arrogant status in the natural world would remain for the rest of his life the cutting edge of his philosophy of nature.

Not only did Muir demand that Lord Man become humbler; humility before nature always marked his own attitude and led, after his conceiving that God and nature were one, to the assertion that nature was essentially benign. While accepting in general the theory of evolution, he rejected "Darwin's mean ungodly word 'struggle'" and the concept of nature as "red in tooth and claw." His position in this respect was paradoxical, since at the same time he recognized that certain animals in the wilds preyed on other animals and that the power of storms, earthquakes, and avalanches wrought untold destruction, but he maintained unshakably that from destruction came creation, and he substituted for Darwinian "struggle" the attribution of repose and "essential kindliness" to nature. In respect to this conviction he jotted in his journal in 1873: "Universal and immovable repose characterizes all the deeds of God. Repose is as visible in the so-called ragings of storms and crash and roar of avalanches as in the sleep of mountains in sun-calm." His claim that even natural catastrophes were fundamentally benign is hard to square with common sense and suggests flaws in his view of nature and a squewed insight into her violence. But again and again Muir affirmed this doctrine in his journals and his published articles and books, as when he remarked in 1875 of the ferocious storm that flooded the Yuba and Feather rivers: "In this great storm, as in every other, there were tones and gestures inexpressibly gentle manifested in the midst of what is called violence and fury, but easily recognized by all who look for them."

A concomitant of Muir's belief in the basic benevolence of nature was his faith in her healing power, especially for spiritual and psychological ills. This Emersonian and Thoreauvian principle he stressed repeatedly in his journals and essays. "Earth," he wrote on one occasion, "hath no sorrows that earth cannot heal, . . . for the earth as seen in the clean wilds of the mountains is about as divine as anything the heart of man can conceive." He urged his fellow citizens to go to the wilds and "gain health from lusty, heroic exertion, from free, firm-nerved adventures without anxiety in them, with rhythmic runs over boulders requiring quick decision for every step." In another statement he paraphrased Thoreau: "In God's wildness lies the hope of the world— the great fresh unblighted, unredeemed wilderness. The galling harness of civilization drops off, and the wounds heal ere we are aware." He made the same argument, essentially, in his chapter on Sierra passes in *The Mountains of California*, beginning with the remark that few places were more hazardous than one's home: "Fear not, therefore, to try the mountain-passes. They will kill care, save you from deadly apathy, set you free, and call forth every faculty into vigorous, enthusiastic action. Even the sick should try these so-called dangerous passes, because for every unfortunate they kill, they cure a thousand."

The perennial source of such healing power was the harmonious unity that Muir had found in nature (objectification of God). It had quickly led him to the perception of the mountains as an organic whole, and to the further perception that the unity of the mountains was but an aspect of cosmic unity, or as Muir put the matter in 1869, "When we try to pick out anything in Nature, we find it hitched to everything else in the universe." And thus, without knowing the term "ecology," at least at such an early date, he had uttered its basic principle.

One important implication of this sense of unity, with its web of interrelationships, was the insight that Bonaventure Cemetery had given Muir into the oneness of life and death. Another attendant idea recognized that the basic unity of nature made for opulent abundance, abundance yet without excess. Still another corollary was Muir's intuition, as mentioned before, that the whole world in its fundamental oneness was alive and sentient, not merely those beings customarily called "living," but even rocks and minerals, which he imbued with mind and soul, however undeveloped. "Plants are credited with but dim and uncertain sensation, and minerals with positively none at all," he wrote in December 1867 or early January 1868, but this common orthodoxy was no sooner expressed than it provoked a major counterquestion: "But why may not even a mineral arrangement of matter be endowed with sensation of a kind that we in our blind exclusive perfection can have no manner of communication with?" The idea implicit in the question, another of Muir's insights during his thousand-mile walk, was more than mere pathetic fallacy. While reviving a conviction universal to primitive societies the world over, it yet informed Muir's approach to all things and all creatures of nature, motivating him to speak to plants and flowers as if they were human beings. "One fancies," he wrote, "a heart like our own beating in every crystal and cell, and we feel like stopping to speak to the plants and animals as friendly fellow mountaineers." It was as if Muir had appropriated the outlook of George Perkins Marsh, who had written that, in his boyhood, "the bubbling brooks, the trees, the flowers, the wild animals were to me persons, not things."

This attitude led to the emphasis that Muir's philosophy of nature placed on the brotherhood of all living beings. Like Thoreau, he assigned inviolable rights to everything that lived, and at the same time denied that any being was made primarily for the sake of humanity. "I have never yet happened upon a trace of evidence," he wrote on one occasion, "that seemed to show that any one animal was ever made for another as much as it was made for itself." On another occasion he made the same point about plants, specifically the twining lily. "Like most other things not apparently useful to man, it has few friends, and the blind question, 'Why was it made?' goes on and on with never a guess that first of all it might have been made for itself." Much of Muir's quarrel with Lord Man was over people's persistently ignoring the rights of other beings in nature.

Seeming at first like paradox, Muir's gospel of nature claimed that her harmonious unity was matched by her streaming flux and flow, incessant change governed by natural law. The poet-ornithologist Charles Keeler underscored this aspect of Muir's thought when he observed that "Muir's eyes were fixed on the ever-changing processes of nature." And how right Keeler was, for the theme of universal flux runs throughout Muir's writing, as when he declared in 1869, "How lavish is Nature, building, pulling down, creating, destroying, chasing every material particle from form to form, ever changing." On New Year's day of that same year, while herding sheep for Smoky Jack Connel, he had addressed the concept in this fashion in his journal: "Everything is governed by laws. . . . But out here in the free unplanted fields there is no rectilineal sectioning of times and seasons. All things *flow* here in indivisible, measureless currents."

Elsewhere he put the matter in a like manner: "The entire universe is in a state of change—flowing like a river"; and during his ascent of Mount Ritter in 1872 he entertained the concept yet again. At first the wilderness seemed without movement, "as if the work of creation was done. But in the midst of this outer steadfastness we know there is incessant motion and change. Ever and anon, avalanches are falling from yonder peaks. These cliff-bound glaciers, seemingly wedged and immovable, are flowing like water and grinding the rocks beneath them. The lakes are lapping their granite shores and wearing them away, and every one of these rills and young rivers is fretting the air into music, and carrying the mountains to the plains." It was a felicitous vision of nature's eternal flow, the myriad changes that held Muir rapt and fascinated. It was no accident that Norman Foerster would find that his prose was most telling when it dealt with change and motion.

Such flow and flux inevitably made of nature, in Muir's perception, an exemplary teacher, more so than any library of books. He heartily seconded William Cullen Bryant's dictum, "Go forth, under the open skies, and list/to Nature's teachings." Therefrom one might learn even about human nature, as he suggested through his frequently quoting Wordsworth's familiar quatrain:

> One impulse from a vernal wood
> May teach you more of man,
> Of moral evil and of good,
> Than all the sages can.

At the same time he pinned down the didactic side of nature even more explicitly when he wrote that "everything [in the mountains] is perfectly clean and pure and full of divine lessons." Many of the lessons that Muir valued so highly were spiritual in essence, but there was practical instruction as well, like his encounter with the ice striae and polished pavements in the summer of 1869 that set him on his course of ferreting out the basis for his glacial theory of mountain sculpture, both in the Yosemite region and in the Sierra at large. He found nature to be, moreover, a spectacular teacher at the Grand Canyon, which impressed him as "a grand geological library—a collection of stone books covering thousands of miles of shelving," revealing "myriad forms of successive floras and faunas, lavishly illustrated with colored drawings."

Nature's practical lessons seemed never-ending, often dawn-

ing unexpectedly, like his discovery that the giant sequoias transformed comparatively arid regions into areas of plentiful water.
It was a similar lesson learned at nature's knee—the necessity of
watersheds for a dependable water supply for the farmlands below—
that gave him a potent incentive to campaign later for the preservation of forests.

Another of nature's teachings was an idea that Muir called
"terrestrial immortality," a concept in harmony with his abandonment of Christian orthodoxy and its doctrine of immortality
as a hereafter of pearly gates and golden pavements. "Terrestrial
immortality" was an eminently Wordsworthian notion, and stim-
ulated by it, Muir wrote that "some of the days I have spent
alone in the depths of the wilderness have shown me that immortal life beyond the grave is not essential to perfect happiness, for
those diverse days were so complete there was no sense of time in
them, they had no definite beginning or ending and formed a
kind of terrestrial immortality." On another occasion he wrote
that "life seems neither long nor short, and we take no more
heed to save time or make haste than do the trees and stars. This
is true freedom, a good practical sort of immortality." How Daniel Muir would have bridled at this unorthodox turn in his son's
thought!

Having crystallized in the late 1860s and early seventies, and
undergoing little fundamental change during the rest of Muir's
life, his philosophy of nature served as his bulwark and support
during the strenuous years of his crusade for the preservation of
wilderness. At the same time certain central implications of his
thought made his point of view a firm forerunner of the biocentric thinking of such later ecologists as Aldo Leopold, ensur-
ing a continued role for Muir's voice in the present-day environmental movement. The enormous esteem in which Muir is held
today was implicit in the regard with which he was held at his
death as crusading naturalist, more than equal to that paid to
John Burroughs, though the number of Muir's books, even counting posthumous volumes, fell considerably short of the total produced by Burroughs.

Any subsequent waning of Muir's reputation abruptly ceased

with the publication in 1945 of *Son of the Wilderness,* Linnie Marsh Wolfe's Pulitzer Prize–winning account of his life, more widely read than William F. Badè's earlier *Life and Letters.* The success of Wolfe's biography encouraged a revival of interest in Muir's own books, and that in turn helped spur a general reversion of the conservation movement to an accent on the Muir tradition and to the ascendancy of his influence over that of Pinchot. "Gifford Pinchot made conservation practical," Howard Zahnizer of the Wilderness Society would soon point out. "It is, of course, John Muir's leadership to which we are more directly committed in our preservation efforts." In 1950 *Studies in the Sierra* appeared in book form under the auspices of the Sierra Club, and four years later Edwin Way Teale's anthology *The Wilderness World of John Muir* assembled chronologically, with provocative commentaries, the highlights of Muir's nature writing. As time went on, additional anthologies appeared, along with new biographies by T. H. Watkins, Tom Melham, James M. Clarke, Stephen Fox, and Frederick Turner, as well as a prize-winning analysis of Muir's wilderness thought by Michael Cohen.

Such a remarkable reassessment of Muir's life, thought, and reputation fueled a vigorous observation in 1988 of the sesquicentennial of his birth, when he was hailed as one of America's most eminent naturalists, the peer of Thoreau as an apostle of nature. It was widely recognized that what Thoreau had done for the natural history of the East, Muir had done for that of the West. Not that it could be claimed that he was Thoreau's equal as a writer; he produced no masterwork to rival *Walden* but to quote Edwin Way Teale, "Never did he get enough of wildness. Of those who have written of nature surpassingly well—Gilbert White, Henry Thoreau, Richard Jeffries, W. H. Hudson—John Muir was the wildest. He was the most active, the most at home in the wilderness, the most daring, the most capable, the most self-reliant." Small wonder, then, that in the light of ongoing reassessments of Muir's historic position, it is not improbable that his legacy for the environmentalism of the future will expand even further.

Bibliographical Notes

IN accordance with the prescribed specifications for entries in the Oklahoma Western Biographies series, *John Muir: Apostle of Nature* is based on published sources, both primary and secondary, including published correspondence of Muir, his several books, a number of his articles, and various works by others that in some way deal with him. Many more sources were consulted than are listed in this statement, but restricted space allows the inclusion of only the most rewarding items. For more expansive listings the reader is referred to two comprehensive John Muir bibliographies. The first is William F. and Maymie B. Kimes, *John Muir: A Reading Bibliography*, 2nd edition, revised and enlarged (Fresno: Panorama West Books, 1986). This work cites all known publications of Muir's writings, with annotations and quotations. In addition it lists all known reports of Muir's lectures and interviews. The second compilation is Ann T. Lynch, "Bibliography of Works By and About John Muir, 1869–1978," *Bulletin of Bibliography*, vol. 36, no. 2 (April–June 1979), pp. 71–80, 84. Lynch lists books and many newspaper and magazine articles by Muir and others, including reviews of Muir's works, reminiscences of him by friends and acquaintances, tributes, memoirs, and biographical sketches.

The present work profited greatly from Muir's correspondence. He was a prolific letter writer, and of the many letters recovered by his literary executor William F. Badè, a generous assortment appears in Badè, *Life and Letters of John Muir*, making it the fullest receptacle in book form of Muir's correspondence. The next fullest compilation comprises Muir's letters to Jeanne C. Carr, collected in *Letters to a Friend* (Boston: Houghton Mifflin, 1915). Six lengthy specimens appear in "The Creation of

Yosemite National Park, Letters of John Muir to Robert Underwood Johnson," in *Sierra Club Bulletin,* vol. 29 (October 1944),
pp. 49–60. Also, "Some New John Muir Letters," edited by
Elizabeth I. Dixon and published in *Southern California Quar-
terly,* vol. 46 (September 1964), pp. 24–58, contains twelve letters to John's brother David and one to his mother. And Muir's
correspondence with his daughter Wanda appears in *Dear Papa,*
edited by Jean Hanna Clark and Shirley Sargent (Fresno: Panorama West Books, 1985).

It is fashionable to call Muir's earlier articles fresher and more
spontaneous than the same material revised and published later
in his books, but for the present work his books were mined with
benefit from being his more mature expression. These books are
listed here in their order of publication. Of *Picturesque California* (New York and San Francisco: J. Dewing, 1888), 2 vols., Muir
was both the editor and a coauthor, and his chapter "Mount
Shasta" contributed to the handling in this biography of Muir's
experience of storms on that mountain. *The Mountains of California* (New York: Century Co., 1894) holds in the chapter "A
Near View of the Sierra" the basic source of the present narration
of Muir's crucial experience on Mount Ritter; and the chapters
"A Wind-Storm in the Forests" and "The River Floods" furnished details for the treatment herein of Muir's experience of a
great gale and a prodigious rainstorm in the Yuba region. In *Our
National Parks* (Boston: Houghton Mifflin, 1901) the several chapters dealing with the various features of Yosemite National Park
yielded details for the present account of Muir's lifelong love
affair with Yosemite Valley and its environs; while the chapter
titled "The Sequoia and General Grant National Parks" (called
"Hunting Big Redwoods" when published in the *Atlantic Monthly*)
is the primary source for the present narrative of Muir's 1875
survey of the groves of Big Trees south of Yosemite.

Stickeen (Boston: Houghton Mifflin, 1909), along with *Travels
in Alaska,* is the principal source for the relation herein of Muir's
adventure on the Brady Glacier with the dog Stickeen, while *My
First Summer in the Sierra* (Boston: Houghton Mifflin, 1911) is
the primary source for chapter six of this biography. *The Yosemite*

(New York: 1912) supplements *Our National Parks* in furnishing information for the reconstruction of Muir's experience in Yosemite Valley and adjacent regions—specifically his witnessing the great earthquake of 1872, his riding an avalanche, and his seeing the "Specter of the Brocken" from the crown of Half Dome. *Edward Henry Harriman* (New York: Doubleday, 1911) helped in working up the chapter on the Harriman-Alaska Expedition; while *The Story of My Boyhood and Youth* (Boston: Houghton Mifflin, 1913) cannot be overestimated as a source, providing as it did the primary basis for the first three chapters of this book.

All the foregoing works by Muir were published during his lifetime. Those that follow were published posthumously. *Travels in Alaska,* finished after Muir's death by Marion Randall Parsons for publication by Houghton Mifflin in 1915, provided numerous details for the present treatment of three of Muir's trips to Alaska, those of 1879, 1880, and 1890. *A Thousand-Mile Walk to the Gulf* (Boston: Houghton Mifflin, 1916) served as the principal primary source for the fifth chapter of this work, whereas the main primary source for chapter fifteen is *The Cruise of the Corwin* (Boston: Houghton Mifflin, 1917). *Steep Trails, Utah, Nevada, Washington, Oregon, the Grand Cañon* (Boston: Houghton Mifflin, 1918) reprints "Mount Shasta" from *Picturesque California* and contains chapters that helped in dealing with Muir's trips to Utah and Nevada in 1877 and 1878 and to Oregon and Washington in 1888. Of greater importance was *John of the Mountains: The Unpublished Journals of John Muir,* edited by Linnie Marsh Wolfe and published by Houghton Mifflin in 1938; it provided rich materials for the narration of many events in Muir's life from 1868 on. Just as significant in its way was *Studies in the Sierra,* seven papers collected by William E. Colby from the *Overland Monthly* 1874–75 and published in book form by the Sierra Club in 1950 (2nd edition, 1960). These essays were essential to a discussion of Muir's investigation of glaciation and mountain sculpture in the Sierra.

Of the various anthologies of Muir's writings the most helpful proved to be the following, listed here by editor(s)—Robert Engberg, ed., *John Muir Summering in the Sierra* (Madison: University of Wisconsin Press, 1984); Robert Engberg and Donald Wesling, eds., *John Muir in Yosemite and Beyond: Writings from the Years 1863 to 1875* (Madison: University of Wisconsin Press, 1980); Richard F. Fleck, ed., *John Muir: Mountaineering Essays* (Salt Lake City: Peregrine Smith Books, 1984); Frederic R. Gunsky, ed., *South of the Yosemite: Selected Writings of John Muir* (Garden City: Natural History Press, 1968); William R. Jones, ed., *The Proposed Yosemite National Park—Treasures & Features* (Olympic Valley, Calif.: Outbooks, 1976); Lisa Mighetto, ed., *John Muir Among the Animals* (San Francisco: Sierra Club, 1986); Edwin Way Teale, ed., *The Wilderness World of John Muir* (Boston: Houghton Mifflin, 1954). Each collection gives, in some degree, the effect of autobiography, and all contain helpful introductions and/or commentary by the editors.

Muir has been fortunate in his biographers, and their works have been indispensable as sources. William Frederic Badè, Muir's first literary executor, prepared the initial biography, *The Life and Letters of John Muir,* published by Houghton Mifflin in two volumes in 1923 and 1924. Badè's work may not be as lively to read as certain of its successors, but it proved to be especially useful for these researches, because of its high proportion of primary material. It has some gaps, but they were admirably filled by Linnie Marsh Wolfe, *Son of the Wilderness: The Life of John Muir* (New York: Alfred A. Knopf, 1945). This work, which won the Pulitzer Prize, has long been considered the standard biography of Muir. Because of their brevity the two library-table lives that followed— Tom Melham, *John Muir's Wild America,* illustrated with photographs by Farrell Grehan (Washington, D.C.: National Geographic Society, 1976) and T. H. Watkins, *John Muir's America,* illustrated with photographs by Dewitt Jones (New York: Crown Publishers, 1976) leave much of Muir's story untold, but both books cont valuable insights, especially that by Watkins. In 1979 came M. Clarke, *The Life and Adventures of John Muir,* a highly able biography republished in 1980 by the Sierra Club. Nine eighty-one saw the appearance of Stephen Fox, *John Muir His Legacy: The American Conservation Movement* (Boston: I tle, Brown), part one of which contains a short but highly sch arly biography of Muir; yet in the main the book deals with the history of the conservation movement in America. The latest full-length biography of Muir to appear—Frederick Turner, *Rediscovering America: John Muir in His Time and Ours* (New York: Viking Penguin, 1985; republished by the Sierra Club, n.d.)—is in some respects the finest life of Muir yet published. All the aforementioned biographies have been useful, and some served as major sources.

Several specialized works about Muir that proved of help are listed below in their order of publication. S. Hall Young, *Alaska Days with John Muir* (New York: Revell, 1915) deals firsthand with Muir's various trips to Alaska, especially those of 1879 and 1880. In 1965 Twayne Publishers issued Herbert F. Smith's *John Muir,* a short critical assessment of Muir's writings, perceptive and rich in insights. In the same year appeared Holway Jones, *John Muir and the Sierra Club: The Battle for Yosemite* (San Francisco: Sierra Club), paying less attention to Muir than the title suggests; but Jones deals copiously and in a highly scholarly manner with the founding of the Sierra Club, the recession of Yosemite Valley to the federal government, and the long-waged controversy over Hetch Hetchy Valley. Shirley Sargent, *John Muir in Yosemite* (Yosemite: Flying Spur Press, 1971) proved a useful source for the Yosemite phases of Muir's life. As for Michael P. Cohen, *The Pathless Way: John Muir and American Wilderness* (Madison: University of Wisconsin Press, 1984), this volume is one of the best and fullest books yet published on John Muir. Though thoroughly grounded in biographical facts, it makes no attempt to retell the whole of Muir's life story, but deals with what the author calls Muir's "spiritual journey," in the course of which Cohen offers a thoughtful explication of Muir's writings, especially those about the Sierra. The following year saw the publication of another specialized book—Richard F. Fleck, *Henry Thoreau and John Muir among the Indians* (Hamden, Conn.: Archon Books, 1985), in which the author traces the progression of Muir's attitude toward Native Americans from ambivalent disgust to the highest respect and finds a parallel between Muir's change of attitude and that of Thoreau.

Several other books, though not explicitly about Muir, must be mentioned for their helpfulness. Dave Bohn, *Glacier Bay: The Land and the Silence* (San Francisco: Sierra Club, 1967) contains an excellent study of Glacier Bay, with accounts of three of Muir's visits there, those of 1879, 1880, and 1890. Paul Brooks' delightfully written *Speaking for Nature: How Literary Naturalists from Henry Thoreau to Rachel Carson Have Shaped America* (Boston: Houghton Mifflin, 1980) presents an effective analysis of Muir's contribution to preservationism; while Michael P. Cohen, *The History of the Sierra Club* (San Francisco: Sierra Club, 1988) admirably supplements Holway Jones on the founding of the club, the recession of Yosemite Valley, and the Hetch Hetchy controversy. Francis P. Farquhar, *History of the Sierra Nevada* (Berkeley and Los Angeles: University of California Press, 1965) contains not only a chapter on Muir's explorations of the Range of Light but also accounts of the history of Mount Whitney, the national parks and forests of the range, as well as the founding and early activities of the Sierra Club.

Norman Foerster, *Nature in American Literature: Studies in the Modern View of Nature* (New York: Macmillan, 1923) includes a glowing tribute to Muir as nature writer. Frank Graham, Jr., *Man's Dominion: The Story of Conservation in America* (New York: M. Evans & Co., 1971) gives a valuable general view of conservation in the United States, with balanced attention to the role Muir played. An even more authoritative treatment of the conservation movement in America, however, is Samuel P. Hays, *Conservation and the Gospel of Efficiency: The Progressive Conservation Movement, 1890–1920* (Cambridge: Harvard University Press, 1959), but as the subtitle suggests, its stress does not fall on Muir's preservationist brand of conservation. Robert Underwood Johnson, *Remembered Yesterdays* (Boston: Little, Brown, 1923) is a *sine qua non* for dealing with the creation of Yosemite National Park, the recession of Yosemite Valley, the National Forestry Commission, and the fight for Hetch Hetchy, intimately involved as the author was in all these matters. Joseph Le Conte, *A Journal of Rambles through the High Sierra of California* (San Francisco: Sierra Club, 1930) offers sharply realized impressions of Muir in

1870. Significant not only for information on the geology of the
Yosemite region but also as aids in reaching a just assessment of
Muir's *Studies in the Sierra* are François Matthes, *Geologic History of the Yosemite Valley* (U.S. Geological Survey Professional
Paper no. 160, Government Printing Office, 1930) and the more
popular version that Fritiof Fryxell prepared from it, *The Incomparable Valley: A Geologic Interpretation of the Yosemite* (Berkeley
and Los Angeles: University of California Press, 1950). C. Hart
Merriam, ed., *Harriman-Alaska Expedition: Alaska,* vol. I (Garden City: Doubleday, 1901) contains John Burroughs' "Narrative
of the Expedition," though a more complete, if secondary, account appears in William H. Goetzmann and Kay Sloan, *Looking Far North: The Harriman Expedition to Alaska* (New York:
Viking, 1982).

    Roderick Nash, *Wilderness and the American Mind* (New Ha-
ven: Yale University Press, 1967; revised edition, 1973) argues
Muir's significance as the publicist for wilderness and the American preservationist movement; the book also contains an excellent though brief chapter on the Hetch Hetchy affair. A later
book on the wilderness theme, with a first-rate reassessment of
Muir's wilderness initiative, is Max Oelschlaeger, *The Idea of
Wilderness: From Prehistory to the Age of Ecology* (New Haven and
London: Yale University Press, 1991). Gifford Pinchot, *Breaking New Ground* (Seattle and London: University of Washington
Press, 1972) is Pinchot's "personal story of how Forestry and Conservation came to America" and contains, among other things, a
detailed account of the National Forestry Commission, from a
minority point of view. Two further books rich in information
about forestry and conservation are Elmo R. Richardson, *The
Politics of Conservation: Crusades and Controversies, 1897–1913* (Berkeley and Los Angeles: University of California Press, 1962) and
Roy M. Robbins, *Our Landed Heritage: The Public Domain,
1776–1936* (Princeton: Princeton University Press, 1942). Michael
L. Smith places Muir in the context of western science in *Pacific
Visions: California Scientists and the Environment, 1850–1915* (New
Haven and London: Yale University Press, 1987); while James
Bradley Thayer, *A Western Journey with Mr. Emerson* (Boston:

Little, 1884) provides interesting details on Emerson's visit with Muir in Yosemite in 1871. Peter Wild, *Pioneer Conservationists of Western America* (Missoula: Mountain Press Publishing Co., 1979) includes Muir among its provocative portraits.

The most useful articles among the many about John Muir include William F. Badè, "John Muir in Yosemite," *Natural History,* vol. 20 (March 1920), pp. 124–41; Clara Barrus, "In the Yosemite with John Muir," *Craftsman,* vol. 23 (December 1912), pp. 324–35; William E. Colby, "Yosemite and the Sierra Club," *Sierra Club Bulletin,* vol. 23 (April 1938), pp. 11–19; Dennis R. Dean, "John Muir and the Origin of Yosemite Valley," *Annals of Science,* vol. 48 (1991), pp. 453–85; Arno Dosch, "The Mystery of John Muir's Money," *Sunset,* vol. 36 (February 1916), pp. 61–63; Samuel T. Farquhar, "John Muir and Ralph Waldo Emerson in Yosemite," *Sierra Club Bulletin,* vol. 19 (February 1934), pp. 48–55; Robert Underwood Johnson, "John Muir as I Knew Him," *Sierra Club Bulletin,* vol. 10 (January 1916), pp. 9–15; and "Personal Impressions of John Muir," *Outlook,* vol. 80 (3 June 1905), pp. 303–6.

Other articles that provided helpful information include John Leighly, "John Muir's Image of the West," *Annals of the Association of American Geographers,* vol. 48 (December 1958), pp. 309–18; François E. Matthes, "John Muir and the Glacial Theory of Yosemite," *Sierra Club Bulletin,* vol. 23 (April 1938), pp. 9–10; C. Hart Merriam, "To the Memory of John Muir," *Sierra Club Bulletin,* vol. 10 (January 1916), pp. 146–51: Samuel Merrill, "Personal Recollections of John Muir," *Sierra Club Bulletin,* vol. 13 (February 1928), pp. 24–30; Merrill Moores, "John Muir in Yosemite in 1872," *Sierra Club Bulletin,* vol. 23 (April 1938), pp. 4–8; Marion Randall Parsons, "John Muir and the Alaska Book," *Sierra Club Bulletin,* vol. 10 (January 1916), pp. 33–36: Theodore Roosevelt, "John Muir: An Appreciation," *Outlook,* vol. 109 (6 January 1915), pp. 27–28; Charles S. Sargent, "John Muir," *Sierra Club Bulletin,* vol. 10 (January 1916), p. 37; and Charles E. Vroman, "John Muir at the University," *Wisconsin Alumni Magazine,* June 1915, pp. 357–62.

In conclusion, two valuable symposia on John Muir in the

Pacific Historian should be mentioned: "The World of John Muir" in vol. 25, no. 2 (Summer 1981), comprising ten articles; and "John Muir: Life and Legacy" in vol. 29, nos. 2 and 3 (Summer/Fall 1985), comprising twelve articles, plus an introduction. An excellent complement to these symposia is Sally M. Miller, ed., *John Muir: Life and Work* (Albuquerque: University of New Mexico Press, 1993), gathering as it does thirteen papers on Muir delivered at a third Muir symposium held in 1990 at the University of the Pacific.

Index